On the Upper Missouri

On the Upper Missouri

The Journal of Rudolph Friederich Kurz, 1851–1852

Edited and Abridged by Carla Kelly

Original Edition Edited by J. N. B. Hewitt and
Translated by Myrtis Jarrell

Introduction by Scott Eckberg

UNIVERSITY OF OKLAHOMA PRESS : NORMAN

Library of Congress Cataloging-in-Publication Data

Kurz, Rudolf Friedrich, 1818–1871.
  [Journal of Rudolph Friederich Kurz. Selections]
  On the upper Missouri; the journal of Rudolph Friederich Kurz,
1851–1852 / edited and abridged by Carla Kelly; introduction by Scott Eckberg.
     p.   cm.
  "Original edition edited by J. N. B. Hewitt and translated by Myrtis Jarrell."
  Includes bibliograhical references and index.
  ISBN 0-8061-3655-3 (pbk.: alk. paper)
  1. Missouri River Valley—Description and travel.   2. Fur trade—Missouri
River Valley.   3. Indians of North America—Missouri River Valley.   4. Kurz,
Rudolf Friedrich, 1818–1871—Diaries.   5. Artists—Missouri River Valley—
Diaries.   I. Kelly, Carla.   II. Hewitt, J. N. B. (John Napoleon Brinton),
1859–1937.   III. Title.

F598.K87 2005
917.8—dc22

                                                                    2004051617

1 2 3 4 5 6 7 8 9 10

This work is dedicated to its author, Rudolph Friederich Kurz.
Without his journal and his illustrations,
there would probably be no reconstructed Fort Union Trading Post
on the bank of the Missouri River today.

Contents

Illustrations

Preface

CARLA KELLY

AT THE TIME THEY are painting or writing, do the artists among us really have an inkling of the longevity and impact of their vision? Could Rudolph Friederich Kurz, a Swiss artist in mid-nineteenth-century frontier America, have had any idea that his impressions of the fur trade and Indians would still intrigue us in the twenty-first century? These two questions frequently came to mind as I took a red pen to Kurz's wonderful journal and abridged it for a modern audience.

I harbor no illusions that Kurz would have approved of this abridgement. Sensitive to criticism, stubborn, passionate about art, and proud, he would probably be horrified if he knew what I have done with his journal. As a professional writer, I understand and empathize; as a historian, I also understand why an abridgement was necessary.

A little background is in order. Kurz wrote a journal describing his 1846–1852 American experiences and took it with him when he returned to his native Switzerland. In the early years of the twentieth century, the Smithsonian Institution's Bureau of American Ethnology acquired a typed manuscript of the German text. Myrtis Jarrell translated it into English, and J. N. B. Hewitt edited the translation. The English version was published by the Smithsonian in 1937 as Bulletin 115. Since 1937, two facsimile editions of the bulletin have been published. Regrettably, both facsimile publications are out of print, as is the original bulletin.

When I started work at Fort Union Trading Post National Historic Site, I read one of the Kurz facsimile editions to familiarize myself with the fur trade. As a writer, I began to understand why the book was out of print. When Kurz described American Indians and the fur trade, his descriptions were fascinating, pertinent, and valuable to historians and fur trade enthusiasts alike.

He became a groaning bore when he wandered from those topics to philosophize about life and art. These meanderings constituted a significant portion of the text.

Artists might argue with me, but I submit that few of them read Kurz for his ruminations on art. His priceless narrative of the fur trade and American Indian life has made him the property of historians. While I struggled through those lengthy passages in which Kurz rhapsodizes about art or topics pertinent to his generation, I became impatient with him. "Look here, Rudolph," I wanted to tell him, "we read you today for your fur trade stories. Get back to the point!"

And this is true. Kurz is extremely valuable today for his insights into the workings of the fur trade. His cogent observations on Upper Missouri Indians are equally important, perhaps even more important. Because of these elements, Kurz *needs* to be in print.

When I finished reading Kurz for the history, I looked at him again with an editor's eye. What if an editor were to start Kurz's journal upriver in 1851 at Council Bluffs, where he began his Upper Missouri adventures with the fur trade? Once she had Kurz upriver, that editor could trim away everything from his journal not related to the fur trade or Indians. Also, since this is translation literature, that hypothetical editor could also gently massage some of those sentences to make them sound more English by eliminating Germanic diction that was inherent even after translation. She would not want to remove the color, but the key would be readability.

I decided that I was the woman for the job. The University of Oklahoma Press agreed, and the results are before the reader. Kurz's wonderful journal is now tighter and aimed at his principal audience of fur trade historians and enthusiasts, as well as readers interested in America's first global enterprise.

After his return to Switzerland, Kurz added a few footnotes to his journal. Because they are all explanatory footnotes, I incorporated them into the text, where they belong. I retained the footnotes found in the 1937 edition that were put there by the editor and translator (and initialed as such). Where Kurz mentions something that would benefit by more detail, I added my own explanatory footnotes, which are not initialed. I kept these to a minimum, not wishing to intrude on Kurz's narrative flow. When a single word or two would do, I inserted it into the text within brackets; the parentheses are Kurz's. Also included are the sketches found in Bulletin 115 and subsequent facsimiles, with a few more illustrations in the body of the text, as well as a much-needed map. I left in some of Kurz's quaint spellings for the flavor, which is why you will see *metif* rather than *métis* and *Herantsa* instead of *Hidatsa*. Kurz spelled "Assiniboin" without a concluding *e*. I left that alone, although "Assiniboine" is the preferred spelling today.

In a perfect world, Bulletin 115 would still be in print, and the reader would have every single word written by Kurz, that child of the Romantic era, student of classicism, and passionate observer of a culture that fascinated him all his life. But this is not a perfect world, and university presses have neither deep pockets nor indulgent patrons. All I can do is assure the reader that I have made every effort to keep this edited, abridged version of Kurz's original journal pertinent to the subject. The good news is that one of the most valuable records of the fur trade is back in print.

This new edition and abridgement would never have seen the light of day without the guidance of key people. I express my appreciation to personnel at the following museums and archives for their assistance in securing Kurz's sketches and illustrations: Bernisches Historisches Museum of Bern, Switzerland; Thomas Gilcrease Institute of American History and Art of Tulsa, Oklahoma; Midwest Jesuit Archives of St. Louis, Missouri; and National Anthropological Archives of the Smithsonian Institution of Washington, D.C. I wish to extend my thanks, especially, to David Burgevin and Daisy Njoku of the Smithsonian for their help. The Fort Union Association of Williston, North Dakota, has my sincere appreciation for their funding to procure these sketches and illustrations.

The book needed a map, and this was supplied by Tracy Rissler and Tom Patterson of Harper's Ferry Center, National Park Service, in Harper's Ferry, West Virginia.

Special thanks go to my friends and colleagues at Fort Union Trading Post National Historic Site for their encouragement and helpful suggestions: Andy Banta, Harriet Carico, Michael Casler, Richard Stenberg, Robert Thomson, and Loren Yellow Bird. Chief Ranger Randy Kane gets separate billing; without his steady guidance and encouragement, this project truly would never have happened. And my thanks go to Scott Eckberg, former chief ranger at Fort Union, for his willingness to write the introduction and share his knowledge of Kurz. This was a Park Service project from beginning to end.

My grateful appreciation also goes to Charles Rankin and Greta Mohon of the University of Oklahoma Press, who recognized that Rudolph Kurz's story of life on the Upper Missouri at Fort Union needed to be retold.

Introduction

SCOTT ECKBERG

FOUNDED IN 1828 BY the American Fur Company, Fort Union established itself as the epicenter of the Upper Missouri fur trade. Its commanding presence near the confluence of the Missouri and Yellowstone Rivers sustained a generation of commerce between the company (and its succeeding incarnations) and the Assiniboine, Cree, Crow, Hidatsa, and Plains Ojibwa people who made their way to it.

To the American Indians, Fort Union represented an extension of ancient bartering traditions, which by the 1850s emphasized exchange of bison robes for an array of manufactured articles. From eyewash and sewing needles to trade cloth and spirits, Fort Union played a part in altering traditional lifeways by instilling a nascent desire for consumer and convenience goods. Borne upriver by company steamboats, trade items were incorporated into indigenous cultures, just as furs and buffalo robes were transported downriver for reconstitution and resale as hats, attire, carriage robes, and wall coverings for homes in America and abroad. This was a big business: during the 1850s, an annual average of between 60,000 and 80,000 robes were consolidated at Fort Union for shipment to St. Louis, along with smaller quantities of bison tongues, beaver pelts, and other furs.

To the resident fur company managers, clerks, and engagés, Fort Union represented not just a business, but also a way of life that was unique even within the paradigm of the nation's westward expansion. The prosperity, much less survival, of a minority of traders in Indian country required a rare ability to live simultaneously in two disparate worlds. Unlike the demands placed on the miners, soldiers, and homesteaders who followed, the fur trade required an unusual level of cross-cultural understanding and tolerance; traders customarily adopted intermarriage as a means of sealing commercial and personal alliances with their tribal partners. In this respect the fur trade community was as removed socially as it was remote physically from the majority experience of Victorian antebellum Americans, white and black.

Nevertheless, while the premise of mutual gain enabled the trade and its unique community structure to flourish, with few exceptions, all who entered Fort Union's massive gates departed retaining the values, beliefs, and lifestyles of their respective cultural upbringing. Whether Indian or non-Indian, each participant understood his particular way of life as superior to that of his opposite, despite the many years spent cultivating and perpetuating the close personal relations attendant to the conduct of business.

For thirty-nine years, those timbered gates opened into a fascinating world; and to the adventurous, Fort Union was mecca. To this polyglot place came explorers, scientists, aristocrats, missionaries, and in particular, artists. Three of the latter were hosted as company guests at Fort Union between 1832 and 1843: George Catlin, Karl Bodmer, and John James Audubon. Their art remains internationally renowned. Each painted and described the inhabitants, animals, and landscapes of a country that in many ways seems alien to the farms and ranches of present-day North Dakota. Each artist left his fleeting, if prestigious, mark on Fort Union. It remained for a lesser-known artist in 1851–52 to leave an indelible impression not only on the trading post as it existed then, but also on the historic site that commemorates Fort Union today.

Rudolph Friederich Kurz was the son of a prosperous Swiss banker who defied family expectations for a respectable career in order to pursue a dual passion for art and for the American Indian. His youthful inspiration was George Catlin, whose famed Indian Gallery toured American and European cities, frequently accompanied by the artist himself, lecturing on the basis of his detailed published letters. Kurz was also directly influenced by his countryman, Karl Bodmer, whom he particularly idolized. Bodmer had accompanied German explorer Prince Maximilian of Wied-Neuwied to the Upper Missouri country in 1833, and Bodmer's lithographs of his Indian portraits and North American landscapes were widely circulated. As a result of meeting Bodmer and obtaining the master's encouragement, Kurz redoubled his resolve to both fine-tune his technical mastery of drawing and make his own artist's journey to the wilds of North America.

"My chief task in the world was to give from my own observation a sincere portrayal of the American Indian in his romantic mode of life, a true representation of the larger fur-bearing animals and of the native forests and prairie," Kurz wrote. An avowed romanticist, Kurz exhibited a passionate and sympathetic inclination toward Indians that ultimately influenced his artistic portrayals of them in classical depictions of savage nobility. Kurz's predilection for antiquity is betrayed in his paintings of Indians and their activities: a group of bathing women, or a warrior in repose, or an encampment in a primeval forest appears strikingly like eighteenth-century paintings depicting fancy epic scenes of daily life in ancient Rome.

In this important respect Kurz the artist veered dramatically from Catlin and Bodmer in both his intent and his interpretation of Indian themes. A reaction to the social and political upheaval attendant to industrialism, Romanticism was influenced by a nostalgic yearning for the comparatively simpler, more pastoral human existence of earlier societies. To Kurz the modern European, Indian people living in America's wilderness evoked that purer era of existence, which he sought to capture and express allegorically in his paintings. A sensitive, opinionated, and driven young artist, Kurz persevered many years against great odds to achieve his goals. Despite all his efforts, Kurz's unique artistic vision failed to connect with his audience upon his return to Switzerland; this was a source of personal bitterness for years to come.

This assessment is not meant to imply that Kurz was a bad artist or that he intended to use his art to deliberately mislead. He was naturally talented, and once his family accepted his commitment to pursue a fine arts profession, they obtained for him the best atelier training available. Twelve intense years of study and practice enabled him to master the technical aspects of the media of pencil, pen and ink, watercolors, and oils. It also sharpened his powers of observation and his ability to capture nuance and intricacy. His sketchbook images of Indian subjects faithfully record ethnological details, from the decorated robe of an Assiniboine warrior to the facial tattoo of a Cree woman. Moreover, Kurz's portraits are seldom insensitive to the humanity and dignity of the people whose images he captured on paper, whether the sitter was an Indian or a non-Indian person.

As an artist, Kurz was neither a Catlin nor a Bodmer, nor would his talent ever have elevated him to their stature. But Kurz's eye was no less precise, and his attention to detail is conveyed not only in his sketches, but also in the lively journal he began upon the start of his long-anticipated North American odyssey.

Arriving in New Orleans in 1846, Kurz immersed himself in American life. That his peripatetic wanderings ever brought him to the Upper Missouri country at all is due to a chance invitation by Honoré Picotte and Alexander Culbertson (agents of Pierre Chouteau, Jr., and Company) to visit, sketch, and possibly clerk at Fort Berthold, a company post. Unlike Catlin, Bodmer, and Audubon, Kurz had precarious finances that made the possibility of a paid situation all the more compelling. In retrospect this was to the good, for few artists could have better captured fur trade life in image and word than one who was actively engaged in it.

Kurz's fur trade journal conveys the ebullience of a young man living his wildest dream. Meeting and drawing Indian people, earning the confidence of fur company employees, and reveling in the country that inspired the artists he ardently sought to emulate, he allowed his enthusiasm to reverberate in his pictures and writings.

However, his employment at Fort Berthold came to an end after a deadly cholera epidemic broke out among the Hidatsa there. In an effort to bolster their own business, competing traders blamed the illness on the artist. With Kurz's life in danger, the company found him a safe haven, employment, and renewed inspiration at Fort Union.

Here he came into his own. Kurz's friendship with his new employer, Edwin Thompson Denig, was manifested in their long discussions about Indian life, the fur trade, and the implications of change both for that trade and for the tribes engaged in it. A hard-featured man with a fearsome reputation for running a tight ship at Fort Union, Denig was a rare intellectual on the frontier. His stories about his long years in the fur business provided ample material for Kurz's journal. Denig went out of his way to provide the young artist/clerk opportunities to observe the ceremony customary to the Indian trade; he also gave or sold Kurz, at steep discount, Indian objects as souvenirs.

Perhaps most significant, Denig recognized the value of Kurz's artistic skills for advancing the trade and enlarging the stature of Fort Union and its manager in the Indians' critical eyes. As one of the conditions of Kurz's employment, Denig commissioned portraits of himself and his dog and other paintings for adorning the Indian trade house and bourgeois house; exorbitantly priced canvas trade banners; and ornamental peace pipes for presentation to important chiefs. A shrewd manager, Denig used and rewarded Kurz's talents. With rare equal shrewdness, Kurz restrained his own outspoken nature regarding what he perceived as his employer's ignorance of the higher purposes of art itself.

In his spare time, Kurz sketched the details of Fort Union and its surroundings. His portfolio brimmed with scenes of the company's impressive stockade, bastions, gates, and bourgeois house as they appeared during his tenure there as clerk. These architectural images captured a weathered yet still-impressive fur post and company depot. Kurz's drawings proved invaluable in documenting for posterity aspects of Fort Union's appearance in 1851–52.

In 1867, as cross-cultural trade was replaced by military conflict, the venerable fur post disappeared, its remains recycled for the construction of portions of nearby Fort Buford, an outpost of the U.S. Army. A century later, the National Park Service acquired Fort Union Trading Post National Historic Site. In 1985, the Park Service undertook a partial reconstruction of the fur post. This reconstruction was based on archaeological evidence and the written and pictorial descriptions of several artists and observers, most particularly Rudolph Friederich Kurz.

Ever the romanticist, Kurz expressed his admiration for Indians on canvas in the form of portraiture of primeval red noblemen. Following his return home in 1852, sick and impoverished from his extended American journey, Kurz was so stung by the critical response to the first exhibition of his Indian artworks that he angrily vowed never to show them publicly again. His dream of emulating the example of George Catlin—whom in his journal he alternately praised, belittled, and despised—only reinforced the high expectations and personal costs that drove Kurz from Switzerland to the Upper Missouri, and back.

At his untimely death in 1871 in Bern, he was remembered and respected primarily as a landscape painter and as a founder and director of that city's first art school. In death there persisted colorful rumors about another side of this quiet, complex man: his abortive marriage to an Iowa Indian girl, his adventures as a fur trader, his collection of Indian articles and furs that lined his small apartment. These stories were as fascinating as Cooper's *Leatherstocking Tales*, ravenously consumed by young art school pupils under Kurz's tutelage.

Although some of his more graphic works, particularly nude Indian women, were destroyed by Kurz's scandalized family after his death, others survived, along with several Indian objects acquired by Kurz. Today, many of those surviving works, sketchbooks, and objects are housed in the ethnology department of the Bern Historical Museum. Also in the museum collections is Kurz's handwritten journal, which he intended as supporting documentation for his anticipated Indian gallery. Kurz may never have achieved the success or fame of his artistic predecessors at Fort Union, but his extraordinary document more than compensates.

As moments captured in time, Kurz's journal is a testimony to the Upper Missouri fur trade society that he both observed and participated in; its reappearance in print is both timely and important. Originally translated by Myrtis Jarrell from a typewritten German manuscript in the Smithsonian Institution's Bureau of American Ethnology archive, and edited by J. N. B. Hewitt, the *Journal of Rudolph Friederich Kurz: An Account of His Experiences Among Fur Traders and American Indians on the Mississippi and the Upper Missouri Rivers During the Years 1846 to 1852* first appeared in 1937. It was published by the Smithsonian Institution as the Bureau of American Ethnology Bulletin 115. In 1969, Ye Galleon Press of Fairfield, Washington, issued a facsimile edition. A year later, the University of Nebraska Press reprinted Bulletin 115 as a Bison Book.

This abridged edition is based on Bulletin 115. Editor Carla Kelly has admirably distilled Kurz's writings to the essential aspects of his experience as an itinerant artist and fur company employee from June 1851 through May 1852. In deleting Kurz's extraneous discussions about art and philosophy, Kelly excises some of the artistic fervor that impelled Kurz to the Missouri River outposts. Nevertheless, this edition by no means detracts from Kurz or does him an injustice. It retains a strong sense of the author's personality and his equally unrestrained opinions and observations on American Indians, art, the fur trade, and life in general as Kurz experienced it. Until Kurz's original handwritten manuscript at the Bern Historical Museum is reexamined and retranslated, this abridged edition remains a sound account; its reappearance will be welcomed by students of the Upper Missouri fur trade.

This highly readable volume makes a wonderful companion to the legacy of that other frank chronicler of the Upper Missouri fur trade, Charles Larpenteur (who was absent from Fort Union during Kurz's tenure there), whose *Forty Years a Fur Trader* is also a must-read for its interpretation of daily life in the Fort Union trade community. It is also a fine adjunct to Edwin Thompson Denig's *Five Indian Tribes of the Upper Missouri*, a collection of essays on Indian life containing information Denig undoubtedly shared in discussions with his eager young Swiss protégé.

Taken together, these firsthand sources are the next best thing to sitting down to a lively dinner conversation with these three men about life and business at Fort Union Trading Post. In reading their words, we must acknowledge that we have only one side of the Upper Missouri fur trade story. The accounts of Indian partners, whose tribal indulgence and trade participation were absolutely prerequisite to Fort Union's commercial establishment and longevity, have yet to be told. Given the oral tradition of American Indian societies, until the day their words may find expression in print, fur trade literature of this kind must be approached with the understanding that the conversation remains one-sided until their place at the table is filled.

Fig. 1. Self-portrait of Rudolph Friederich Kurz. (©Ethnographic Collection at
the Historical Museum Berne, Switzerland)

Prologue

From Switzerland to Council Bluffs, 1851

RUDOLPH FRIEDERICH KURZ was born into a prosperous merchant family on January 8, 1818, in Bern, Switzerland. From an early age, he expressed an interest—an obsession almost—in "primeval forest and Indians."[1] Earlier, more idealized ages fascinated him; the turmoil of incipient nationalism that swept Europe after the downfall of Napoleon held little charm for Kurz. He longed for both the dignity and the nobility of classical Greek life and art, as well as the simplicity and peace of nature. Kurz was a true child of the Romantic movement in art.

When this artistic, sensitive youth decided that his medium of expression would be art, he wrote, "My life purpose was fixed: I would devote my talents to the portrayal of the aboriginal forests, the wild animals that inhabited them, and to the Indians."[2] Kurz's parents were not thrilled with his choice of vocation. They preferred that their son embark on a career in business or civil service, as was expected of one in his social stratum.

Finally, after a period of "perseverance and untiring patience" on Kurz's part, Johannes Kurz gave his son grudging permission to study art, first in his native Bern and then in Paris. In 1838 Kurz went to Paris, where he spent four years learning his craft from various French artists. He was classically trained to see the ideal in the human form, which would be reflected, incongruously sometimes, in his Indian studies.[3]

Impulsive, eager Kurz would have left for Mexico in 1839, except that Karl Bodmer, fellow Swiss artist and one who had traveled in the Americas quite successfully, encouraged him to improve his abilities first, hence the four years in Paris. In true Kurz fashion, those were four intense years. Throughout his life, Kurz wrestled with his vision of the artistic ideal and his level of technical and creative ability. His frustration with this conflict occasionally got the better of him. During one eight-month period, he worked at his craft from seven in the morning until ten at night, with only evenings and Sundays to rest. Dissatisfied with the results of all that labor, he bundled up his sketches and studies, bound them to a stone, and tossed them into the Seine.

He followed this impulsive act of destruction with a four-month sketching tour of France, which restored his artistic equilibrium and set him on a rational course of action. He regretted his rashness but learned from it: "Never again [would I] bring about by overfatigue such a wretched state of mind."[4]

Kurz returned to Bern in 1842 when his money ran out, and he secured the position of drawing instructor at a local school. After the death of its founder, the school struggled for a few years, then closed in 1846. This event, his subsequent inability to support himself with his art, and increasing political turmoil in Europe convinced Kurz that the time was ripe for him to journey to North America. In November 1846 he booked passage on the *Tallahassee* and arrived in New Orleans on Christmas Eve.

His first inclination was to begin his artistic adventure in Mexico, but the United States was at war with that nation. He saw no future in "comfortably sketching scenes in the war zone" or in waiting out the war in Texas, which friends informed him was a haven for "lawless ne'er-do-wells."[5] New Orleans did not hold his attention long, either. A brief stay convinced him that the climate was unhealthy. In addition, as a true child of enlightened Europe, he felt nothing but disgust for the practice of slavery.

He left New Orleans on New Year's Day in 1847 and went to St. Louis aboard the steamship *Amaranth*. In St. Louis, he came in contact with Alfred Michel, a Swiss expatriate and successful businessman, who invited him along on business trips up and down the river. Michel also provided employment; one venture was to manage a tavern for Michel in St. Joseph, a frontier town on Missouri's western border. Kurz remained in St. Joseph between April 1848 and the spring of 1850. During this time, he apparently managed the tavern and met Witthae, a sixteen-year-old Iowa woman, whom he married in the Indian way in January 1850. The romance was short-lived; in less than six weeks, she had returned to her people. Kurz never married again.[6]

Disappointed and disillusioned, and probably frustrated by his inability to begin a serious study of Indians, Kurz concluded his business in St. Joseph and moved north to Savannah, Missouri. He considered and discarded several schemes to get himself farther into the West, including a venture to take a herd of horses to Salt Lake City and sell them there. At the last minute, a partner who was to have accompanied Kurz changed his mind, so Kurz sold the wagon and team.

He finally resolved to go up the Missouri River by steamboat, if he could arrange passage. On May 11, 1851, Kurz left St. Joseph on board the *Sacramento*, bound for Council Bluffs, Iowa. He decided to remain there and see if he could journey upriver with one of two steamboats that made annual trips to fur trading posts in the Upper Missouri region. In Bellevue, Missouri, he stayed with trader Peter A. Sarpy and found himself "living at present in a trading house; sleep[ing] on a buffalo robe, . . . again in the midst of Indians."[7]

His luck turned on June 10, when Honoré Picotte and Alexander Culbertson (veteran agents for Pierre Chouteau, Jr., and Company), whom Kurz had met previously, arrived in Bellevue. Culbertson suggested to Kurz that he accompany them upriver on the company steamboat. He assured the financially insecure artist that there was the possibility of a clerk's position at one of the company's fur trade posts. If not, he could at least sketch Indians, animals, and landscapes and return downriver when the summer was over.

On June 16, Kurz boarded the *St. Ange* to begin his journey to the Upper Missouri. He had spent a lifetime preparing for this event. Armed with a telescope from his brothers, a sketch pad, pencils, watercolors, and his journal, the Swiss artist with classical European training and the soul of a romantic took his place in the tumultuous life of the American fur trade. His ambition was to publish an account of his experiences that would complement a series of paintings. Ironically, that journal—published long after his death—became a priceless window to a world on the edge of enormous change.

Journal of Rudolph Friederich Kurz,
1851–1852

Foreword to the Original Edition

J. N. B. HEWITT

THE ACCOMPANYING NARRATIVE Journal of the noted Swiss artist Rudolph Friederich Kurz of Bern, Switzerland, was recorded in the German language during the years from 1846 to 1852, which the author spent in the western trading posts of the great fur companies on the Mississippi and the upper Missouri Rivers, from New Orleans to St. Louis and Fort Union.

Through the interest of Mr. David I. Bushnell, Jr., a typed copy of the Journal in the German language, and a script and a typed translation of it into English by Myrtis Jarrell,* are now in the archives of the Bureau of American Ethnology, Smithsonian Institution, Washington, D.C.

The typed German text consists of 455 pages (inclusive of three supplements), large legal cap in size; the English translation of 780 pages of ordinary typewriter size (including the appendices).

The original German manuscript of this interesting Journal is now in the Historical Museum in Bern, Switzerland.

Rudolph Friederich Kurz was born in Bern, Switzerland, about January 8, 1818, and he died there in 1871. From his Journal it is learned that he had two brothers, Louis and Gustav.

Through the courtesy of the staff of the Legation of Switzerland in Washington, D.C., the following biographical note concerning Mr. Kurz has become available for use here—namely, from

---

* TRANSLATOR'S NOTE—Owing, no doubt, to omissions in the copy of the Kurz manuscript, references in the manuscript proper to certain additions in the supplements have no corresponding references on the pages of the latter, so I was unable, in every instance, to verify the references in the manuscript.

"Dictionnaire historique et biographique de la Suisse," to wit:

"Kurz, Rudolph Friederich, 1818–1871, peintre anamalier et paysagiste, vécut quatre ans chez les Indiens du Miscissippi supérieur; maitre de dessin à l'école cantonale de Berne 1855–1871; membre fondateur et premier directeur de l'école d'art.

Références:

Sammlung bernischer Biographien, volume I;

Dictionnaire des artistes suisses;

E. Kurz: Aus den Tagebucheren des Malers F. Kurz;

Volumes d'esquisses au Musée historique de Berne."

From evidence which the Journal itself supplies it appears that at least portions of it were recast and rewritten as late as the year 1856, so that his comments on events and persons of the period covered by the manuscript express his own matured opinions and observations.

Mr. Kurz witnessed a number of historically important events in the valley of the Mississippi River. While in this great western region he learned much of the final westward migration of the Mormon people resulting from the bitter hostility of the white people with whom the Mormons came in contact.

He likewise witnessed the great rush westward of the money-mad to California after the reported discovery of gold there. His comments on these events are sometimes rather caustic, but they appear to be based on his own observations. Mr. Kurz is especially critical in his remarks on the causes and the conduct of the Mexican War, which had broken out just before he reached this country.

Mr. Kurz lived at several of the great trading posts of the fur companies on the Missouri River, being occupied at times as a clerk, especially at Forts Berthold and Union, and so came into direct contact with the daily lives of the Indians, of the carefree traders, and of the officers of these trading posts.

It was this intimacy with the private lives of these several classes of people which supplied him with the data he so interestingly incorporated in his narrative, since he witnessed conditions which have long ago passed into oblivion along with the buffalo.

At all times he evinced a deep sympathy for the Indians in their struggle against the destructive encroachments of the white man, and so he willingly excused the Indians for their foibles.

Mr. Kurz indulged in severe criticism of Mr. George Catlin, the artist, even charging that Catlin did not hesitate to victimize "Uncle Sam" in the sale of his paintings.

Mr. Kurz, in explaining his presence in America, writes in his Journal: "From my earliest youth primeval forest and Indians had an indescribable charm for me." He continues: "Man's habitations spread over the whole earth; there are churches and schoolhouses without number; yet where are men found dwelling together in unity? Where does sober living prevail, or contentment? I longed for unknown lands, where no demands of citizenship would involve me in the vortex of political agitations." Continuing, he remarks: "Twelve long years I spent in preparation for my professional tour."

Such considerations, among others, moved Rudolph Friederich Kurz to leave his homeland to seek in an unknown country for the attainment of his ideals.

So, Mr. Kurz sailed from Havre on the *Tallahassee*, commanded by Captain Hoddard. His objective was Mexico, although he knew that war had broken out between that country and the United States. Notwithstanding this information, he kept on to New Orleans, under the impression that Mexico would submit as soon as General Taylor crossed the disputed boundary, the Rio Grande.

But upon his arrival in New Orleans on December 24, 1846, he learned that, according to the plans of President Polk, the war was to continue. This knowledge caused Mr. Kurz to change the field of his proposed operations. So, on January 1, 1847, he embarked from the city of New Orleans on board the steamer *Amaranth* for St. Louis, which place he reached January 17.

The editor has not felt it incumbent upon him to make any material change in the text of the Journal, except to make the spellings of tribal names in it conform to the standard of orthography adopted in the Handbook of American Indians, Bulletin 30 of the Bureau of American Ethnology. He has, however, in one or two places expunged passages reporting mere hearsay which might be held to be obnoxious to certain bodies of people. In all other respects the Journal has been left in the language of the translator, Myrtis Jarrell.

ONE　　　　　　*June 1851*

June 10—Just as I was beginning a portrait of an Omaha youth, three gentlemen came in, two of whom I knew already, William [Honoré] Picotte[1] and Alexander Culbertson.[2] They are agents in the Upper Missouri region for the great fur-trading company. The third gentleman was chief pilot of the Mackinaw boats and also a trader. I talked with Mr. Picotte about my plan to take advantage of their steamboat, if possible, to study Indians and wild animals in the regions of the Upper Missouri. He said I should be able to see little or nothing from the boat. Owing to the noise a steamer makes, animals were very shy about coming near the shore.

On a steamer I should see little more than a few gaping Indians, nothing of their woodland exploits, their dancing, or anything of their sports. He said I should have to spend two or three years at a fort to see what was really of interest concerning Indians. I knew that beforehand; however, I had not the means to take up quarters in a fort at my own expense. I asked him whether it were possible to get a position as clerk.

"I will see," he said. "In any case, come on board. If you find that you can see as much as you desire voyaging up the river, then you can return on the boat."

Mr. Culbertson will take me as far at least as Fort Benton, where the Blackfeet live.

June 11—The two agents went downstream in their boats, met the company's steamer, and accompanied it up the river. Heretofore the firm (Chouteau, Jr., & Co.) had operated their own boat, the *Assiniboin*, and, after that was wrecked by fire, the *Yellow Stone*. Since the latter was wrecked, they have had their goods transported on boats owned by other people. So far, all has gone well!

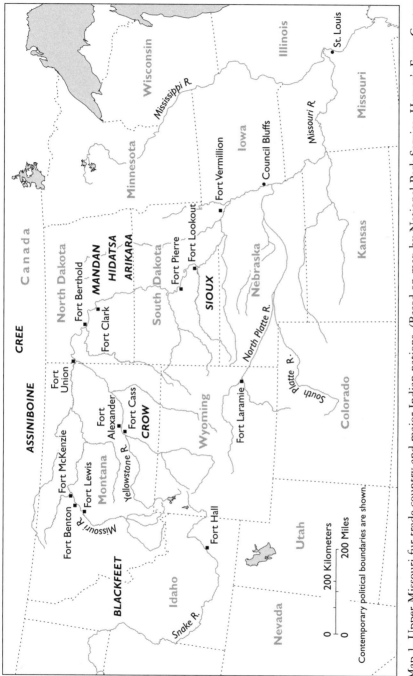

Map 1. Upper Missouri fur trade country and major Indian nations. (Based on map by National Park Service, Harper's Ferry Center, Harper's Ferry, West Virginia)

I made a portrait of Tamegache, son of the well-known Waschinga. He became lame and surrendered his claims as chief in favor of the young "Elk." I also made a sketch of Tanini, a most beautiful 14-year-old girl. She began to cry from fear (of some charm of witchcraft?). Only the promise of a calico dress could induce her to dry her tears.

June 12—I rode with Joseph La Fleche to the Omaha village and witnessed a buffalo dance around the wounded Tecumseh Fontanelle, a medicine dance to cure him. The dance of the buffalo troop was held in a large, roomy clay hut. In the most natural manner, ten dancers arranged in pairs imitated the way buffaloes drink, the way they wallow, how they jostle and horn one another, how they bellow—and all the while, the performers sprinkled the wounded man with water.

All the dancers wore decorated buffalo masks and buffalo tails fastened to their belts in the back. With the exception of the never-failing breechcloth, they were nude. A throng of people looked on. Only the "jongleur," or Indian doctor, danced alone, without mask and tail.

In the event that the captain on the company's boat that we are expecting cannot take me with him, [Stephen] Decatur[3] offered me a clerk's position at their trading post with the Pima on the Fauquicourt.[4] Sarpy's trader, Descoteaux, is there. The fact that he is a man of bad reputation makes the offer unattractive to me.

June 13—Bought all sorts of materials that I can barter on the boat for Indian relics to add to my collection. Money would be of little use in such trading, because the Indians themselves have no idea of values. All commodities at the forts farther on are very much more expensive.

June 14—Decatur told me a good joke that old [Joseph] Robidoux[5] played many years ago on Manuel Lisa,[6] a competitor of his in these parts. Both were traders with the Pawnee. Each of them tried to acquire by trade as many pelts as possible for himself, without being at all squeamish what means he employed. For that reason, they often quarreled. In order to prevent such wrangles and under the conviction that neither had the power to ruin the other, they pledged reciprocally to be "loyal"; that is, if a band of Indians arrived at their trading posts for the purpose of exchange and barter, neither would attempt to take advantage of the other.

Manuel Lisa had no intention of trading on honorable terms for any length of time. Accordingly, upon an occasion when both of them expected a band of Pawnee, he tried to circumvent Robidoux. When he ordered his post supplied in secret with commodities to barter with the Pawnee, he went over to see Robidoux, with the purpose of putting him off his guard by his own presence there to hinder preparations, and to see what was really going on in the other storehouse.

Robidoux played the part of unsuspecting host just as well as his opponent played his role, acting just as though he had really allowed himself to be duped. He invited Lisa to drink a glass of champagne to the success of the prospective trade. Regretting that on account of his gout he was not able to stoop down, he asked Lisa to fetch the flask from the cellar himself. The latter obligingly raised the trapdoor in the room and went down the steps. Joe let fall the door, rolled a cask upon it, and with mocking words left his opponent imprisoned, in order that he might trade alone with the Pawnee.

On this same occasion, I related a story to Decatur that I had often heard in St. Joseph about old Robidoux. He had a son, Joe, by his first marriage, who inherited so many building lots in St. Louis from his deceased mother that according to the current prices of city property, he was worth about $90,000.

Joe, Jr., a confirmed drunkard, gave his father a great deal of trouble, on account of his bibulous habits. Some years ago he went into the Catholic church dressed like an Indian, i.e., practically naked, to the amazement of the assembled worshippers. Being in rather poor financial circumstances because of his great number of children and his unfortunate addiction to cards, the old man took advantage of this opportunity to confine his drunken son in his cellar for several weeks as a punishment. Old Joe refused to release him until Joe, Jr., put in a favorable mood by a glass of whisky received after a long fast, signed a deed, already prepared, transferring the property to his father.

June 16, Monday—Early this morning Decatur waked [Fred] La Boue [the pilot] and me with the shout, "The company's boat!" I read the name *St. Ange* with my telescope. There were our two gentlemen, Picotte and Culbertson. The vessel came to land. A steer was slaughtered at once to provide meat for the boat's crew; the doves and cats that were to be taken to the ports were caught and put in their cages; some freight was unloaded; and I was granted my request to take advantage of the boat trip up the Missouri.

The steamer was really a hospital for victims of cholera—the sick and the dying! My cabin is filled with the effects of people who have died. My box now serves a sick person for pillow. Shall I take this risk? But the boat is already under way in midstream. "Goodbye, Decatur!" Two engagés took advantage of the boat's stop at Council Bluffs to abscond, after they had already drawn their wages in advance.

June 17—No doctor on board; two more deaths since yesterday! Evans, a professor in geology, prepared the remedy (meal mixed with whisky) that I administer. Father Van Hocken[7] bestows spiritual consolation. Father Pierre Jean De Smet[8] is also not well, but he is not suffering from cholera. The engagés drink too much whisky. The deck hands or sailors remain sober; therefore they are in good health.

June 19—In the evening we were forced by a violent tempest to lay to near Black Bird's grave. Such raging wind! Such a flood of rain! Such vivid lightning! The cages containing the doves and cats blew into the river.

June 20—Anchored the entire day on the right-hand shore, in order to renovate the boat, to air clothes in the sunshine, to take better care of the sick, and to bury the dead.

June 21—Father Van Hocken is dead. Dying as a Christian, he had been sick only two hours. It was about 4 o'clock in the morning when I was awakened by his calling me. When I found him half-dressed on his bed in violent convulsions, I called Father De Smet. We anchored in the evening and buried him by torchlight. Father Van Hocken was to have gone as a missionary to the Nez Percés. And I had not sketched his portrait for Father De Smet.

June 22—Stopped a moment at Sergeant's Bluff (Floyd's grave) to greet "La Charité" and "La Verité." This is Iowa [Indian] territory. They say a city is to be founded here later on [Sioux City, Iowa, 1854].

June 23—We travel slowly; there is no need of haste. As Louis has died, I am now installed as Mr. Picotte's clerk. I am obliged, therefore, to be up early in the morning and wake the engagés, see to the woodcutting, weigh out rations to the cooks: coffee, sugar, crackers, bacon, etc., for each day's "mess." These are my prospects for a good position. At least I get my traveling expenses free of charge.

June 25—Fort Vermilion[9] is abandoned. Schlegel, the bourgeois, came with bag and baggage on board our steamer, to proceed 60 miles farther up the river and establish a new post. His company is forbidden to sell whisky and could not, therefore, compete with trade in the nearby Iowa [Indian] territory, where whisky can be had. This is an example of the effect of civilization upon the fur trade. Civilization under the advance of the whisky flask!

June 26—The Prussian Schlegel drank all my French brandy as a preventive for cholera on the sly and became intoxicated. Mr. Picotte called me to account. Schlegel and his native mistress were put ashore with all their goods and chattels at the Isle de Bonhomme, where he intends to establish a new trading post in the land of the Sioux. Toward sunset we passed the estuary of the Rivière á Basil [Basil River], with its strikingly picturesque scenes.

There are a great many fallen trunks from which firewood can be cut. That night we stopped not far from L'Eau qui Court to have wood cut and also to put off an engagé with Mr. Sarpy's cargo. We had an unexpected visit: a troop of Ponca warriors who, in the deep shadows of the primeval woods, gave us a most welcome concert of their war songs. Then they came on board, and after an exchange of harangues, coffee was served.

June 27—Cedar Island.

June 28—We met a flotilla of laden Mackinaw boats belonging to our company. We dropped anchor. Fred La Boue assumed chief command at the wheel; he directs the course of the first boat. All of the others must follow in his wake. I saw several Indian women with their children near the helm. Their husbands are coming back again in the autumn on horseback. Most of the others remain in the States and are replaced by our engagés on the *St. Ange*.

June 29—As we were nearing Fort Lookout[10] this morning, Campbell (together with Schlegel, who had come aboard) wished to take the shortest route thither on his favorite horse, for he is a trader there. Owing to the elasticity of the long planks, however, the beautiful bay, in attempting to go ashore, fell into the water. Instead of swimming toward the land, he turned his course midstream in an effort to cross to a pasture he knew. They had to go out in a rowboat to catch him and keep fast hold until we could take him aboard the steamboat, which we were forced to land on the other side of the river.

TWO $\mathcal{July}$ 1851

July 2—While we were voyaging along the right bank this afternoon I noticed the walls of a fortification on shore. I thought at once that I had found some remains of ancient Indian origin and hastened to Mr. Picotte to question him concerning this remarkable discovery. The earthwork dates back to earlier traders, from whom the big company purchased it.

When wood was to be cut, those places in the forest were chosen principally where leafless cottonwood trees were found in great numbers. At that time I took for granted that those bare tree trunks were denuded of bark and foliage through decay due to age. [John James] Audubon[1] and [John] Bachman,[2] on the other hand, attributed that condition to another cause: one of Audubon's companions discovered that the porcupine is the evildoer. This condition had never been observed before, even by such an experienced traveler as Audubon.

July 4—We came in sight of Fort Pierre while we were at an extra lunch in honor of the Fourth.[3] After our midday meal, we reached the fort, H. Picotte's chief trading post for the Teton Sioux. Painted and decorated, a dozen braves guarded the wares that were unloaded from the ship. Most Sioux women still wear their traditional waistcloth. I sketched the fort and the settlement from the deck of the *St. Ange*. Many people and a large part of the ship's cargo were left here. A splendid bull of Devonshire breed is kept at this place for breeding purposes. He is said to have overthrown buffalo bulls more than once.

July 5—We left Fort Pierre at 10 o'clock, with the Teton warriors giving us a parting salute. For the purpose of using poles and beams for firewood, we demolished winter huts in several abandoned Indian villages. Since we no longer meet farmers along the river, we have to cut firewood ourselves and carry it aboard.

July 7—I saw buffaloes today for the first time. One hundred and eighty years ago they were still to be found in the state of Ohio! Good-by buffaloes, Indians, and fur companies. We came upon several buffalo bulls standing on a sandbank. Owing to the direction of the wind, they did not get our scent. We approached them so close that we were actually startled and gazed with eyes and mouth agape. One was killed; he ran quite a distance, however, before he fell dead. By means of a long rope he was pulled onto the deck by the engagés with a loud hurrah, and immediately quartered. I had my first buffalo steak.

July 8—Reached Fort Clarke,[4] the Arikara (Riks) village. As Mr. Picotte expected the grandees of this settlement and wished to serve them sweetened coffee and crackers when he presented gifts, I had to remain on board to issue orders, etc. In the village, Mr. P. and company were invited to partake of roasted dog as a choice dish. (I should not have exchanged courtesies.) From my station behind Père De Smet's wagon I watched what was going on there as well as at the fort and observed the people with the aid of my telescope.

Had an interesting view of about 50 girls and women bathing. As they thought themselves well concealed, they were sportive and animated in a natural way. There were several dainty figures among them—so slender yet round, so supple yet firm. How they splashed and romped behind the partly submerged tree that they thought screened them from observation.

Others dreamily dried themselves in the sun in postures and movements so natural and unrestrained, and yet with such grace! If only that dog feast had continued until night I should not have been sorry. Mr. P. was escorted back on a pony that had been presented to him. I was obliged to go down to the office and see that the Indians were properly cared for in the main cabin.

Several Mandan accompanied us to their nearby settlement. Fourteen huts, most of them empty; a poor remnant of a tribe.[5] A windstorm drove us so violently shoreward that we were compelled to halt near those huts. The boat was actually driven to the riverbank. Several Mandan and Minnetaree [Gros Ventre, or Hidatsa] remained on board and journeyed with us to Fort Berthold, which they regarded as a great favor. The village now inhabited by the Arikara belonged formerly to the Mandan. [Maximilian] Prince [of] Neu Wied,[6] spent a winter there, and [Karl] Bodmer[7] has a good drawing of it.

July 9—Early this morning Mr. P. told me that I was to be prepared to remain at Fort Berthold.[8] He had just heard that Mr. [James] Kipp,[9] the bourgeois there, wished to spend the autumn in Canada, and therefore a clerk must be left in charge. However, I might go on to Fort Union if Pierre Gareau, the half-breed interpreter, should care to take charge of the fort himself. At midday we saw from afar the white palisades of an Indian village gleaming in the sunshine.

We enjoyed a joke with our redskins on board. From the deck they could discern in the distance several members of their race whom they declared at once belonged to a hostile tribe. They began their war songs, loaded their muskets, and fired at the foe. We were rounding a neck of land or "bend," as "the lurking enemy" came bounding into view. We found them to be friends.

Commodities consigned to this post were already disembarked when I received the message to take my luggage and go ashore. The steamer departed. I remained on guard near the wares until they were taken in a two-wheeled cart to the fort. At a little distance off, shy children peered curiously from behind piles of merchandise and made comments on the strangers. In the course of time I went myself to the fort and met my new bourgeois, or chief. I had seen Mr. Kipp before in St. Joseph, Missouri, where he was trading horses. I observed him, especially, as he was leaving there for Savannah in a two-wheeled vehicle drawn by two beautiful animals.

After supper with Alexis I took possession of my new quarters: a dark room, lighted only by a tiny window, the panes of which seem never to have been washed. There was a large fireplace and two wooden bedsteads, which I found upon closer inspection to be inhabited by bedbugs. I was immediately induced to spread my buffalo robe on the floor and sleep there.

July 10—What I saw and heard today offers me a rich harvest of sketches. In the neighborhood in which I now spend my days is an Indian village of 80 clay huts surrounded by palisades and frequented by billiard players, idle lookers-on, horse traders, and Indian women engaged in daily tasks.

There are also throngs of troublesome mosquitoes; only by smoking them with "sweet sage" (*Artemisia*) can one think of getting any sleep in the house. They say this fort is always alive with Indians, except in winter, when they hunt the buffalo in surrounding regions. That is another sight that I shall enjoy.

There is little traveling to and from this post. The Minnetaree, or Gros Ventre [also Hidatsa], as they are called, never go far from their stockades for fear of the Sioux. They are too few to have the protection of different bands of their own tribe. The Indian women here plant fields of Indian corn (maize), and after the harvest, Crow Indians, a related tribe, come to the village. Now that a treaty of peace is concluded, Assiniboin also come to barter for corn—or rather, to beg. The Minnetaree are so reduced by wars and pestilence that in return for 100 buffalo hides, Mr. Kipp enclosed their habitations with palisades, so that they might be secure against surprise attacks and consequent extermination. Now no huts are visible until one has passed through the entrance to their barricade. Bellangé holds out to me the prospect of witnessing a combat, notwithstanding. He says the Sioux renew their attacks every year.

July 11—I made a trade with Bellangé for two Indian pipe bowls, seven pairs of moccasins, and other things.

July 12—The river shore was all astir after breakfast. Hunters and horses were ferried across by Indian women in flatboats made of raw buffalo hides.

One could see a shifting dark spot on the plain in the distance—buffalo. The assembled hunters had to surround them on horseback and procure fresh meat enough to last for a time. While a few of the animals might escape this danger, they would fall into the hands of the lurking Sioux. Mr. Kipp had provided his runners with excellent marksmen, who undertook the hunt for him in return for a share of the game. They came back soon, their horses laden with fresh meat. They had come upon five buffaloes apart from the herd that the huntsmen intended to surround. They selected the youngest and fattest, overcame him at once, and brought back the meat we were so much in need of. For 2 days we had had nothing at all; furthermore, only two meals a day, at 6 o'clock in the morning and 4 in the afternoon, is an order of things that brings on the discomfort of an empty stomach. In exchange for a blue blanket and a knife, I got from a Mandan a buffalo robe elaborately trimmed with vertical stripes of porcupine quills.

July 13, Sunday—In the afternoon, while I was industriously sketching, a Mandan came hurriedly into my room and begged for my double-barreled shotgun, because one of his comrades had been shot by an enemy. I refused to let him have it, as I might need the weapon myself.

I went out immediately to the village to find out what was going on and found the place like a swarming beehive. Warriors and young men in arms were hurrying across the plain; others were mounting their horses; a crowd of women was hurrying in haste from the fields where they had been grubbing [prairie] turnips; other women were going out; curious onlookers were standing in groups, eagerly gesticulating, anxiously chattering.

They said an Indian called Le Boeuf Court Queue [Short Tail Ox] had been shot by one of the Sioux. He had been at the fort about breakfast time. I wished to trade with him for an old-style tomahawk (an elliptic stone attached to a very tough dried tail of the buffalo bull). I sat on the roof of our house and scanned the village and plain with my telescope. Though it was a gable roof, it was covered with earth instead of shingles, so I could easily walk around up there.

The scene before me was most interesting: an increasing number of women and children were returning across the plain, some on horseback, others on foot, some with their sumpter (burden-bearing) beasts, others driving loaded travois drawn by dogs. Toward sunset, I saw the escort of the dead approaching. Nearer and nearer across the plain they came in a golden shimmering light that soon deepened to violet, then to gray, throwing the dark forms into relief. The nearer they came, the more dull and dead appeared the heavens, until, in the dusk of the twilight, they arrived at the village.

First came the mourning widow, leading the horse across whose back lay her dead husband wrapped in his blanket. Mourning relatives followed, encircled by restive braves whose blood was hot. Now we got some information concerning the coup. Le Boeuf Court Queue had gone with his family out on the prairie 3 miles north of the village and had lain down on the ground beside his grazing horse, while his wife and child were grubbing [prairie] turnips. Suddenly the wife was aware of something moving in the tall grass in front of her, and knowing that they were on the extreme boundary of their fields, where danger might be lurking, she called her husband's attention to it.

Bow and arrow in hand, the Mandan swung himself at once upon his horse to investigate the suspicious movement of some low bushes. Hardly was he in range of the enemy's arrow when he dropped dead from his steed. The woman screamed for help. The enemy fled without the scalp—in fact, without having touched the Mandan. The deed, therefore, is not counted a coup. To shoot a person from a distance and kill him is not regarded as a heroic act among Indians. One must scalp the person attacked. One of the five men who admit having witnessed the deed reports that the enemy took away the Mandan's swift-footed horse.

Having arrived at the burial ground, the dead warrior was taken from his horse and laid on his blanket, his head and chest raised. Relatives sat around him wailing and howling, jerking out their hair, pounding their heads with their fists, tearing their flesh with knife and arrow points until their blood flowed as sacrifice.

Friends brought blankets, garments, cloths of bright colors as funeral offerings. Meanwhile a scaffold was constructed of four stakes held together with crossbeams. Upon this structure the fallen Mandan, attired after the manner of Indian warriors and wrapped in his robe, was laid beneath the covering of a new red blanket. His medicine pouch was fastened to one of the posts. The crowd dispersed—only his widow and his mother remained to wail.

Indians on the prairie do not put their dead underground. In the first place, they have no implements suitable for digging graves and, second, the bodies would have to be buried very deep to be secure from wolves. The sight of these scaffolds erected for the dead is often horrible, even loathsome, when after a time, the wind loosens the wrappings, and crows and ravens ravage the body. Bits of putrefied flesh fall below. In the end, the posts themselves give way and the remains of the dead, once so respected, so much beloved, so deplored, lie scattered on the ground, the prey of magpies and mice.

July 15—Whenever I might be sketching in my room, the Mandan are always in the way; they never weary of smoking with their friend Alexis. The latter is here for the purpose of demanding back his horses that the Minnetaree stole, because they thought the horses were the property of the Sioux. The fact is, Alexis lives in the domain of the Sioux (Yankton) at Fort Medicine.[10] On that account and for the further reason that through his marriage with a woman of that tribe he is allied with those enemies of the Minnetaree, he will find it a difficult matter to get his stolen horses back, though he has identified them.

I see so much that is picturesque, so many striking groups that follow one another in quick succession. I wish to sketch them while the impression is fresh in my mind, but I cannot endure being so much disturbed and inconvenienced. To make matters worse, the Mandan and Minnetaree as well are extremely superstitious and look with dread upon an artist as the forerunner of pestilence and death. They regard drawing and painting as "bad medicine." This is not to be wondered at, when one considers the singular coincidences that have confirmed them in that belief.

For instance, it was the misfortune of these tribes to suffer their first epidemic of smallpox 20 years ago, when Catlin made his journey to this region. They suffered an affliction equally disastrous from cholera immediately after Bodmer's visit here with the Prince von Neu Wied. Fifteen people were carried off by cholera on our boat this year. Though in recent years no devastating pestilences prevailed, coincident with my arrival that dreadful disease made its appearance among Indians in the regions south of us. I was warned by Mr. P. even while in Belle Vue and forbidden to paint any portraits in their territory, for the reason that I should be held to account for the least misfortune.

It might be that I should have to atone with my life for any untoward occurrence and might bring upon the company, as my protectors, complications equally disagreeable. Accordingly, I had been on my guard. I had not asked any Indian to sit for his portrait but had studied them covertly and only made sketches. Despite their mistrust, they were so impelled by curiosity that they would stand in wonder before the drawings and took great pleasure in looking at them and in recognizing Père De Smet, Picotte, and Captain La Barge from some rough sketches I had made of those gentlemen without sittings.

Mr. Kipp installed me today as clerk. I was charged with the task of compiling, according to his pronunciation, a dictionary of the Mandan dialect for Colonel [David] Mitchell.[11] I kept the rough draft for myself and gave him a copy.

After supper—I cannot say what time it was—I was in my room waiting, when I heard shots and outcries in the village. A woman, who peered through the small window and saw me there, made the sign for throat cutting, across the river. The enemy upon us again already, I thought. A moment later I was on my way to the steep riverbank. A crowd was assembled on the landing below to see two skin boats come to land. Two young braves were returning with their first scalps! What exultation among the spectators! Everyone was eager to extend the first welcome. The warriors came ashore. Their faces were painted black with the exception of the tips of their noses (sign of their having performed a coup).

Immediately upon landing, they presented their weapons to those standing nearest them on shore, in token of the first congratulations. One of the bystanders so honored fastened the two scalps (there was no skin attached) to a long pole and strode into line just behind the victorious braves, singing their song of triumph. Proudly they moved forward, betraying no sign of emotion, totally unresponsive to the embraces of their people.

Before I slept I found out all the particulars about that heroic exploit. The two young Indians were 19 days on the warpath. They went as far as Fort Lookout, ostensibly on an expedition for scalps, but in reality to steal horses. They had already seized four horses when they saw two well-clothed Indian women bending over their work in a cornfield. They rode swiftly by, flying an arrow at the women, and in an instant the deed was done. The older woman attempted to draw a pistol from her belt but did not succeed, because her blanket got in the way. In her great haste she could not extricate the weapon (rash resort to a pistol had long been a matter of scorn among our Indians). As the attack was made in sight of the wigwams, the two heroes satisfied their greed for glory by scalping the unfortunate, shrieking women, and fled to their horses. They were hotly pursued and were finally obliged to abandon their stolen booty, because the horses were too much exhausted to swim across the river. The two scalps were placed beside the dead Le Boeuf Court Queue as an expiatory offering.

As a goodly number of half-breeds live in the vicinity of Fort Lookout it is possible that the two luckless women were of that caste. Judging by the good clothes and the fact that Zephir's wife is the only woman to have a pistol in her possession, one may very well suppose, as Alexis himself did, that the women must have been Zephir's wife and daughter.[12] Zephir is now enjoying a pleasure trip on the *St. Ange* in recognition of his long service as interpreter for the company. I am well acquainted with both mother and daughter. In my position here as clerk, I have had to measure out to them a great deal of coffee, sugar, etc. Quite recently the daughter bartered her white shawl for 20 pounds of New Orleans sugar. How delighted she seemed that day when she caught sight of the high-priced luxury!

July 16—The Mandan dictionary is finished—600 words. I bought some rare antiquities from Mr. Kipp: a bear's claw, a chaplet, and a crossbow made of elk horn, for which I paid $5 each. Mr. Kipp is getting ready for a journey to Liberty, [Missouri] on a visit to his white wife and children, a trip he has been undecided about for quite a while. In the meantime his Mandan wife and papooses will stay with her parents in the Mandan village.

He did not like my bringing a large trunk filled with wares for the barter trade, because he prefers to have the advantage of all profits made in that way. When he saw that I had only ornaments, weapons, and clothing, the sort of articles his company does not carry, he said no more. In fact the two gold pieces he received from me today put him in a good humor.

Heretofore he has always been brusque with me, regarding me, it seems, as the fifth wheel of a wagon. He has assigned me no work to do. Not once has he verified the receipts for goods brought on. He complained constantly about having so little to do and was sure he should die of ennui without some employment. He acted in a way I thought queer. Finally he said plainly that I would serve my purposes better at another fort. He was talking in that vein when I applied to him for work. I felt uncomfortable to see myself regarded as superfluous when I knew perfectly well how the time could be profitably spent.

Now he has decided to go. He will stay at least three months and return about the time of the first snowfall. Meanwhile Pierre Gareau will have charge of the post. That man can neither read nor write. Neither does he know how to enter sales to the Indians and to the employees on the books, nor to credit the amounts that are received. In fact, he does not know how to reckon.

At noon, just as we were going to watch the war dance around the two scalps in the village, we discerned on the horizon, beyond the distant forest, clouds of smoke ascending from the steamer *St. Ange*. The boat from Fort Union was arriving. Indian women who are engaged to carry packs of 10 buffalo robes were summoned from the dance, painted and bedecked as they were. The dance itself was interrupted. Indian women in this region carry bundles on their backs by means of broad leather bands that cross upon the breast. Iowa women carry their packs by means of bands across the brow. The difference may be due, however, to the greater weight of the burden here; 10 robes weigh at least 100 pounds.

Mr. Kipp came in utmost haste and gave over keys and books to me, with no special directions. He put on his hat and coat. The boat was already at the landing. Mr. Picotte came hurrying up to us without coat and hat and bade us bestir ourselves. He was much vexed because nothing was in readiness. The bill of lading should have been at hand when the boat landed. Without the shipping bill, either for the boat's clerk or for himself, how could he tell how accounts stood at the post? He bade me give presents to this and that Indian and charge the gifts to his account. I did not know where they were to be found.

"What have you been doing all this time?"

"Mr. Kipp would not assign me any duties."

"And yet he will go away. Has he those bills of lading himself? Where can they be?"

At that moment Pierre Gareau and his two wives came upon the scene, prepared also to go aboard the *St. Ange.* "Where in heaven's name are they setting off for?" I asked myself. Pierre informed me in passing that, if Mr. Kipp should have to stay, he was going on a visit to his kinsfolk in the Arikara village. He also gave over his keys to me. Mr. Picotte came out of the house without having found the bourgeois. The fact is, the latter's yearning for an inspiring drop or two had attracted him to the boat.

"You have a fine state of things here."

I would have liked to creep away somewhere and hide, for he was certainly right. Nothing was in order, so far as business affairs were concerned. There I stood alone, in a state of absolute unpreparedness, with all the keys in my possession. Every one else was busy either with the ship's lading or on the boat. Alexis came and told me that Bonaparte would give him back his horses, and he went away. Mr. Kipp was not going aboard, but Pierre Gareau was.

The boat has gone, and I am here for at least a year. The bourgeois says cholera in the States south of us hindered his departure. He must look after the Indians who are suffering from influenza, he says, else they might become wild. If he went to the States he might die himself. The true reason for his remaining here, however, is Mr. Picotte's dissatisfaction. He is now unpacking; comes immediately upon valuable articles, such as castoreum, which he had forgotten to dispose of. That makes him peevish.

July 18—To the accompaniment of a tambourine played by an old man, young Indian women and girls gave a dance in full dress in our courtyard. They formed an ellipse, facing one another, and with feet close together they skipped forward and back to the rhythmic call of *"eh, eh."* Their cheeks were painted red. A few wore feathers in their hair. One carried a cavalryman's sabre in her right hand. The dress of Herantsa women (Herantsa=Hidatsa) consists of their traditional shirt of deerskin or of blue-and-white-striped ticking or some other cloth made according to their ancient style.

The Crows follow the same mode. Their house dresses are usually very greasy and dirty. Their full dress shirts or smocks are trimmed with rows of elk's teeth. A hundred teeth cost as much as a good horse. This high valuation is due to their being so rare: it is well known that elk have only six incisors in the lower jaw. I am indebted to old Totano for the pleasure of witnessing the dance.

July 19—Pierre Gareau is back from Fort Clarke. He declares that the Mandan have cholera and attribute their misfortune to Pale Faces, who so frequently bring them ravaging diseases. "The whites must have buffalo robes, but the Indians can get along perfectly well without the whites." Mr. P. has bestowed bounties to appease them. P.G. has fever now. On his return journey he ran down and killed a bison, and he drank a great deal of impure water while overheated.

An Indian offered me five robes for my telescope—a good price, but I cannot spare my glass. It does me invaluable service by enabling me to enjoy scenes at a distance that I could not get a view of close at hand. Besides, being so nearsighted, I could not go out on the prairie without it, in this land where I never know what I may come upon. Furthermore, my telescope was the last gift I received from my brothers, Louis and Gustav.

The 67 Assiniboin warriors who were put across the river on Thursday, the 17th, have marched home on account of bad weather and want of shoes—most probably! They took the field against the Arikara but have come back empty-handed. I went to walk on the prairie in hope of finding a certain beautiful person. There were too many people about in the neighborhood taking care of horses. Scalps in plenty at the place of sacrifice. The

Herantsa, as the Gros Ventres call themselves (that name is foolish; they have not large paunches), are mistrustful of my sketching; they say it brings the pestilence. What would they think if they should see the scalp of one of their relatives in my possession? I should have to declare it was taken from an enemy; then they would be eager for it themselves.

Many Indians are sick—afflicted with dry cough and pains in the head. Mr. Kipp and family, P. Gareau, and others are also very ill at the fort. Only I, the evil genius ("bad medicine"), am well. My art is to blame for those deaths on the steamer. In reality, the dry cold wind that has been blowing continuously for 14 days causes this epidemic of colds. Since I came I have enjoyed only 2 warm days. Wind south, southeast, cool and brisk.

Chatted for a long while with Bellangé. He has been here many years—knows everything. He is smith, wheelwright, farmer, trapper, interpreter, and trader. He would like to take the position now held by Pierre Gareau, whom he cannot endure. If he could read and write he would be ambitious to supersede me also.

July 20—While I was making a study in my room of a droll shabby dog, Le Nain [Dwarf] came in and gave me instruction in the Herantsa dialect. I wrote down the words—sharp pronunciation even for a Dutchman. Half of our Indian huntsmen rowed across the river to get fresh meat. We have had only dried meat for several days now. Not many from the village are on the hunt; most of the people there are suffering from cold in the chest and from headache (influenza).

Bellangé related many of his adventures. His desire is to distinguish himself, especially as a beaver trapper. The fellow claims to do too much; I don't believe half of what he tells me. He says that beaver pelts will not bring $6 a pound this year. What a power fashion exerts, even in the most distant, out-of-the-way land! Now that beaver hats are no longer in vogue, the price of beaver pelts has considerably declined. There are said to be a great many of them not far from here, but trapping them is too dangerous for Indians. Besides, as the prairie so frequently swarms with warlike bands of Arikara, Crows, Cree, Cheyenne, Sioux, Assiniboin, and even with members of the Blackfeet tribe, the Herantsa [Hidatsa] dare venture out only in large numbers.

July 21—As there were few Indians about, I made sketches of their dogs, of which there is an endless number here. Most of them look like wolves.

Moreover, they do not bark but howl dolefully. If one dog begins a chorus, 100 strong immediately join him. Continuous cold rains. Our huntsmen rowed across the river. I have worse prospects than heretofore for work in the storehouse, but I will at least show good will. Bellangé gave me further instruction in the Indian sign language.

July 22—The epidemic grows constantly worse. Hardly an Indian seen outside the village. Fever patients now and then jump into the river in spite of their coughing and sweats. Kipp and Gareau complain constantly of headache, aching bones, and twitching muscles. Kipp held out no hope of my remaining immune from the disease now so prevalent. He repeated this so often that I began to believe he wished me to have influenza. It would relieve his mind to know that meals need not be cooked for me alone; if I were ill, I should have no appetite.

Again made studies of dogs. I realize more and more what an advantage it is to be so well prepared in the art that I can readily grasp characteristic features of the landscape, of animals, and of the human figure. Mosquitoes unendurable. Excessive heat, then tempest.

July 23—How fortunately I am placed! What favorable opportunities for studying the Indians! I am quite contented to have found such excellent models among the Indians. The Herantsa Wirussu are a magnificent people—the women possess little beauty of face but are splendidly formed. These Indians have a noble mien that is classic—all about me are living models of the antique. Draped with their blankets, they offer the best of subjects for the chisel. I often wish that I were a master sculptor, but then I would have to forgo the pleasure of depicting grandeur in landscape. Terrific hailstorms, in the midst of which these red children eagerly rush out and gather the hailstones, as many as possible, in order that they might have clear, cool water to drink. That is a luxury here, where one is dependent upon muddy, lukewarm water from the Missouri.

July 26—The 2 days just past were of absorbing interest. A dozen Metisse de la Rivière Rouge (half-breeds from the Red River) arrived with a Catholic missionary. They wanted horses, either in exchange or by purchase. They had come from their large settlement, a day's journey from here. All were dressed in bright colors, semi-European, semi-Indian in style. Tobacco pouches, girdles, knife cases, saddles, shoes, and whips were elaborately decorated with glass beads, porcupine quills, feather quills, etc., in an artistic work done by their wives and sweethearts, but their clothes were of European rather than western cut.

The young priest, Father Charles Lacombe, began to preach. At once, he found much with which to reproach us. Mr. Kipp, living here with squaw and children, had a white family in the States. His half-breed son was not baptized. P. Gareau, living here with two squaws, was sire of several children equally regenerate. Bellangé has a troop of half-breed offspring not yet baptized. As for me, I was not a Catholic. Things were in a sad state. Every one of the children must be christened forthwith. And that was the utmost thing that he accomplished. He was told that the conditions under which a man had to live in this region were not his concern; white women would not live here. As the black-robed priest was quartered in my room, I did not escape a lecture. I cut him short, however, with the remark that there was too wide a divergence of opinion concerning such matters and too great a difference in age and experience between him and me to justify his calling me to account. When he found out that I was not a Romanist, he refused to sleep in the same room with me. Went to his flock encamped outside.

The priest was sent here by the Bishop of Chicago for the purpose of founding a mission. He wishes to begin that work, but if he desires success, he must not set out by antagonizing respectable people whose support in this place he must necessarily depend upon.

I found a smith among those half-breeds who had whisky in his possession. P. Gareau drank until he was intoxicated, then began insulting and fighting everybody who refused to drink with him. He attacked Indians as well as others, pulled off his shirt, and was of a mind to go into the village and challenge his enemies (members of the opposition) to combat. He was stopped by the soldiers (highly respected braves entrusted with the duty of keeping order in the village or settlement) and brought back. Then I shut the gate.

Now these Metisse are half Chippewa and half Canadian, Scotch—even Swiss—from an earlier colony of Lord Selkirk's.[13] Early this morning we received news that a band of Sauteurs (Ojibwa, Chippewa) would come from their settlement and make us a visit. The Ojibwa who used to live in the region of Sault Ste. Marie were called Sauteurs. Finally, after all members of the group had their festive array in order—according to Indian custom that is of the highest importance—they emerged from a grove of trees and marched forward toward us. There were perhaps a hundred of them, some in trappings of war, some on foot, while others, on horseback, flanked the column.

Five chiefs formed the vanguard, carrying ornamental peace pipes, or calumets, and prominently displaying their trophies in recognition of "coups." The soldiers marched behind them in platoon formation, singing martial airs, beating the drum, and firing their guns. Upon occasions of visits on the part of Indians, the firing of a volley from their muskets to announce their arrival betokens that they come on a mission of peace. Then came three women dressed in one of the several costumes worn by Indians in this region: a skirt of blue cloth that extends to the shoulder and is held in place by 2 broad bands or supporters over the shoulders and a girdle about the hips, both girdle and bands elaborately decorated. Last in the procession came a chorus of young men who had not yet won distinction for themselves.

Behind the fort, Quatre Ours [Four Bears], the Herantsa chief, and La Longue Chevelure [Long Hair], the celebrated speaker, awaited their coming. Both chiefs looked particularly self-satisfied in their black dress coats. They wore black suits, European in style, without the traditional shirt or smock, but with breech-cloth. They wore long hair, no gloves, and they carried fans made of eagle feathers. When they came up, the Sauteurs paused long enough to hear the speaker's address of welcome. Then singing together they withdrew with swift, proud step to the village and sat down in an open space on a narrow strip of dry ground that bordered what at that time was nothing more than a large, ill-smelling pool of slime inhabited by thousands of frogs.

The five chiefs laid their pipes on the ground in front of them in such a way that the pipe bowl pointed to the hut occupied by Quatre Ours and the stem to a wooden fork stuck upright in the earth nearby. The pipes were not lighted. Magnificently ornamented articles of clothing were brought to the chiefs and laid on the ground in front of their pipe bowls. The garments were for the most part so-called *habits de Cheffre*, i.e., sort of gay-colored military coats of red, blue, or green cloth and shirts of soft white deerskin, either laced or richly embroidered with colors.

There were no presentation speeches, but much dignity of port. There was continual singing during this performance. I had more than enough of it. As I wished to make purchases from those half-breeds I betook myself to my room, where I bartered for some beautiful work at a reasonable price, according to what the same articles would bring today.

The Sauteurs overtook that Sioux who shot Le Boeuf Court Queue and killed the man and his wife. The woman was so tired she could go no farther. The man remained with her, while the other three took to flight, riding the horse in turn.

This evening the Sauteurs are off to pitch their camp farther on and hunt buffaloes—*courir la vache*, as the Canadians say. One of the Metisse brought a white buffalo robe to sell and received two good racehorses in exchange. Such a skin is very valuable, for white or dappled buffaloes are very rare. There are sometimes crossbreeds that are said to be very large, splendid animals.

July 27—The Metisse have also taken their departure. Our Indians are over the river again to ensnare buffaloes. As soon as they catch sight of the animals in the distance the "soldiers" assemble in their hut (so-called assembly lodge), to consider whether they will go on the hunt. A crier reported their decision from the lodge. Nobody is allowed to take his own course contrary to the decision of the "soldiers" on the buffalo hunt, because, according to the rules of the sport, everyone is to enjoy equal opportunities.

I bartered a plug of tobacco to the Metisse for a beautiful bridle; a plug of tobacco and a pound of candy kisses for a knife of odd design with a broad, tapering blade, together with its embroidered sheath; a red coverlet for a most beautifully ornamented pouch and whip; a pound of coffee and a pound of candy kisses to the Sauteurs for a feather ornament; a knife for a boy's tomahawk; and from Bellangé I got six pairs of children's shoes, three pairs of larger moccasins, one pair of gloves for winter lined with beaver, and two *ceintures* [sashes].

July 28—All the talk of this day is about the disappearance of the young and beautiful wife of Nez d'Ours [Bear's Nose], one of our "soldiers," i.e., one of the braves who are entrusted especially with the protection of the fort and never allowed any transactions with the opposition.

While he was bartering with the Metisse during their stay here for the white buffalo robe, a young Mandan buck took advantage of the opportunity to escape with this young woman in a buffalo boat to the Mandan, who live near the Arikara village. The girl is hardly fifteen years of age, rather small, to be sure, but beautiful, graceful, and to all appearances modest and unassuming in manner. The elopement of a wife with her lover is a dangerous venture, but nevertheless frequently occurs. However much he may care, Nez d'Ours must treat the matter lightly, else he will be scorned by his comrades as an unworthy brave. At the same time, he has the right to demand the return of all gifts and horses that he had bestowed for his unfaithful wife, as well as all that the young Mandan possesses, if he has anything at all, and to give the latter a sound flogging whenever the opportunity is offered.

In the presence of several Herantsa I killed a young chicken snake that had the evident intention of crawling about the floor under my bed. Hardly had I struck the reptile when one of the Indians fell in my arms and indicated to me that it was for his medicine (talisman). Then he slowly picked it up with two sticks and carried it solemnly to the door. Had the Indian brought the snake into the room? Be that as it may, his superstitious belief had received a rude shock. Chicken snakes are not venomous; neither are they very often seen. In St. Joseph I saw an unusually large one, 6 feet long, with a body 2½ inches in diameter. Once one of the Iowa came to me wearing a dried snakeskin of this sort around his neck, the head and tails of which were decorated. I purchased it just as a curiosity.

July 29—This evening the steamer *Robert Campbell* arrived, bringing commodities for the opposition's company (Primeau, Harvey, and Joe Picotte). Their fort is situated on the other (eastern) side of the village. The boat has gone farther up the river again. It left St. Louis on the 2nd of July and had met the *St. Ange* on the way at Fort Pierre. Last year, the *St. Ange* made the voyage from St. Louis to Fort Union and back in 32 days. This year, two months were necessary. Why? Because $100 a day is charged instead of a fixed sum for the entire trip.

Mr. Kipp is talking again of his desire to travel on the *Robert Campbell* to St. Louis. The old man does not know what he wants to do. At last it occurred to him to unpack his goods and examine them. Summer is not the season for trade in furs. Animals shed their hair or fur at that time; their coats are thick and beautiful only in winter. If I am to remain here, I shall have a great deal of free time for my studies. The bourgeois says he must go to Canada and attend to some pressing business with his two sisters. That arrangement would require my remaining here a year at least. In the meantime I should learn the Herantsa dialect and become acquainted with the people and the business. Perhaps I might remain here altogether, or at another post.

I should have to order my effects that I left behind in St. Joseph sent on to me; otherwise I should lose them. I am not conscious of the least yearning for so-called cultured societies. Here one lives much more at ease, is more free than in the civilized States. The so-called savage is not always disputing about the teachings of religions, about political matters, the rights of man, etc., principles concerning which men should have reached some uniform understanding long ago. With the savage, the sound sense with which Nature endowed him has settled all such matters. Cursing, quarreling—such as one hears constantly among us—is never heard among the Indians. Let one but look on when they are playing billiards; the strokes are so nearly equal, the game so close, that the players themselves cannot easily decide which one wins (and they always play for a stake, oftentimes quite high). They then appeal at once to the bystanders as arbiters. There is no swearing, no contention—they lack even expressions for such. Furthermore, insult would inevitably bring definite results: deadly revenge from the person insulted, involving even bloodshed and death. With us, affairs of honor are either passed over without punishment or satisfaction is demanded at great cost; the duel is forbidden.

I exchanged two good linen shirts with Pierre Gareau for a most beautiful saddle pad. While I was taking a walk on the prairie today, I met a number of interesting children playing in groups near their grazing horses. Several little girls, who had made a shelter from the blazing sun with their blankets, were singing to the rhythm of drumbeats and tambourines. Their song practice soon enticed one of the boys who were also guarding horses, and he taught a little dwarf to dance. Quite frequently, I saw small boys at their first shooting practice. With grass stalks for arrows they aimed at the leaping frogs and, when they hit the mark, laughed with delight to see the little white-bellied creatures turn somersaults in their swift movements to escape.

July 30—Today Mr. Kipp gave me a packet of newspapers that he had received by boat. The dissension and discord in Europe sicken me. How peaceful life is here!

THREE

August 1851

August 1—Children come frequently to see me, now that they know I gave several of them sugar. My tiny window is often quite filled with cheerful faces that watch me and entreat for *"mantsiqua"* (sugar) as I write or sketch. A girl of 14 crops up repeatedly; she attracts my notice more than the others because her hair is entirely gray, and this, with her young, pretty face, gives her an extraordinary appearance. Gray hair is said to be quite general among the Mandan—a sort of family misfortune, not due to severe illnesses.

In this village, men set more value on personal adornment and good appearance than do the girls. They take especially good care of their hair and may even wear false hair glued to their own, but that is done only by those men who are accredited with "coups." The hair of the Herantsa Indians is not smeared with grease and has therefore a rough, reddish brown look. The men wear their hair either hanging loose or coiled in a knot above the brow. La Longue Chevelure, as his name implies, is distinguished by his own unusually long hair. I saw him only once when he allowed it to hang down, and that was the time he delivered the address to welcome the Sauteurs. He wore black clothes throughout and a black hat—not even a white shirt. He let his hair loose over his dress coat. In fact, aside from a uniform, Indians think that black clothes, such as are worn by the President of the United States, are most fitting for ceremonial occasions.

Since Indian women are accustomed to the nudity of Indian men and look upon that condition as in the nature of things, to be taken as a matter of course, no immoral effect is produced on them; while the men, who have opportunities all the time to see naked women, children, and girls in bathing, are just as little affected. It is certain that half-concealed nakedness excites the senses more than a completely nude condition. They regard clothes as protection from sun and weather. Girls go naked even to their third year; boys, to their sixth. Often both are also sucklings at that age.

August 4—Between 9 and 10 o'clock, the *Robert Campbell* returned from Fort William.[1] Mr. Kipp did not leave on that boat, although he has often spoken of going. The old man does not know what he will do. Mosquitoes are still unendurable; unless a man wears clothes of deerskin, they drive him raving mad. Unless one makes a Hades of one's room every evening, one cannot possibly sleep at all. Do these pests prefer the blood of a white, unsmoked body?

August 7—The weather is getting cooler again. One is already sensible of the lengthening of the evenings and the nights. I long for the winter, that I may observe the hunting in this region. Such a little adventure would not be undesirable, as a variation from my usual life here.

August 8—Have been thinking much about the past—how much I have endured. My aims are nearer their fulfillment. At last we began unpacking and verifying commodities consigned to this post.

August 10—For some time I have been occupied with the thought of painting an especially beautiful buffalo robe, but not with the intention of depicting my "coups." On the contrary, I will paint thereon Indian scenes in my own manner. Today I have the plan complete: across the robe at the top, an Indian village; below, a fort; on one side at the bottom, the outstanding periods in the life of an Indian brave, from youth to old age; on the other side, the life of an Indian woman; in the center, "coups" of my heroes. Heroic exploits and adventures of my heroes will include, necessarily, the most important wild animals of the chase. Not a bad idea!

I gave an order to Pierre Gareau for a complete and whole hide of a buffalo bull, including the head, tail, and legs. Such hides as that rarely come into trade for the reason that, on account of their size and thickness, they are too difficult for the women to handle. Furthermore, such hides cost as much as three of the usual size, because the hunter, when flaying the animal, has to be so extremely careful that twice the usual amount of time and trouble is required. Bellangé is of the opinion that a buffalo hide may offer good material on which to sketch, if it is shaved perfectly smooth. Perhaps that is true of cowhide, but the hide of a buffalo bull?

August 11—A cool, brisk wind from the west this afternoon has considerably lowered the high temperature of the morning. Yesterday I swapped coffee and sugar with a young girl for a queer sort of embroidered needle case. Today the same girl brought a friend with her who had what seemed to be a bodkin case; I swapped with her also. The girls wore these as ornaments pinned on the front of their deerskin shirts.

I passed the time bartering goods I had brought with me for objects of Indian make. I gave a bolt of calico to Pierre Gareau for a man's buckskin shirt, elaborately ornamented, and a woman's shirt-dress made of two whole bighorn pelts; each of these, at the current price, was valued at $12. Bellangé's Assiniboin wife will supply me with a similar garment, made more simply and untrimmed, for 18 pounds of coffee. From Bellangé himself I bought a pair of ornamented trousers made of buckskin, for $10. They are cut according to European mode and trimmed in Indian fashion. Finally, I received six beautiful arrows from Mr. Kipp for my elk-horn bow. I gave him a flask of cherry brandy in return, and two pounds of candy kisses for his Mandan woman. I shall probably pay the further price of a sleepless night, due not only to my joy in my new possessions but to the possession, on the part of the boss and his wife, of the flask of cognac!

Ugh! How the rain pours.

August 13—Toward sunset yesterday I heard an outcry from the direction of the village, followed, as usual, by the howling of all the dogs. Everything was in commotion. I hurried to the gate, curious to know what was going on. The trouble was that someone from Yankton had carried off four horses belonging to an old Crow Indian. He could not find them anywhere. In a trice, young braves, mounted and armed, were galloping across the prairie. By the time they reached the forest, night had fallen; it was impossible to follow any trace. Until late at night they were heard singing and firing off their muskets as they returned home. Today they say the horses have been found. Only a little excitement for the Indians and me. There has been rain and nothing but rain this entire day.

August 14—La Grande Chevelure [Great Hair] paid me a visit today, bringing one of his friends with him. With signs, he entreated me to open my sketchbook for them, that they might see with their own eyes and decide whether my sketches were really the cause of the sickness so prevalent among them. Owing to the absence of Quatre Ours, who is with Mr. Culbertson and the Assiniboin chiefs at Fort Laramie,[2] La Grande Chevelure is now chief of the Herantsa.

He is distinguished for his intelligence as well as for his gift of eloquence; Quatre Ours is accredited with more "coups," having 14 to his account. La Grande Chevelure finds in my drawings nothing in the least to warrant suspicion. He will talk with his people.

He is a middle-aged man of dignified and imposing presence, with fine eyes, a well-arched chest, and small hands. He usually wears an old buffalo robe and carries an eagle wing for a fan in his hand. His breast and arms have tattoo marks. As president of the council he is regarded as the most notable personage in the village, and as the war chieftain of Quatre Ours, he is most influential.

While he was looking at my drawings I studied his interesting features, and as soon as he left, I immediately made a sketch of him from memory. I must get a more exact likeness. Here with Mr. Kipp, I shall have the opportunity to do that, for I can see him almost daily. Of the two chiefs he is superior to Quatre Ours, who is not distinguished for personal force and valor. By the way, Quatre Ours has a perfectly beautiful wife, with the most finely chiseled features that I have seen for a long time.

August 15—I hear daily that Schmidt, the bourgeois at the opposition company's trading post, dins into his children's ears continually that the great company brings among them all the devastating diseases so prevalent and that the painter is especially to blame, for all those whom he sketches fall ill. That is perfidy, pure and simple, and may in the end place me in a most undesirable situation.

What will trade envy not contrive! A girl of doubtful character stole my last Regensburg pencil from me today. She committed the theft in revenge because I was indifferent to her. This is the second time articles belonging to me have been purloined by women. The pencil with which I made sketches was "medicine" for the Indian woman.

Pierre Gareau put me on my guard concerning "the blonde," i.e., the gray-haired girl, because he sees her so frequently here and she is said to be married. She is certainly not yet 14 years old, and already a wife. Indian girls in America mature at a very early age. I know Creoles in St. Louis who were married at 14; one, in fact, at 11 years old. Her husband (Marey) played the role of doctor when the Americans occupied Santa Fe [1848]. The gray-haired girl belongs to an old man who brought her up in order to have about him a young, invigorating person. If he finds out anything about our

relations, he may rightly claim all that I possess, and I may indeed be satisfied if that is all he demands. A jealous man, really outraged in his love,
might make an attempt upon my life. For me, that would be a pleasure
dearly bought. In reality, perhaps this is a trap the old sinner lays for me,
after having seen the contents of my boxes not long ago. Who would have
thought that so young a girl could be his wife?

I have not sought its companionship hitherto, but this fragrant blend
pleases me well. My pipe will not get me into trouble. And as I am for
politeness' sake to smoke with men who visit me, I can also resort to the
same means of passing the time when alone.

August 16—The wife of La Longue Chevelure is suddenly dead from
cholera, I am told; she suffered violent spasms of colic and vomiting. Is it a
coincidence that cholera should first make its appearance here now, just after
we have opened those bales of goods that we brought with us?

Mr. Kipp says that heretofore, the attacks were caused by the eating of
too much unripe fruit, by that ill-smelling pond in the midst of the village,
and by breathing stagnant air confined within the stockades, through which
the wind never blows freely. Hot sun and cold wind may be the cause of
some illnesses. On the other hand, Schmidt tells the superstitious Indians
they have cholera, a disease they have caught from the great fur-trading
company. I am inclined to believe that Schmidt is right this time; the conditions I have mentioned above would produce cholera any time.

Bellangé seems moody. On one evening he cannot have enough of relat-
ing his adventures and will talk to me until late at night; on another day, he
will not say a word. It is a matter of indifference to me; besides, it is not for
one in my position to be familiar with him and pay no attention to my chief.
Day before yesterday he was quite content to conclude some advantageous
bargains with me; yesterday he hardly recognized me, for fear, most likely,
that I might decide not to trade. Today he wishes my double-barreled shotgun at any price. As long as I live in this region, however, I cannot let him
have my gun. He offered me just such a buffalo head as the most famous
warriors appear in when they perform the buffalo dance. He will, however,
have great difficulty in getting one, for they are very highly prized; so he
must himself order such a head made ready for me by his Assiniboin wife.

All at once Bellangé has a desire to learn reading and writing, in order
that he may, in the course of time, displace P. Gareau and perhaps steal a

march on me. He says I can see all that is of interest to me here in one year; every year is merely a repetition of those gone before. Skirmishes and affrays will most likely end once and for all when these Indians agree to the treaty with Uncle Sam. Oh yes, I smell the rat!

August 17, Sunday—This recent epidemic is getting the upper hand—not a day goes by but somebody dies in the village. The Indians have such a dread of the disease that they have determined to hurry away to the hills. They would like to take their families with them and live in the huts they build for the summer on the Knife River. This would afford me an opportunity to sketch the village as well as the place of sacrifice and Indian catafalque. Take advantage of everything, even that which is unfortunate.

August 18—Diable! I am confined to the house! At 9 o'clock this morning, Mr. Kipp came and begged me to put my drawings away, to allow no Indian to see them ever again. They talked in the village of nothing but my sketches. I immediately put them under lock and key; then I went out to help Reith, one of our engagés, with the tedding of hay.[3]

Soon Le Corbeau Rouge [Red Raven] came to me and, with signs, made me understand that I was to go to my room and stay there. He said that my looking at everything and writing down what I saw was the cause of so much sickness and death in the village. His signs were unmistakable. I replied that though he was a most highly esteemed brave, he was no chief, least of all my chief, i.e., he had no authority over me. Nevertheless I went later to the bourgeois, who said my own safety demanded that I remain in my room, or at least inside the fort.

The entire blame for the cholera epidemic was cast upon me. Relatives of some of those who had died were exasperated, almost frantic, and when and where I least expected it, an arrow might pierce my ribs. While the trading company would not regard it as a matter of principle to revenge an injury done me, by exposing myself to danger I should, if attacked, be the cause of much disturbance and ill feeling. He might forbid their eating raw pumpkins, turnips, berries, and green maize as much as he liked, but superstition was deeply rooted in the Indians. The old wives were constantly telling of earlier cases that they could account for in no other way than in the remarkable coincidence of my having sketched portraits of the persons dead. In doing that, I had necessarily taken away their life, otherwise the drawings could not be such exact likenesses. His supplies of medicine had aroused their anger. I hope all of them will go up on the plateau; otherwise I shall be obliged to leave, sooner or later.

Traveling down the river alone in a buffalo-hide boat would be most romantic, it is true, but since the Arikara and Mandan are even more incensed against me than the tribe here, such a venture would be too dangerous. I have some friends to defend me here, but there I have none. Once I was on the river, the Arikara would receive news of it before I could reach there and would watch for me.

I no longer have the least doubt that the disease is really cholera. I doubt just as little that this outbreak of the epidemic is due to the opening of those bales of goods that were packed in St. Louis while cholera was raging there. That I did not catch the infection in St. Joseph, on the *St. Ange,* nor yet here I ascribe less to regular diet than to lack of fear and, most of all, to a happy frame of mind due to my having realized the aims for which I took the journey: to the joy of being at the work I had long desired to do.

After dinner I told Mr. Kipp that I was ready to leave at once if the interest of the company or his own interest, in particular, made my departure advisable. All right, he said, but wait a week longer and see whether the disease spreads or not. It is to be hoped that out on the open prairie the epidemic will lose its force. In that event, nothing more will be said.

If the worst comes, then something can be done at once, if I hold myself in readiness. In any case, I am not to go outside the fort. If I do, he has no means either to protect me or to avenge an attack on my life. The sick who were left behind will by-and-by recover or they will die. In either case, the people who are taking care of them will go away, and I shall again enjoy liberty. Let us have a smoke; time brings good counsel. I find it strange that cholera broke out here for the first time upon unpacking those bales of goods, yet the same disease was prevalent sometime before among the Arikara south of us. At least none of the boats had anyone on board suffering from cholera when they landed either at Fort Clarke or at this place.

August 19—The wind has shifted from east to west-southwest; it brought us fine cool weather. The sick people are better; those in good health and the convalescent are going away. In violation of orders and against my own conscience, I yielded to the desire to draw. The morning was so insufferably long; it was hard to endure the thought of having to leave the fort, to say adieu to the Upper Missouri, perhaps even in the next hour.

Quickly I drew the water tub against the door, and through my grimy windowpane I made some sketches of the interior of the fort. A large tub filled with water is kept in all of the rooms that are occupied, for daily use and also as a means of protection in case of fire. There are neither fountains nor cisterns at the forts. Once when Mr. Kipp, the bourgeois, went on a visit to the Blackfeet, his fort burned down. Water is brought from the turbid Missouri, which is within easy distance of the fort, yet too far away to supply water without the aid of a fire-engine hose. This lack of water near at hand would be much more serious in time of war, because most of the forts are on heights and can be cut off from all approaches to the river without the least difficulty.

My two sketches finished, I put everything very quickly in place again. Le Loup Court Queue [Short Tail Wolf] comes with his nephew to ask that they sleep in my room in order that they may not have to see his mother die. He may have no fear of me, but he asked with signs whether I were sick. Did I cough? Have violent pain? Convulsions?

Made a drawing of the inner construction of a skin boat. Catlin tries to prove from the similarity of these boats to the Irish coracle that the Mandan derive their origin from Madoc's colony.[4] That this boat made of buffalo hides belongs peculiarly to the Mandan is just as unlikely as that winter huts are of Mandan origin. All Indians who dwell on the prairies make use of skin boats on account of the scarcity of wood.

What Catlin calls blond hair among the Mandan is nothing more than sun-burned hair that is not continually smeared with grease. Black horses become somewhat brown if they are not well cared for and are exposed to all kinds of weather. I may mention, also, that the lighter color of some Indians' skins (not only Mandan) is easily traced to the "whites."

August 20—Of all the occupants of the fort, only Reith and I are in good health. When he went after stovewood, I assisted him with the flatboat, with loading the carts, and with the bags, as he brought the loads up the steep riverbank. Mr. Kipp consented unwillingly to my serving as clerk. I replied to him, according to his own statement, that with nothing to employ my time, I should become peevish and ill. I told him I had expected to be of some service here, not to live as a lord. He assured me that he understood perfectly well and that I should soon find quite enough to do, when he went away. In winter, moreover, I am accustomed to have a horse at my service, by the hour, so that I can take part in the hunt and extend my opportunities for observation and study.

My willingness to remain here disposed him so far toward liberality that he added what he had neglected to mention, that if I should get hungry between meals I was only to go into the kitchen and order something to eat. That may be done. The married engagés receive so much meat for their families and they always find time to eat this during the interval between meals, while I have nothing at all from 6 o'clock in the morning to 2 o'clock in the afternoon, a condition which my empty stomach often cries out against in protest.

Mr. Kipp speaks of undertaking a journey to the States on horseback in the autumn. Not at all probable.

Our courtyard is crowded with old men and women who were unable to go along when the others departed. Concerning their age, they can estimate at least that they are certainly more than a hundred years old. I would better say a hundred winters, because they can reckon more easily by snows that have fallen. They do not attempt to count more than 60 or 70 years, for they have not the least interest in knowing their exact ages. These old crones are disagreeable creatures. I look upon them as sentinels; each possesses, unfortunately, one or more pet dogs—some young, some old—that make the night hideous with their continual howls. Sleep is impossible. Bill, the cook, rose up in his wrath and sent an arrow through the body of one of these canines and then threw him over the palisades. That rash act made an enemy of the old woman; she is now quarreling unceasingly about us.

Toward evening Jim Hawkins, a Negro from Fort Union, arrived here. Mr. Culbertson intended at first to take him as cook to Fort Laramie but left him behind temporarily at Fort Union, where he was also obliged to serve as cook. He says Dennik [Denig], the bourgeois there, is a hard man, liked by nobody, not even here. He keeps two Indian wives, Jim says, and squanders all that he has on them; he begrudges anything paid to the employees, oppresses the engagés with too much work, is never satisfied, etc.

Jim ran away, taking a boat that belonged to the great company. He must have related his story to Mr. Kipp with highly pleasing embellishments, for the latter put him in the kitchen forthwith and sent Bill, who has been our cook hitherto, to the hayfield.

At one time, Jim was in the employ of Mr. P. A. Sarpy in Belle Vue, where I knew him quite well. He squandered all that he earned there on old immoral Indian women; consequently he could not be kept longer. He is really someone's slave in St. Louis and is required to pay a certain sum to his master every year; the balance of his wages he may spend as he likes. It is true he is free here, but the company must be responsible, more or less, for his life.

Jim had bad luck today on the Missouri. Having been already nine days on the river, his provisions were exhausted. He was obliged to go hunting but dared not trust himself far from his boat, so shot nothing. He found instead an abundance of wild cherries and carried a goodly portion to his skiff. This morning, in perfect ease of mind, he was gulping down one handful after another, stones and all, when his boat struck a snag ("*gigot*" in French) and was upset, throwing him, his stolen booty, and his rifle into the water.

Luckily he swam to the shore on this side of the stream. After shaking his wet clothes and looking sorrowfully but in vain for his lost belongings, he was then obliged to work his way through a wood full of bogs, from which he emerged at last on a hill and saw in the distance the glimmer of something bright. He rightly took that to be our palisades and wandered on in this direction.

La Queue Rouge [Red Tail], my language teacher, comes along with Le Loup Court Queue to share my room with me. Just for the fun of the thing, he put on a superb military cap adorned with all sorts of horns and plumes in order that I might have a model for a sketch. His friend wrapped a costly mantle of otter skin about his bare legs, which made a sorry appearance in conjunction with his richly ornamented leather shirt and the imposing headgear. At first I was reluctant to make a sketch of La Queue Rouge. I asked him whether he was not afraid of falling ill. What was I talking about? He laughed at the idea of such a thing! Extraordinary, what different views these people take. I wonder, did he wish merely to give proof of his bravery, his fearlessness?

August 21—Le Loup Court Queue has gone. The only men from the village now left here are La Queue Rouge and a brother of Quatre Ours; the former is nursing back to health his convalescent wife, who is so weak she can scarcely stand. Her fever rages to such a heat that she wears no clothes at all.

After she had lain perfectly nude for a long while today on her buffalo robe in the shadow of the palisades, she wished to come alone into the courtyard. Fortunately I met her just as she grew dizzy from weakness and was about to fall. I assisted her to her relatives in the courtyard. Two more people have died in the village (one of them the mother of my language teacher), else I might make a sketch of the settlement. I will steal away to the river shore instead and sketch the boat landing, the watering place, and the bathing pool.

Jim was tortured today by cherry stones. He suffered so terribly from griping pains and cramps that he lay down across the corner of a packing case in the courtyard, then fell to the ground, writhing like a wounded animal. He was relieved by means of a very strong emetic.

August 22—There is no fresh meat since our Indians went away. We have only cured meat. I am entirely dependent for what I have to eat upon the mood of the bourgeois. Though P. Gareau is keeper of the meat house, I am less dependent upon his humor, for the reason that he orders his two wives to cook what he likes. If Mr. Kipp has a good appetite he searches for the best of everything in the storehouse and we live in luxurious abundance, such as one would not dare expect in these wilds.

On the other hand, if he is not well, he assumes at once that the rest of us need no more to eat than he does. A short while ago we were served a heavy soup with rice or beans, excellent rib roast, fresh griddle cakes, buffalo tongue, and in addition, cakes with dried peaches or apples. Now, a sudden change of menu: cured meat and hard crackers—so hard that in an attempt to bite one, a man can easily break his teeth. Nothing more.

August 23—Dorson and Beauchamp of Fort Clarke arrived here. Those women killed at Fort Lookout were in reality Zephir's wife and daughter. For 30 years Zephir had lived happily with his wife. The Yanktonai will avenge that deed when the Herantsa and Mandan are on the chase next autumn. They would find the present their best chance to wreak vengeance, but even Sioux are afraid of contagion.

Today has been the hottest of the entire summer. All the mosquitoes and flies in the village have come over here for what they can find to nourish themselves. Neither by day nor by night do we get any relief from mosquito choruses and mosquito bites; furthermore, the pests bring the stench of the village slough with them.

Aged Indians and the sick are encamped in front of our fort in tiny huts constructed of boughs and twigs. They make use of these shelters at the same time for taking their vapor baths. They produce steam by heating stones red hot in a great fire prepared in front of the huts. Then, having tightly closed the one they wish to use, they carry the stones inside and pour water upon them. As soon as they have converted the place into a sweating box at a high temperature, the sick people (sometimes those in good health also take vapor baths) crawl naked into the midst of the heat and steam, whereupon a profuse perspiration ensues. Indians think this is highly conducive to health. It appears to be their only treatment for cholera—at least, I have heard of no other remedy—and yet all their cholera patients have not died.

For want of other medicine, Mr. Kipp served out small doses of whisky at first. His supply was soon exhausted, for the reason that he is so very fond of that remedy himself (greatly to his own hurt, for he has had already the chance of two fortunes and of being regarded a rich man in the States but has ruined himself by immoderate drinking).

Our surroundings have the appearance of a hospital—eight decrepit old women squat beside one another in the sunshine along by the palisades, pick off the lice from their bodies, and eat the flesh of wild animals with relish. The young sister-in-law of Quatre Ours lies naked in a corner of the bastion, while her husband continually goes to and fro, bringing her fresh water from the river. A blind girl, convulsed with cramps, pounds her abdomen with her fists in an effort to get rid of the dreadful pain. I met her today tottering along the palisades toward the gate. Suddenly she sank to the ground and I hurried forward to lift her up, wrap a buffalo robe about her nude form, and carry her inside the fort. Her body seemed to me of too bright a color for "pure Indian." If an old woman dies, there is nobody to bury her except ourselves. We have already sent two down the river in perforated skin boats, left there to go to the bottom.

August 24—Another aged woman is dead. She starved herself to death because she saw that she was a burden to her family. Though she did not lack food, she obstinately refused to eat. This hospital of ours, our fare of dried meat, and the mosquitoes prove too distasteful to Dorson and Beauchamp; they intend to leave this morning.

August 26—Have made a sketch of the great place of sacrifice dedicated to the sun and moon. A painted buffalo skull, set on the summit of a small mound, is encircled by other skulls of buffaloes and of enemies. In front of every skull a bit of white down is placed on a small stave. Beside the circle of skulls stand two posts to which bearskins are hung. Bundles of fagots are fastened to the posts above. Above one of the bundles lies a fur cap to indicate the man, while the other is to represent the woman—that is, the sun and the moon. Made a sketch of the Indian catafalque, or scaffold for the dead.

A violent, cold east wind is blowing; two young Indian women have taken up quarters with me to avoid exposure to the weather. As night came on, a heavy rain fell and the good women did not know where they might find shelter, for they would not go to the village. One of them is a sister of Loup Court Queue and the wife of Tete Jaune [Yellow Head], who left her and his boy here so that she could take care of his mother, now dead. The other is the blind woman whom I have mentioned already, a young wife deserted by her husband, since she lost her eyesight during this illness.

August 28—This morning the sight of seven buffalo bulls on the road leading to Fort Clarke somewhat relieved the monotony of our existence at this hospital. We noted their age with our telescope. According to the current expression, they were *"cayaks."* That means they were thrust out by the young bulls and nevermore allowed to approach any herd of cows. Excluded from the herd, such animals range in small groups by themselves; their flesh is not used for food. Later in the day great droves of buffaloes appeared, coming down to the river from the distant western hills. P. Gareau and Bellangé mounted their horses forthwith to go in pursuit of them. Mounted huntsmen followed with pack horses to bring back the meat.

Meanwhile, herds came continually into view on the other side of the river, emerging from glens and valleys and descending slopes on their way to the river. Having been left undisturbed for 2 weeks or more in this region, they dared come within a short distance of the fort. At 4 o'clock our hunters returned from the chase laden with meat. P. Gareau shot a cow, and Bellangé wounded a calf, which Gareau killed after it had been driven about for a long while by Mr. Kipp's small hunting dog, Schika. Forthwith, everybody began to roast meat. After our recent scanty fare we found delicate, tender rib roast an unrivaled dish; nothing could be better, we thought.

August 29—Today old Gagnon of the opposition fort came back from a visit to the Arikara. He says eight people died there in one night from the same disease that is prevalent here and called cholera. The symptoms are violent cramps and vomiting, and death usually results in a few hours. Gagnon was guilty of a mad act in running his Arikara woman away from here to Fort Clarke. By so doing, he spread the contagion to the Arikara village. Dorson thinks as I do, however, that cholera was brought in those bales of goods that we opened. Perhaps he welcomed the occasion that Gagnon's arrival afforded him to throw blame on the opposition. Gagnon had to make his escape by night when he realized the results of his imprudent act. The Arikara have also abandoned their village for the most part and are seeking another distant location.

For the first time, I saw a young wolf running about here that an Indian youth drove out on the prairie last spring with a cord tied tight at the end of his backbone to accustom the brute to pain. The animal's movements— now leaping about, now standing still, now bounding away, now trying to squirm himself free—can give some idea of the pain inflicted. In addition, another was made to drag eleven buffalo skulls a mile over the prairie.

Behind the fort stands a queer sort of scaffoldlike contrivance from which men are suspended, tortured, and starved, on occasions when sacrifices are offered to invoke good fortune on the hunt or in war. Thus, young lads are prepared for bloody undertakings by enforced endurance of pain and by deprivation.

Toward sunset, four buffalo bulls came out on the sandbank with the evident intention of crossing the river. As the river shore on this side is high and steep, they fell down several times while attempting to ascend, and sank deeper and deeper into the mire. While I was amusing myself watching their floundering, I heard a rifle shot. Turning my head, I saw an Indian on a dun-colored horse coming toward me at a gallop; it was La Queue Rouge. His wife is dead, his daughter is still sick, but this does not seem to have put him in a particularly melancholy state of mind. The Herantsa have divided their people into three bands and are said to have gone far north, even as far as the Knife River and regions lying contiguous thereto.

The old people in the encampment on the river below us are said to be in good health. They were left there because they could not travel to the new settlement on foot and the horses were needed for other purposes. While reloading his gun, La Queue Rouge told me about a "banneret,"[5] or young Indian, who, upon finding a group of wild cherry trees, began to sing their funeral dirge, jeered at them as enemies, then bang! he shot at them.

He fell to eating cherries greedily, under the impression that his "medicine" had robbed them of any harmful effect. That same evening he was a corpse. Seventeen more have died among the Herantsa since they went away.

August 30—My prospects for a longer stay at this place do not improve, as our sick people increase in number rather than diminish, on account of the return of old women and little girls from their camp on the river below us. I went to the upper cornfield to get a good view of the fort for a sketch, and I finished the drawings I had begun of the place of sacrifice and burial scaffold. If I could only have studied buffaloes, stags, elk, and bears, I should not trouble myself about the rest. For the present, I have enough of the antique.

FOUR

September 1851

September 5—Fort Union. I was obliged to flee to this place 3 miles beyond the mouth of the Yellowstone; perhaps I shall have to travel farther still—as far as I like.

The Sabbath is not distinguished from weekdays here by the ringing of church bells and the preaching of sermons, but merely as a rest day for the engagés. Last Sunday I took Bellangé with me to the upper cornfields to shoot ducks among the inundated willow bushes. He succeeded in killing only a pair, even though for 6 hours we waded about in the water—oftentimes up to our chests—in our efforts to steal up on the ducks.

On the way, Bellangé came near to shooting me. He was pushing through the thick willow growth just in front of me when one barrel of his double-barreled gun was accidentally discharged, the entire load just passing my left ear. When we returned at 2 o'clock in the afternoon we heard bad news from the settlements both above and below us. The Herantsa are dying in great numbers, fifty deaths already estimated: a proportion of one person in every fourteen—seven hundred souls in 84 clay huts. Some of them, they say, are in a rage about my presence here, because so many of their people are dying. Two bannerets have come from the Arikara also and report an even worse condition there than here. Arikara and Mandan are said to be dying like flies under the first winter frost. Those who survive swear that they will be revenged on all whites.

Dorson has closed his fort, so I am told. The opposition is without fear, because they are the instigators. At evening, Bellangé came to me and said that the "old man" had the intention to send him and me to Fort Union.

I was to remain there. He was to conduct me thither and at the same time get a new supply of medicinal drugs and bring them back. What he did not especially like was the necessity of making the return journey alone. As the crow flies, the distance by land is about 170 miles; by the river route, more than twice as far.

On Monday, September 1, everything was in readiness to start in the evening on horseback with just as little luggage as possible. As I was obliged to leave my boxes behind, together with the goods I had bought with them, I began to exchange on the spot or to barter on credit whatever articles I was unable to take along, and yet could not leave packed for an indefinite time. At evening we mounted our horses and bade our acquaintances heartfelt adieu. I was of the opinion, however, that my departure was due less to considerations for my own safety than to the desire to be rid of a superfluous man, since the bourgeois could no longer consider taking his journey.

Queue Rouge was greatly astonished when I said good-by and gave him some tobacco as a farewell gift. We were provided with the worst horses at the fort, which did not by any means guarantee my safety. We laid our double-barreled guns, heavily loaded, across the saddle in front of us. We were well provided with powder and shot, and each of us carried a scalping knife stuck in our belts. My cloak, together with a sack containing some changes of linen and a zinc drinking cup, all fastened to the back of the saddle, made up my total equipment.

In place of underwear, Bellangé carried our provisions, our coffeepot, and a blanket. We rode across the prairie into the West, cutting off the circuitous route of the Missouri. The first day we saw nothing but prairie chickens, blackbirds, and in the evening several shy antelopes. Here blackbirds (Brewer's Blackbird) take the place of sparrows and finches. We camped at night beside a spring, tethering our horses to tufts of tall grass. A deathlike silence reigned, except for the howling of wolves and the chorus of mosquitoes.

Before sunrise on Tuesday morning we saddled our horses and resumed our journey, always riding at a slow trot. About 8 o'clock I enjoyed my first prairie breakfast, cooked by a fire made with buffalo chips. Bellangé forgot the meat, so we had only biscuits and hot coffee. He consoled me by saying he had his gun, which would keep us supplied with game. I allow myself to be easily comforted when I am enjoying myself. When on an adventure and in a happy mood, I disregard hunger. If our pads [horses] had been better travelers, the sense of my romantic situation would have sustained me beyond any specified limit.

Constant danger from lurking enemies; the vast prairie, bounded only by sky and sea; buffaloes and bears in prospect; perhaps a violent storm by way of variety; fine health and tense anticipation: what more could I desire? Every dark spot amid the green might be a wolf, an antelope, or a deer. My glances wander everywhere. My telescope brings within my range of vision what my eyes cannot distinguish. I would not have exchanged this journey for the one I had in mind to Salt Lake. There I should not have seen any fur-bearing animals and not nearly so many Indians as at Fort Berthold. Nude Indians, with their beautifully proportioned figures, their slender yet well-formed limbs, their expressive eyes, their natural, easy bearing—that is what I am seeking, and not the painted types well-nigh overburdened with excessive decoration.

We started our first buffaloes on that day. Bellangé wished to be sure of having the Knife River (Rivière aux Couteaux) behind us before the evening in order to get out of the Gros Ventres' district, so we had to cut across the Big Bend: Grand Detour—a bend in the river 50 miles in length; direct route hardly 10 miles. Finally Bellangé found the trail, which our Indians had marked out with their tent poles. Traces of a wandering band of Indians are essentially different from similar trails left in the wake of white travelers, for the reason that the former have no wagons.

The tracks of a wagon and team make one road; the travois forms three deep paths or furrows parallel with one another, that is, a middle path along which the beasts of burden, whether horse or dog, travel, and two outer paths furrowed by the tip ends of the carrying poles. This trace we followed from the prairie down toward the river, then for a time along the bank of the stream until we came again into a plain. Near a "cut-off"—a lake (frequented at that time by great numbers of pelicans) which was earlier the bed of a river that had now taken another direction—we found skeleton twig huts, over which the Herantsa had merely thrown blankets, and abandoned fires.

This was a trace somewhat too fresh for Bellangé's comfort. He began to fear for his skin. Turning from the river, we left the trails and trotted off to a distant prairie surrounded by a chain of hills. After a time my horse refused to trot longer, while La Vieux Blanc [Old White], a well-seasoned traveler, steadily kept his even gait. In order that Bellangé and I might remain together while traversing the wide stretch of country that we had yet to cross, I was forced to urge my jade forward with a hazel rod. After we had forded the Coquille [Shell] at noon, we dismounted and lay down for a little while in the tall grass in order to stretch our legs and to allow our horses to recover their breath.

Our midday meal consisted of half a biscuit. We were in the Herantsa's own hunting ground. We dared not fire a shot or even show ourselves too openly for fear of unnecessarily attracting an attack from the so-called enemy. Besides, hostile Indians frequently approach such places by stealth in order to number yet another "coup." We might be in more peril of the Sioux than of the Herantsa.

As we were proceeding across the plain in a direction that cut off the Big Bend, I called Bellangé's attention to a graceful *cabri* buck (prong-horned antelope) that came trotting forward from a glade and peered cautiously about without getting scent of us, because we were traveling against the wind. Bidding me to be still, Bellangé slipped off his horse, took my double-barreled gun, and aimed at the fat fellow, which had approached near enough to have been killed with an ordinary pistol. The beast paid not the least attention when Bellangé fired, but trotted gracefully about us, still without gaining any warning from the wind. Bellangé's second shot was aimed much too high. Now alarmed, the buck fled swiftly away with prodigious leaps and bounds. By way of excuse, Bellangé said that as a matter of course, the gun was too heavily loaded for hitting an object at that distance. I did not think it necessary to inform such an excellent huntsman as he represents himself to be that one can hit a mark whether distant or near with the same charge, according as one takes high or low aim. As a sportsman, he has rather lost my good opinion.

He is wont to console himself with this saying of people derisive of Canadians (who, when among strangers, speak in such exalted commendations of their country when there is, after all, nothing to warrant such exaggeration):

> *Je suis du Canada* (I am from Canada)
> *Je me font de ça* (I am a part of it)
> *J'ai des pommes de terre* (I have potatoes)
> *Por passer l'hiverre!* (enough to pass the winter)[1]

In the evening we had to climb the *coteaux*, or hills, near the Knife River. They were so steep and so often intersected by deep-lying brooks that we were forced to lead our horses. From these heights, we had a magnificent, far-reaching view of a range of hills beyond the Missouri, where the land swarmed with buffaloes. The sun was setting as we waded the Knife River. In the distance, we saw the former village that the Herantsa inhabited before they chose their present abode near Fort Berthold, which—to say the least— is much better situated for defense. On a high, steep river shore in a wide-spreading plain, they are much more secure from surprise attacks than here in the midst of so many deep, narrow valleys.

At length we reached the high woodlands that are usually found along the banks of the Missouri. We unharbored a herd of white-tail deer. They paid no attention to the approaching horses until they saw man, that most dangerous of all animals, quite near them.

We selected a spot on the riverbank for our camp in order to have water and, in the second place, to get rid of the mosquitoes by means of the strong breeze that was almost continually blowing toward the stream. A mug (tin pint cup) of coffee and a cracker (biscuit) was all we had for our supper. We extinguished our campfire to avoid attracting enemies, either by firelight or smoke. We kept no watch. Wrapped in our blankets we slept peacefully with our saddle for pillows, while our nags grazed, tethered with long halters (lassos). We had been in the saddle 16 hours that day.

As we were in constant danger while crossing this hunting district, we mounted again before sunrise. We were deprived of much enjoyment by the utter weariness of our horses. Riding a lamed nag that has to be constantly urged on with the aid of a rod and with digging one's shoe heels into the sides of the beast takes one's attention away from the beautiful surroundings. On the other hand, when one's horse travels willingly without whip or spur, stamps with impatience when told to stand, neighs and snorts when allowed to run, one's spirits become exuberant—one could shout for joy.

We found a piece of sole leather (parfleche) and a bow lying beside it, evidence of Indians having but lately passed this spot, while we imagined they were behind us. We camped for breakfast on the Rivière Blanche [White River]. Afterwards we crossed a steep, rocky ridge of hills that would have given an enemy thousands of opportunities to catch us unaware in an attack or to shoot us dead from ambush. We saw cedar trees that had turned to stone, trunk and branch. How very, very old they must have been! As we descended these hills and came into the outskirts of a forest, we saw great quantities of fresh dung—in fact, we were evidently following quite close upon a number of bison. We put our loaded rifles in position under the left arm, so that we might bang at a buffalo the instant he allowed us a glimpse of him within range of our guns. At length we caught sight of several dark humps in motion directly before us, but we were unable to bring our weary nags to a gallop. The beasts escaped; we could only make ourselves merry over the peculiar rolling gait of the galloping buffalo bulls. At every step we were crossing paths that had been traced by those animals from the hills to the Missouri.

We traversed another range of hills that were peculiarly unlike any other in one particular, i.e., red clay soil. From a distance they had the appearance of brick-colored eminences. Entering a deep and narrow ravine that opened upon the plain, we noticed three buffalo quietly grazing about 200 feet ahead.

We dismounted at once. I held the horses in the ravine, standing in the dried bed of a stream, while Bellangé crept forward to shoot a buffalo. He took most deliberate aim before he fired, notwithstanding that the beasts were standing perfectly still, grazing. Finally he pulled the trigger, raising dust beneath the paunch of the bull nearest him. The animal looked about him with surprise. Bellangé fired again, this time frightening the buffaloes to the extent that they flaunted their tails angrily and took to flight. As they saw no one in pursuit, they soon stopped again.

Not one of them was wounded. Excellent marksman! With his own well-tested rifle he missed a buffalo bull standing perfectly still at a distance of 100 feet. No evasion would serve this time, and Bellangé was not a little abashed. First shot was far below the mark; second shot, much too high. After a time, he did make a sort of excuse by saying that at this season of the year the flesh of buffalo bulls was not fit for food. "But surely," I answered in scorn, "some parts of the animal are eatable—the heart, the tongue."

We came in view of several very large herds of cows encircled by the bulls, their defenders, and followed by the old, worn-out, cast-off members of the herd. At this season the bulls fight, stamp, paw the ground, and bellow so loudly that they are heard for quite a distance away. However great the numbers, all these herds fled the moment they got wind of us. We could not follow in pursuit. We dared not stray too far from our course for fear of losing our way and of fatiguing our weary nags too much.

We found a cow recently killed, from which only the tongue and some of the ribs had been cut—evident proof that the hunters were living in abundance, when they had cut from their quarry only choice bits and had even neglected to take off the hide. As the animals seemed to have been but lately killed—no vultures, ravens, or wolves in sight—I was inclined to slice off a piece of fresh meat for supper. Considering our scant traveling provisions thus far, I could not be blamed if I were sensible of my animal appetites and found the meat inviting. But Bellangé pushed on farther; Indians were in this vicinity. He said we should be obliged to leave the open plain and seek out a more sheltered way through thickets and along the dry bed of prairie brooks. As there were multitudes of wild animals here, it was hardly possible that meat would be wanting for our evening meal.

We rode on into grazing lands that extended farther than the eye could see and over the wide extent of which were scattered the dusky forms of bison, ranging in herds. This will give an idea of the great numbers of those animals that in an earlier period roamed the plains of Indiana and Illinois. All the droves we had met with on that day were coming from the Missouri, whither they had gone to quench their thirst; all the prairie streams were dry.

The sight of buffaloes was nothing new to my guide; he was on the alert for Indians, because he feared them. Those immense herds were altogether novel to me, and my keen pleasure in seeing them made me heedless of any danger whatsoever. Besides, I was in no hurry to reach Fort Union, uncertain what condition of things awaited me there. Perhaps I should again be regarded as a superfluous guest. I was constantly wishing to stop and observe more closely the motions and capers of the playful calves, how the cows were cared for by their lovers, the bulls, and to study the old stragglers. Bellangé persisted in hastening forward, perpetually belabored Vieux Blanc, and peevishly called out for me not to lag behind. My only thought was for the buffaloes on the prairie; I was enjoying the sight that I had wished a thousand times I might behold!

Then all of a sudden we became aware of a herd coming swiftly toward us over the crest of a hill in the direction of the river. We simply could not resist running them. Buffaloes move slowly forward when grazing. They lie down only to chew their cud or to sleep; hence, they never remain long in one place. Just as I was pressing on to catch up with Bellangé and call his attention to the unusual speed with which the animals were moving, we both saw, at the same moment, a number of Indians on horseback galloping along the flank of the fleeing herd. The leader caught sight of us, wheeled about, and all the wild huntsmen disappeared at once behind the hill. The buffaloes swept by. Another mounted Indian appeared at the hill's edge and turned around immediately when he saw us.

"They have discovered us! We are lost!" Bellangé exclaimed anxiously.

He had been apprehensive the entire day of our meeting with some misfortune, because his left elbow had been constantly itching. I counseled him to put his confidence in those balls of lead that, in defiance of superstitious Indians, he wore around his neck as a talisman—his "medicine." What is more, they were said to have been consecrated by a priest for the purpose of preserving him from peril. For my part, I relied more on my own courage and the double-barreled shotgun.

We were on an open, perfectly level prairie. It was probably about 4 o'clock; the sun was glaring and hot. The grass was not sufficiently high to make a surprise attack possible. For my part, I was not at all concerned about danger—least of all from the Herantsa. Even though we were beset, has not danger a part in every romantic adventure? Even love dissociated from risk and hazard would lose the charm of romance. My guide now took my telescope to spy out any suspicious signs of the Indians' approach, either openly or by stealth. The terrain to our left was distinctly to our disadvantage: there was the Missouri, several miles distant, bordered with thickets and copses where the enemy might conceal themselves and get the start of us, or else keep watch upon us, note what course we took, and take us unawares by night.

At last we neared a group of low hills, which we had long seen through the distant blue mists ahead and which Bellangé had mentioned as our camping place for the night. In their vicinity, he said, was an old house, where, at an earlier date, Mackenzie, clerk at Fort Union, had traded with the Assiniboin.[2] We were now in the hunting grounds of the latter tribe, which I assumed was all the better for us. We had nothing more to fear from the sick and afflicted Herantsa. As for the Assiniboin, they were friendly redskins whose language Bellangé had learned from his wife.

Speaking of this, he was telling me how he had first seen his Assiniboin wife at Fort Union, where he was employed as engagé. He had later bought her, a prisoner, from the Crows because at the sight of him she had wept for joy. While talking together in this way we came unexpectedly to a steep bluff and saw with astonishment that two Indians were standing on the other side of a small stream at its foot. We were still more surprised when they waved their red blankets, a sign that we should come over and join them.

They called to us, *"Maregna! Maregna!"* (Friend.)

Bellangé answered, *"Oui, oui, crapauds, pas cette fois ci."* (Yes, yes, you toads! Not this time.)

He shouted to me that they were Sioux who were watching this place for Gros Ventres. He whipped up his white horse and off we went at a gallop. My mare wished to follow, but I was not of the same mind. While I was forcibly holding her back, my portfolio was wrestled out of place, and as a result, sketchbook, paint box, writing utensils, journal, everything, lay scattered on the ground. Abandon my sketches and drawing materials—never! To dismount and pick up the most important articles required only a moment, but my portfolio was all awry. I was obliged to keep hold of the horse's rein with the same hand with which I was holding my rifle.

Finding that I could not get the sketchbook in, I thrust it under my arm. My riding cloak, which had also fallen off, I threw again across the saddle, whereupon the confounded jade sprang back, jerked the rein out of my hand, and off she went at a gallop. "Ah, I see now you can travel quite well," I said. "Just wait!" The sketchbook with my colors, brushes, drawing paper, compass, etc., all restored, and the portfolio put properly in place, I threw my cloak over my left arm and cocked the rifle. Holding it with both hands ready to attack, I awaited the "savages" that were now coming speedily forward from different directions, all armed and riding bareback. Instead of holding their hands to their mouths to make the war cry resound, the leader called to me again, *"Maregna! Maregna!"*

Meanwhile, Bellangé had seen my mare running around loose, and he came galloping back in order that he might share my danger. He found me surrounded by acquaintances of the Herantsa tribe, with whom I was shaking hands and making much sport about his having run away. While he was greeting Le Tete de Loup [Wolf Head] and Le Tete de Boeuf [Ox Head], I tried to find the rest of my belongings that were scattered about on the prairie. Some Indian lads rode after my horse and brought her back. The Herantsa found our meeting most edifying; not so Bellangé. He was exasperated with me because I had not followed him at once.

Now we must go with the Indians to their camp. I could see Tete de Loup was bent on mischief. All of us rode together down the bluff and through the stream to the camp, which consisted of a number of shelters built of twigs over which blankets were thrown. We dismounted and sat down before the fire in the circle of our red friends—or foes. Bellangé bade me keep my gun in my hand; otherwise, I was lost.

Several children who knew me, and to whom I had frequently given sugar in my room, came bounding forward and offered their hands in the friendliest manner. Indians greet one another neither by shaking hands nor by expressing good wishes. Upon meeting, they talk together or give some sign, either by outcry or by a movement of the hand. Iowa say *"hou,"* which white people in their neighborhood often imitate instead of wishing one "good day" or "good night." When an Indian offers the hand in greeting, it is in imitation of our custom.

Though I did not believe we were running any risk, I laid my gun across my lap. The Herantsa told us how they had been watching us for a long while as we approached across the prairie, and they laughed at us for the way we constantly looked about us—they called attention to my metal water flask that glistened so; it had dazzled them at a great distance. It was plain that if they had had evil designs they could very easily have put an end to us with an arrow while totally unobserved.

There could be no question as to their chances of overtaking our weary nags with their fresh runners on which they were mounted to hunt buffaloes. We could only have concealed ourselves in a dense coppice and have halted there, but we could not have relied on that protection for any length of time. Herantsa knew something of our weapons from an earlier time: Tete de Boeuf had often admired the arrangement of my gunlock—a smaller hammer, like the cover of the priming pan, covered the fuse, in order to protect it from dampness and at the same time to prevent any untimely discharge.

The pipe was passed around, each of us taking several whiffs. In the meantime, Bellangé related to his friend Tete de Boeuf, who always called the former's wife "sister" in token of the great friendship existing between the two families, that the purpose of his journey to Fort Union was to take me there to stay; to get medicinal drugs for "Ikipesche" (for Kipp; the Herantsa called P. Gareau "Mi"—Stone—from his name, Pierre); and to carry them back on his return. He entreated him to do us no harm, for I was much too fond of Indians to have any will to destroy them by pestilence. Bellangé heard that some of them intended to put me to death, but he hoped to be treated as a friend by the brother of his wife. Tete de Boeuf answered, for his part, that they were on their way to the Crows to pay a visit to their relatives. I had nothing at all to fear from them, though they believed me to be "bad medicine."

The Indian women brought choice bits of fresh meats, a great quantity of which was hanging out to be dried by the sun. In return we gave them coffee to boil, and sugar with which to sweeten it, so that all might have a share in our luxurious repast of juicy tender meat and sweetened coffee.

After the meal was over, although the two men invited us to spend the night and ride the rest of the way to Fort Union with them, Bellangé insisted upon pressing forward. He gave as excuse that he was in haste, but he was really urged on only by fear. I cut for my use a jolly good willow switch with which to teach my mare how to behave, for I was much provoked with her for running away from me. Our friendly hosts gave us enough meat to last several days longer, and just after sunset, we took our leave. Bellangé conducted me to a beautiful spring 2 miles from this camp, where we had clear, cool water and good pasture near at hand. After we had secured the horses with long halters, we lay down to sleep, but not before I made clear to my guide the disadvantageous situation of the place he had chosen, and warned him that if he did not really trust the Herantsa, he should not have selected that kettle-shaped burrow.

Here we were virtually entombed in the midst of encircling heights, behind which the enemy could creep up on us, themselves unseen and unheard, and shoot us dead. There was no longer any cause for fear, he replied. Bellangé was wholly contradictory with regard to our danger. He would not keep watch at night; he fired his gun as opportunity presented itself, yet he forbade me to do so, though every shot from his rifle was just as easily heard as from mine. He was wanting in courage, bad humored, and much inclined to give himself airs.

Shining gloriously in a clear sky, the moon was mirrored in the quiet water of the fountain spring. From far and wide came subdued sounds of the bellowing and pawing of combative bulls. An old "cayak" passed near the grazing horses, grumbling and shaking his shaggy mane. How was it possible for a person to go to sleep? The moon was so brilliant that I could read by it. I looked into my portfolio to find out what articles I had lost: my seal, a valued gift from my brother Louis (in Paris, 1838), a small inkhorn from my friend F. Studer, some percussion caps, pencils, compositions on loose paper, and other trifles besides. Only one pencil remained for my use during the remainder of my journey, not a comfortable state of things if Fort Union offered me no better supply of paper and pencils than I had found at Fort Berthold.

At last I lay down, wrapped in the riding cloak I set so much store by. Hardly had I fallen asleep when my mare sent forth a loud neigh. As I looked up, Bellangé said he had long ago heard talking. "Those toads of Indians *(ces crapeaux de sauvages)* are following us. The mare has the scent of their horses and is calling to them. I hear distinctly the crackling of the boughs," he said.

The mare neighed again, but the old white horse was silently grazing. Though I heard nothing, I thought Bellangé was probably right. My hearing had been much affected during my service in the artillery at an earlier time in my homeland. "Cayaks" continued to pass quite near us, bellowing and lowing. Finally the moon went down; it was dark! When the sky began to brighten in the east, we saddled our nags, mounted, and rode across the brook that flowed from our spring. Then we heard the voice of someone behind us calling "*Maregna*" again. Without halting we turned and saw on the height the shadowy forms of Tete de Boeuf and his boys. He called for us to wait for them; they wished to make the journey with us. Bellangé replied, "Adieu, barbarians!" We went swiftly forward, for our clothes were damp and we were chilled by the night mists.

Thursday. The sun rose brilliantly upon a vast rolling prairie over which innumerable buffalo herds grazed. Several times we came quite near fighting bulls. In their rage they did not see us, but only ran away when they heard the report of a gun. Covered with dust and foam, they fled swiftly in the wake of the herd, their tails lashing their flanks or else raised vertically aloft, as a threat that they were about to begin the struggle anew.

I should have thought that under circumstances such as these, the bulls at least would be inclined to stand at bay upon the approach of men, but all of them fled from us. On the prairie, they escape the moment they catch the scent of human beings, unless the herd is too large to evade hunters. It is only in narrow woodland paths that they try to run over people or knock them down. If on the hunt a person comes in close contact with a buffalo, the animal butts against his pursuer. Buffaloes never attack; a bull defends himself valiantly against bears, but a cow has less courage. It appears odd to me, therefore, that these animals are not tamed. Our breeding bulls in the meadow are much more fierce and angrily attack strangers.

We found a little pond inhabited by a multitude of ducks. Here we dismounted, watered our horses, looked about for buffalo chips—though we might search far and near, we found not the slightest sign of wood or straw—and lighted a fire to boil the last of our coffee. We wished to fry the meat that was given us, for it was not yet dry enough to be palatable uncooked. We found the taste of it by no means impaired by our having used buffalo chips for fuel; on the contrary, we ate it with good relish.

We hurried on after breakfast. Saw a great many antelopes and wolves. Passing through a little valley, we noticed, as we rode by, a young grizzly bear in his den and frightened him out. Bellangé called him "Ours Jaune [Yellow Bear]," because his hair was yellow and he had a bright ring around his neck. That is the color of one-year-old bears only. This fellow ran from us, too, but we could easily have overtaken him and peppered him with shot if, unfortunately, our horses had not been such poor beasts. However, even though they had been good travelers, it would not have been wise to run our horses for such a purpose.

Opportunities to test their fleetness of foot were too frequently tempting. For instance, as we were slowly climbing a hill, we noticed the dark hump of a buffalo moving along the edge of the summit. He was a powerful fellow and hardly 100 feet distant. Bellangé was now to have the final test of his marksmanship. We stopped. I was eager to have a crack at this bison from my horse's back; his heart offered a near and sure aim. But Bellangé sprang down, crept forward in order to get nearer him still, *a bout portant* (with muzzle clapped to his breast). He fired. I could see plainly where he wounded the animal's shoulder. As the beast was escaping I took aim and fired, just that I might say I had one shot at a buffalo.

His movements showed that I hit at least his hinder parts. No shot that missed the heart would kill. Bellangé had so badly acquitted himself this time that I could not refrain from remark. In retaliation he made some observation concerning my lack of skill in horseback riding, because I was not able to keep up with his white steed. I asked him whether his idea of horsemanship was to bruise his beast with blows?

After fording the Bourbeuse[3] we came to a prairie that was utterly barren, flat, rocky, and sterile. Not an animal showed itself, not a bird was to be seen throughout the entire extent of this plain, which seemed endless to me. Finally we caught sight of hills again in the distance. Behind them rose still another ridge we should have to cross before we arrived at Fort Union. I asked Bellangé whether we should not have done better to spend the night on the Bourbeuse and allow our horses to rest. He replied that he still hoped we might sleep in the fort that night, for the region we were traveling through was very dangerous ground. Blackfeet were said to be often roaming stealthily about, lying in wait for Assiniboin who passed this way constantly, one by one, as they went back and forth between the forts and their various settlements. We had to make haste. I would have been glad to sleep one more night in the open. The weather was so enticingly clear, and we still had some meat.

My guide became more timorous and more hurried, the nearer we came to Fort Union. He did not even halt at midday. In order to allay thirst as well as hunger, I thrust a piece of half-cured meat in my mouth to chew on. My arm was tired from beating the mare, but we still had 25 English miles to cover before reaching our destination.

Becoming more and more disquieted, Bellangé alighted to exchange mounts with me. He bade me ride the white horse with all the luggage, whereupon he whipped the mare unmercifully and away went the poor beast, trotting with a limp. He laughed at me, saying the only trouble was, I was no horseman. In reply, I asked whether it was his habit to ride with one stirrup shorter than the other. He had not noticed that one stirrup strap was shorter by two holes than the other; in consequence, I was forced to sit sidewise. In order not to be delayed on that account, I rode with my legs hanging free.

Our way led through plains that became constantly less broad and were more frequently traversed by streams that had worn a deep bed but at the same time contained little water. On our right there were always hills; on our left flowed the Missouri. Evening came on apace; to me it seemed no longer possible to reach the fort that day. At length we came to a prairie at the verge of which Bellangé pointed out a bright spot.

With my telescope I discerned a white bastion. That was Fort William, trading post of the opposition. Five miles farther, 3 miles above the mouth of the Yellowstone River, lay Fort Union. Bellangé smacked with his tongue and licked his lips. The reason for this was his anticipation of a drink when he delivered a letter he carried from Schmidt to Joe Picotte,[4] bourgeois at Fort William, nephew of our Mr. Picotte but employed by the opposition company. The letter and my close acquaintance with Joe gave Bellangé hopes of getting a dram.

Soon we came upon the track of a wheel. We were at Fort William. Roulette, clerk and interpreter, received us, took possession of the letter, and thanked us in behalf of his bourgeois, who at the moment was on the river fishing. Without dismounting, we continued our way along a good smooth road to our fort. The sun went down and a golden shimmering light spread over the landscape. Soon the stockade was visible and the white bastions, over which appeared the top of a tall flagstaff that stood within the courtyard. At length we rode up to the gate. Bellangé was immediately surrounded by his many acquaintances. I was most heartily glad to stand once more on my own legs.

Bellangé delivered the letter he brought to a small, hard-featured man wearing a straw hat, the brim of which was turned up in the back. He was my new bourgeois, Mr. Denig.[5] He impressed me as a rather prosy fellow. He stopped Bellangé short, just as the latter was beginning a long story he wished to tell. He ordered supper delayed on our account that we might have a better and more plentiful meal. A bell summoned me to the first table with Mr. Denig and the clerks. My eyes almost ran over with tears! There was chocolate, milk, butter, omelet, fresh meat, hot bread—what a magnificent spread! I changed my opinion at once concerning this new chief. A hard, niggardly person could not have reconciled himself to such a hospitable reception in behalf of a subordinate who was a total stranger to him.

After we had eaten he apologized for not having a bed in readiness for me. That night I must content myself with buffalo robes in the interpreter's room; better arrangements would be made the next day. The inside of the room presented an appearance rather like an Indian's habitation. On the floor near me were three beds for three couples of half-Indians and their full-blooded wives—visiting "barbarians." The wife of Spagnole [Joe Dolores],

Fig. 2. Bourgeois House, Fort Union, September 1851. Built as a one-and-a-half-story structure with dormer windows in the 1830s, a full second story and gallery were added between 1847 and 1851. Kurz's watercolor is the first to show two full stories. (Midwest Jesuit Archives, St. Louis, Missouri)

the horse guard, was Mandan. Smith's wife was a Cree, and Cadotte's an Assiniboin. Both hunters were Cree half-breeds and at that time absent.

The last two men had been obliged to accompany, as guides, the transport of goods to Fort Benton in the territory of the Blackfeet and had not yet returned. In spite of this promiscuous company I slept quite well. I dreamed of milk, for the reason, I presume, that I had been so long deprived of it. Until that evening, I had not even tasted milk since I left Belle Vue. No cows were kept at Fort Berthold on account of the cornfields. The law prevailing there gives Indian women the right to kill any animal that strays into their fields. Once I saw a splendid 2-year-old colt half killed by an Indian woman because it had escaped from its keeper and was bustling about in the midst of the growing corn. There is no Indian village near Fort Union. The Assiniboin are roving hunters without fixed abode. The tribe is separated into various bands that live apart from one another, for the reason that a great number of people move slowly from place to place and find greater difficulty in providing sufficient food.

That night after supper, Joe Dolores, the horse guard, played the leading role in a comic action. He galloped up to the gate shouting, "Blackfeet! Blackfeet!" R. Mack and Pattneau swung themselves at once upon the backs of their respective runners in order to corral the grazing horses and assist in defending the fort.

Everyone was keen to help. Blackfeet were reported to be sneaking secretly about the garden coulee (dry gully). With great trouble the men got all the horses together just as a man emerged from the spot where the enemy was suspected to be in hiding. Who should it be but our Negro Auguste! He had been looking for berries, simply as a means of diversion. Joe was so ridiculed that he took refuge in flight.

This morning after breakfast, the room in which I am now writing was put in order for me and furnished with a bedstead, two chairs, and a large table. Here I am alone, always the more agreeable arrangement for me. I do not find company a necessity. I have always something at hand with which to occupy myself, so I am not lonely, though I may be alone. What is more, Mr. Denig has found some work for me to do. He has many oil colors here (neither very good nor complete), with which I am to paint the front of the house. Then I am to decorate the reception room with pictures. At the same time, I shall not fail to execute a life-size portrait of him that is to hang in the office, where it will strike the Indians with awe. All this work is to be done before Mr. Culbertson returns from Fort Laramie. Mr. Denig wishes to prepare a pleasant surprise for his chief, and he expects that Mr. Culbertson will take me to Fort Benton.

All colors, crude or ground, were searched for in the principal building, in the warehouse, in garret and cellar. A marble slab with a grinder was put on a special table, five measures of oil were procured, and all spare shaving brushes were collected in order that the painting may begin tomorrow. Today I am still free to do as I like. I employ the time writing.

A young grizzly bear and a war eagle, both alive, are confined behind the powder house. A number of Indian trinkets are displayed in the reception room and there are, besides, a stuffed Rocky Mountain sheep (female bighorn), black-tailed deer, a large white owl, prairie hens, and pheasants, all of which will afford me sufficient models for sketches and studies.

September 6—Before breakfast Bellangé began his return journey to Fort Berthold. Denig was provoked with him because he had to leave two good-for-nothing nags here and wished to have in exchange a thoroughly good traveler. He received a pack mule with the notification that his commission had been executed. Bellangé wished very much to be allowed to take my telescope with him, but I could not spare it. I must give him something later, as a return for the fear he endured.

This entire day I have been painting the balcony and reception room, with the assistance of two clerks, Owen Mackenzie[6] and Packinaud [Charles Paque-naud]. He was called Packinaud, which is said not to be his real name. As he can neither read not write, he is himself not sure. I have ground some colors.

September 15—Morgan has gone again to the "Chantier," a place in the forest up the river where workmen and laborers under his direction are getting beams ready for the palisades. The palisades of this fort are not driven into the ground, as in Fort Berthold, but are fitted into heavy beams that rest upon a foundation of limestone. At this place palisades are further secured by supports of crossed beams on the inside, so that they cannot be blown down by the wind. It happened once during my stay that on the western side, where the supports were badly decayed, a violent wind forced them down before the new beams were ready.

Morgan was only on a visit here and therefore was lodged in my room. Now I am again in quiet possession. Last week I worked hard: ground colors and painted the pickets in front of the house. Mr. Denig expressed the wish that I also paint a sideboard in the mess hall. It was not sufficiently glary when finished, so he decided to improve its appearance himself. As paint of that sort is an abhorrence to me, I praised his work highly in order to be rid of it once and for all. I was interested in painting the entire outside of the house to his satisfaction, for he is most kind and agreeable in his associations with me. Every evening he sits with me, either in my room or in front of the gate, and relates experiences of his earlier life. As he has held his position in this locality for 19 years already, his life has been full of adventure with Indians, particularly since the advent of the whisky flask.

He also wishes me to paint a portrait of himself and his dog, Natoh (bear), a commission I am very glad to execute. In return he promises, in the interest of my work, to enable me to have the best opportunities for studying wild animals. Now that I have found out what I need to know about Indians, I would like to vary my investigations by making just as thorough a study of wild animals. My plan is not to write a book on the history, religion, and customs of the Indian race, but rather to depict the romantic life of Indians, either in oil paintings (my gallery) or in prints. Therefore I find it necessary to study animals of the chase, although that is by no means my chief purpose.

I may regard my recent transfer to this post as the most fortunate event of my life in this country. I am indebted to Herantsa superstition for my removal from a most unpleasant situation and for a highly interesting journey to this place, where I find congenial surroundings and where I can make myself useful and not be regarded as the fifth wheel of a wagon. As to the personality of my new bourgeois, who was represented at the fort below as being a disagreeable person, I find myself most pleasantly surprised. Kipp is a man approaching old age, forced by necessity to begin life anew for the reason that he had lost a good fortune on account of his addiction to strong drink. This makes him unhappy, dissatisfied with himself, and morose. On the other hand, Denig, his former clerk, has come rapidly forward, owing to his commercial knowledge, his shrewdness, and his courage at the posts where he was earlier employed. Therefore, he has aroused the jealousy of his former chief, whom he now disregards. Fort Berthold, which is really under the control of Fort Pierre, is not a trading post of much consequence. Trade is carried on with one tribe. For the most part, business is done on credit, which frequently results in loss.

Assiniboin, Crows, Crees, and half-breeds do their trading here. Fort Union is the depot or storage house for the more distant posts, Fort Benton and Fort Alexander.

It goes without saying that a bourgeois who occupies the position of responsible warden, chief tradesman, and person in highest authority at a trading post far removed, where he has fifty men under his direction, may regard himself of more importance than a man who directs five men. To conduct such a post as this requires more ability. In winter there are established from three to four byposts. In this region, where there is neither the rule of law nor an established police force, it is necessary for one to know these engagés in order to understand the difficulties of managing them. They are workmen employed by the year, representing all nationalities—Canadians, Americans, Scotchmen, Germans, Swiss, Frenchmen, Italians, Creoles, Spaniards, Mulattoes, Negroes, and half-Indians—who come, for the most part, from St. Louis, where they have found no means of earning a livelihood. Canadians are in the majority, but these men are not to be mistaken for those commendable sailors mentioned earlier, the *"coureurs de bois,"* who were fitted for their employment under the strict discipline of the Hudson Bay Company.

The men here are called *"mangeurs de lard,"* because their chief occupation is the eating of pork. According to their talk, there are no workmen more capable, but when it comes to work they are neither industrious nor skilled. It is no small matter to make such people work, when one has no recourse to police control or to any outside assistance. One has to manage them with ability, courage, and tact. The more capable of these engagés advance immediately to better positions. If they are really skilled craftsmen, they are employed as such, their wages doubled and better board and lodging provided. If they are qualified in the mercantile line or in languages and prove to be honest and shrewd, they are advanced to clerks, bourgeois, or agents. In this region every man works up from a lower position, for many years' experience among Indians—to become familiar with the Indian character, habits, and tongue—is required at the more important trading posts.

One has not much respect for the ordinary engagé. One has to be constantly at hand when he is assigned work, for he takes no interest in the success of the fur trading company and runs away upon the least suspicion of danger. Our smith (Gagnon) and Zimmermann gave us, more than once, evidence of their spirit. Both were thrifty fellows and tried to earn some extra dollars as trappers. One evening in winter they were together in a nearby thicket to set traps for wolves or foxes. One of them saw, in the distance, a person descending a hill. Immediately he abandoned both friend and trap and ran breathless to us, crying, "Indians! Indians!" The approaching foe proved to be merely an Indian woman accompanied by her dog!

As a matter of course, Denig keeps the subordinate workmen strictly under his thumb. What is more, he has to, if he is to prevent their over-reaching him. He feels that one man alone is not sufficient to enforce good order among these underlings, for every one of them is armed and though not courageous in general, they are touchy and vengeful. For purposes of order and protection he has attached [to himself] the clerks, who stand more nearly on the same level with him in birth and education, and afford the only support—moral as well as physical—upon which he can reckon. In his turn he just as willingly provides some diversion for all of them when they have performed services satisfactory to him. On the other hand, he limits their victuals when they are idle or lazy. For instance, last week under Morgan's direction a supply of hay for next winter was mowed 9 miles from here and piled up in stacks (conical heaps). Nearly 15,000 pounds of cured meat was purchased at an Assiniboin camp, and both clerks have returned with their men and teams. Today they had another laborious and difficult task, the felling of trees and the preparing of lumber for palisades at the fort.

On Saturday evening, Denig gave a ball, to which he also invited Joe Picotte, his family, and the people who work with him. We decorated the room as brilliantly as we could with mirrors, candles, precious fur skins, and Indian ornaments. Denig himself had the hardest work of all, because he was the only fiddler and did not stop until everybody had tired himself out with dancing.

Indian women and men were dressed according to European mode. From my point of view, the ball on that account lost much of its character and the picturesque interest that one might have anticipated in this region and under these conditions. Only the spectators, who were in Indian costumes, gave one to understand in what part of the country the dance was taking place. The cotillion, which the squaws went through with much grace and far more correctness than I should have expected, seemed to be the favorite dance.

Indian women manifest the same preference for dancing that is common among our white women, and most of them have had much practice in the art with their white husbands. Figures of the cotillion represent what is most pleasing to me in the way of a dance. To me, the waltz seems like nonsense. It corresponds in no way to the purpose of dancing, i.e., developing a graceful body, suppleness, and ease of manner. As I do not dance myself, I beat the tattoo on the drum.

It is odd—yet worthy of note—that just such savages, engagés, clerks, and even bourgeois cannot have enough of distinguishing themselves as "Mountaineers" on their return to the States or when they go back there on visits. They attract attention in their highly ornamented buckskin clothes, by performing Indian dances and imitating Indian war cries, in order that they may be regarded as the hardy, fearless, jovial "Mountaineers," a name synonymous with famous huntsmen, distinguished warriors, bold and crafty trappers such as are described in books. While they take pleasure in making themselves conspicuous among their white brothers as savages, they try to make a forcible impression upon their red brothers here as white men. He knows—at least, the usual engagé knows—that he is unable to do this except in the matter of clothes, which the poor Indian cannot get, for the former has none of those qualities one ascribes to the "Mountaineer." On the other hand, the Indian possesses them all in high degree.

I must mention here that since beaver pelts have fallen in price, that far-famed class of trappers is almost nonexistent. The trappers are no longer found at all throughout the entire territory of Blackfeet, Crows, Assiniboin, Cree, Chippewa, Herantsa, Arikara, and Dakota.

Beaver skins used to be their principal branch of industry. Other pelts like ermine, fox, muskrat, otter, and Alpine hare, are either too rarely obtained or else not sufficiently profitable to justify risking so many dangers. The risks, deprivations, and adventures of trappers have been enough related by storytellers and most excellent authors. The same fault is committed almost universally: They treat the Indians, the rightful owners of these lands and all beasts of the chase—the redskins' only source of food found therein—as robbers and murderers if they defend their property against hunters who are not entitled to poach there. On what authority do huntsmen and lovers of the chase base their right to follow that sport in Indian territory, to rob Indians of their only means of providing food and clothing? Do they first ask permission? Not at all! But if the Red Men make reprisals, either by cunning or by force, then there is raised an outcry, both excessive and unjustified. So it comes about that the writers who relate those stories treat first one nation and then the other as arrant knaves, as the meanest plunderers, just as they have frequently shown themselves to be among the Pawnee and the Crows. Is that just? Moreover, the same can be said concerning the behavior of the emigrants.

In many cases they could make necessity their excuse, it is true, but the greater number of animals they killed not from necessity but merely from love of sport. If, then, the right of the strong hand is to prevail, let the same right be granted the Indians, and with whatever measure one metes, let it be measured to the other. Indians defend their domain as it is distributed among the nations according to fixed boundaries, and they maintain their supply of food, their existence, as well as they can. Are not fruits of the field, grazing herds, even beasts of the chase, protected in civilized states by laws? Furthermore, is it not lawful in many Christian countries for the owner of land to fire upon a trespasser?

In return for Mr. Denig's kind invitation, Joe Picotte invited us to his fort the next day (yesterday). As I can neither dance nor play any musical instrument, I looked forward to the visit with little pleasure, especially as I am just now occupied with ideas other than amorous adventures. I would much rather have spent Sunday studying the young bear than to have gone to a party at 10 o'clock in the morning, but Joe Picotte seemed so much pleased to see me again, I thought mere courtesy required me to go.

Though I was well acquainted with him in St. Joseph, I had perceived already on the *Robert Campbell* that he did not like seeing me with an opposition company. At about 11 o'clock at night we returned from the ball as merry as it is possible for people to be who have indulged in such gaiety without the enlivening effects of love and wine. The ride home in brilliant moonlight was splendid, a real delight. Firing off his pistols, Morgan rode in front with his dogs. Mackenzie rode on Toku, his superb courser, whose plunging and rearing, as well as the great speed at which the spirited animal galloped home, made Mac's wife, riding behind, anxiously clasp him round! Denig's younger wife [Deer Little Woman], riding a pony behind Smith's wife, followed with me. I was mounted on a pony belonging to Denig's older wife, who expressed a wish to drive back. The two women were constantly trying to tempt me to run a race with them and see which could first reach the vanguard. They would remain behind a moment, then shout, "*Oppaheh! Oppaheh!*" to me, whip up the pony, and away they would go. Behind us came the two-wheeled cart, drawn by two mules, carrying the bourgeois and his family and the musical instruments. Pattneau, astride the pony, brought up the rear.

Today Joe Picotte came over to ask how we had passed the night. At the moment I was engaged in no duties, so Mr. Denig said I might paint a portrait of Joe in watercolor. I immediately set about it. In return for the portrait, Mr. Picotte promises me something rare in Indian design. He possesses elk horns of remarkable size and attached to the skull. If I could get such a pair I should have quite an addition to my collection. The difference in the size of elk horns is so considerable that I attributed the smaller pair of horns on our bastion to a smaller species. On the contrary, the hunters maintain that they were taken from young elks whose antlers up to a certain age have only a given number of tines, and afterwards increase both in weight and in size.

Today I received a [buffalo] cow's hide most excellently prepared and decorated as a gift from Mr. Denig. The hair is as fine as silk, the underside like velvet. Across the middle of it runs a broad band, decorated with beads, porcupine quills, and tiny bells that hang from rosettes. He got it from the Crows. Though it is so smooth, I found it impossible to adorn it further with fine drawings, still less with drawings on a large scale. Mr. Denig says I shall not be able to paint my robe after my own style.

Since I came here I seem to be at perfect peace with myself. In the first place, I am quite unexpectedly so much nearer the accomplishment of my life purpose that I have little more to worry about. In reality, I have enjoyed my youthful dream of journeying in strange lands, of horses, Indian women, and collections of Indian rarities. If I can spend my later life in the painting of pictures that portray the American Indian, if time and strength remain to me until I have realized my ideal, then my cherished aims will have been fulfilled.

September 16—There was a downpour the entire day; in consequence, no work out-of-doors. I spent the time sketching the head attire of a Cree chieftain captured by Blackfeet. This Cree partisan and eight of his braves were attacked by a superior force of Blackfeet. When the former saw that they were going to be overtaken, they quickly dug a hole with their hands and knives in the side of a low hill. That was their only means of shielding themselves. All died valiantly, fighting to their last breath.

The chief's headgear is estimated to be worth as much as a pack horse. Not being in a position to buy it, I content myself with making a true copy. My funds are spent; my merchandise has been disposed of; my credit with the company is good only for wearing apparel. At this place the cost of necessaries is very high, out of proportion to the increase one might expect on account of the distance things have to be transported. The price of coffee is 100 cents a pound; brown sugar, the same; meal costs 25 cents a pound; seven ship biscuits cost 100 cents; one pound of soap costs the same; calico is 100 cents a yard; to get one shirt washed costs 25 cents, etc. On an average, prices are nine times as dear as in the States. If I had bartered my wares at such prices in Fort Berthold, I should have done a better business than I could have managed with cash. The value of a dollar is insignificant; what one receives for it is of no consequence. Even in the States, 20 cents is not worth reckoning. In the western States there is no smaller coin than a 5-cent piece.

September 17—Worked at painting the house this morning. Began a pen sketch of the house this afternoon for Mr. Denig. A band of Assiniboin came from their settlement on horseback, bringing dried buffalo meat for sale. They were invited to partake of sweetened coffee, which must now replace the whisky that used to be served. Mr. Denig thinks a portrait worthless unless the eyes follow a person who gazes upon it, no matter on which side the beholder stands. Furthermore, a portrait must be drawn life-size and painted in oil, he says, otherwise it is of no value as a true representative. A watercolor, it appears, has no worth.

Mr. Denig came up the river in the same year [1833] in which the Baron von Barneburg, alias Prince [Maximilian] von Neu Wied, came. Then it was that he and Mr. Culbertson arrived in this region for the first time.

I have several anecdotes from them concerning the Prince and my friend Bodmer, also in connection with Catlin. This last-named painter is regarded here as a humbug. He is said to have compromised the gentlemen who were then at Fort Pierre with a book of stories that they had written. Catlin took the steamer only as far as this point and went back on the same boat to Fort Pierre, where he remained three months and painted pictures of the Indians. Could never paint at all unless he were perfectly comfortable with easel, camp stool, etc. During the three months at Fort Pierre he requested the bourgeois and clerks to put down in a book, over their own signatures, accounts of interesting moments spent in that region. Many of them related their adventures in the Indian territory as he had asked them to do. Later on, so it seems, he published the book, retaining the names of the writers but greatly distorting the narratives for the sake of effect, i.e., to make the interest of the reader as tense as possible. I had heard Mr. Kipp complain of Catlin. Though the painter knew hardly a word of the Sioux language, he is reported to have given lectures in New York on the subject. Yankee humbug!

Since writing the above I have read the book myself. With the exception of several instances where the author talks big, the book contains a great deal that is true. On the other hand, the drawings are for the most part in bad taste and to a high degree inexact, especially the buffaloes. Indians never go on the hunt as if arrayed for war. That scene where wolves surround the dying bull is a silly make-believe. That one of the Indian vaulting upon a single bull is another. (The latter may possibly occur in a thickly crowded herd, when the hunter is hemmed in on both sides.) His buffalo herds consist of nothing but bulls—no cows and calves. Bodmer makes the same mistake. What astonishes one in Catlin's sketches, particularly in the English originals, is that the faces are grotesque. What is more, they are faces of the same Indians whom he extols constantly, and justly, in the text for possessing the rare beauty of the antique.

He is said to have sold certain paintings of Indians to the United States government with the understanding that no copies would be made. Far from keeping his word, he copied them in secret before they were delivered and exhibited them later in London.

September 19—I had a most interesting ride to the Little or Upper Bourbeuse and back again. Yesterday, after our midday meal (here we eat at least three times each day), the bourgeois sent me with Carafel on a horseback ride to the little stream mentioned above, in order that I might have a chance to see my comrade set his beaver traps. Carafel is a skilled beaver trapper, an occupation that requires much patience and cunning. A ride of 10 miles over prairie, steep slopes, and many rivulets brought us to the Upper Bourbeuse, where we saw several beaver dams.

While I made a drawing of the one most solid and complete, my companion, with the least possible noise, laid three traps nearby in the water and baited them with castoreum he carried in a small horn. We took a farther ride about that neighborhood later with the hope of coming upon some buffaloes. Our horses were not prepared for a run. Carafel was riding my former mount, Vieux Blanc. Though "Old White" is no racer, he is nevertheless a most useful animal. He has no bad faults. He is capable of great endurance and can be left standing untied at any place where he finds forage.

As the few buffaloes that we could find were too far away, we went in search of a comfortable place where we could camp for the night. We found such a place in high grass between two beautiful ash trees. I went immediately to work on a drawing of that spot, while Carafel lighted a fire and made tea. There were mosquitoes in great numbers, but we enjoyed our meal in merry mood, just as well-proved hunters and trappers are wont to do, because they are content with little and blessed with good appetites. While our horses grazed nearby, we chatted together until it was dark, then wrapped ourselves up and went to sleep, dreaming the dreams of lucky mortals. We ate breakfast this morning at our camping place, saddled the horses, took a drink, mounted, and rode again to the stream where the traps were set.

I finished some sketches, but we caught no beaver. They are too shy, having been too frequently disturbed by Indians that pass that way. We saw several of the animals, but they disappeared underwater at the slightest sound. We came home at a quick pace; saw nothing more of interest except a fat buck that we scared away from his lair, and an arrow cut at its upper end in the form of a bird. Around the arrow was a wide circle, where the ground bore the impress of dancing warriors.

Toward midday we arrived here, full of enthusiasm for life in the bush; for horseback rides over stock and stone, through clear streams and across the plains; for dreams of the night, as we lie wrapped in our mantles beside a crackling fire, while our horses are grazing beside us and our loaded rifles lie near at hand. But I lack the keen eyes of a hunter, his principal asset.

Of all the situations at the fort, Morgan's appeals to me most. To be sure, when he is out in the wilds he does not have the benefit of meals as good as we enjoy here, but what advantage have we in comparison with his free roving through meadow and forest, over mountain and vale, hunting deer, buffaloes, bears, ducks, and geese, trapping beaver, foxes, and wolves in the service and under the protection of the company.

He sleeps and dreams in his tent of skin. His life as hunter offers a much more varied existence than even that of the huntsmen regularly employed at the fort; the latter go on the chase only once a week, when fresh meat is needed. Even then, they hunt only buffaloes or elks, shoot and kill as many as they have need of, and load the pack horses that are taken along for the purpose. They quickly flay the beasts, cut off the best portions of meat, which they bind together and lay across the pack saddle, the weight equally balanced on both sides, and hasten home, not taking time even to smoke a pipe.

Morgan was talking about going next year to visit "auld lang syne" and see his mother and sister. Who knows whether his leaving might not give me an opportunity to remain here as overseer of the engagés? For that purpose I do not need an especially keen eye or any knowledge of the Indian speech. On the contrary, European languages and tact suffice for association with such people as they. I feel so well here. I am no sufferer of nostalgia. If I can only sketch here and there, I am happy.

I should be perfectly satisfied where I am if I could have my two boxes. One of them is 2,500 miles distant (at St. Joseph), the other 170 miles away, and both in danger of being gnawed to pieces by mice and moths or else of being lost.

In appreciation of Mr. Denig's many kindnesses, I copied my sketch of the interior of the fort for him.

September 20—Mr. Denig has again contrived some employment for me: to paint the picture of an eagle, life-size, on cotton cloth, then to sew thereon strips of red and white cloth in alternating stripes about 15 feet long, thus providing flags for Indians. They are to pay the handsome price of 20 robes apiece for these standards, so only the wealthiest among them can afford to enjoy the distinction of possessing one.

Mr. Denig likes to look on all the while, and he talks to me continually about Indian legends and usages. As he writes the best of those stories for Père De Smet, by whom they are published, there is no need of my preserving more than some bits of memoranda.

After a few studies from life and further understanding as to the position the eagle was to have in relation to the peace pipe, I set to work at once.

Not the golden eagle, but the white-headed or bald eagle is the national emblem of the United States. The last-named bird is not known on the Missouri. The first is a brave well-known to the Indians. Whether the fur traders, like [Benjamin] Franklin, thought the noble golden eagle a more desirable emblem for the coat of arms of the United States than the common bald eagle, I do not know.

Denig said today that he never wears anything at all that belongs distinctly to Indian dress, for the reason that Indians can take pride in procuring for themselves clothes according to our mode and have an ambition to appear dressed as white men, because they regard our garments as more fashionable and expensive. A white person in Indian costume inspires no especial respect among the tribes; on the contrary, he rather lowers himself in their estimation. Furthermore, if he is a white man in Indian garb of a different tribe, he runs far more risk of being killed, because he may not be recognized in that disguise as a paleface. That is possibly Mr. Denig's real reason for discarding buckskin clothes, which are certainly more serviceable against sun and mosquitoes when one is on horseback. However, he rarely goes outside the fort anymore.

The clerks, who will stay here for years, endeavor to oblige the latter. They wear clothes made of materials that the company carries in stock and on which a considerable profit is realized. For that reason, such an arrangement is acceptable to them. Most of the engagés bring with them quantities of clothing for which they paid much less at the place whence they came and which affords them a good article for trade amongst themselves.

The "Mountaineer" costume in which they array themselves in St. Joseph and St. Louis, they have made before their departure for the purpose of distinguishing themselves. Such suits of clothes are made up and sold at Fort Pierre. Buffalo hides are said to be prepared there and marked for sale.

September 21—Have finished the eagle. This is my first oil painting during the entire 5 years I have been absent from home. The smell of the paints gave me both pleasure and pain. I brought no oil colors on the journey with me, because they occupy too much space and take far too much time to dry. Watercolors are much more practical to take along when one is traveling. Otherwise, I should greatly prefer colors in oil. In the first place, I might have more practice, and second, I find that objects covered with hair, like animals, are portrayed in a much more lifelike manner when painted in oil.

I gave general satisfaction with my eagle and am therefore content. If I had refused to paint the bird because of the lack of necessary materials, I might have been thought ill-natured, and that would not have been well.

It might perhaps also have been whispered about in secret that I could not paint the eagle and had evaded the task by a subterfuge.

Mr. Denig has been reading to me again from his manuscript, which is extremely interesting. He is very well educated, and he has made a thorough study of Indian life, a distinct advantage to him in trade. He is so fond of the life in this part of the country that he is averse to any thought of going back to his Pennsylvania home in the United States. Not for the reason, as he says, that he may have 2 wives here, but to avoid political carryings-on that disgust him. Owing to an accident, his old wife is of no service. According to customs in this part of the world, he might be divorced. For the sake of his kind feeling toward her and of keeping her here as a companion for the younger wife, so that the latter may not seek amusement at the homes of the clerks' or engagés' wives, he will not cast her off. Furthermore, he has a son and daughter by her. His boy is being educated in Chicago, but the girl is at home with her mother.

September 22—Yesterday, the thought never once entered my mind that it was Sunday, and yet I keep a journal with great regularity. Rain fell in such streams all day and all night, and penetrated through the roof and ceiling into my room in such quantities, that I was forced to the constant occupation of placing a water basin and empty paint pots beneath the leaks in order to prevent an inundation.

Today I painted a good-sized picture of my bourgeois' pet, Natoh, whose image I represented so true to life that his master was perfectly satisfied and the women especially delighted. I took pleasure in the work, because it has been so long since I painted in oil that I feared I might get out of practice. I have always found that by varying the kind of work I do, by allowing my several senses or faculties some relaxation, I invariably gain.

September 23—This has been a splendid day in my experience. I have been on the chase for the first time and shot my first buffalo. Sketched my first buffalo from life.

After breakfast, old Spagnole, our cattle herder, brought news that huntsmen from the opposition fort were running buffalo on the lower prairie. We called them Dobies, from the word "adobe," because their fort is built of sundried clay. With much kindness, Mr. Denig offered me the pacer so that I could chase buffaloes with Owen Mackenzie and so have the opportunity to study them. Mackenzie rode Condee. We were therefore admirably mounted, and having no orders to bring meat back, we followed the hunt with no other object in view than our own pleasure. Mackenzie was to kill a fine specimen so that I might have the chance to make a sketch.

My equipment consisted of my sketchbook, carried in my pouch, which was swung over my shoulder, a rifle laid across my lap, hunting knife stuck in my belt at the back, and a bullet pouch hung beside the powder horn, also suspended from my belt. Mackenzie had returned only this morning at breakfast from a buffalo hunt of several days in another region. It was most kind of him to ride out again with me before he had taken any rest.

We could not have chosen more beautiful weather—warm sunshine, clear air, a cloudless sky, and the wide, wide horizon in the far distance, merged in blue haze. The ground was dry; no dusty stretches, no bogs or fens. We had to go 5 miles at a brisk pace before we reached the herd we were in pursuit of. We were beginning to think that the "Dobies" had spoiled our sport when, near the so-called Butte de Mackenzie (named for the father of my companion on the chase), we came unexpectedly upon a small group of both old and young bulls. Some of them were lying in the grass near a spring at the upper end of a coulee. Others were comfortably grazing around them. We changed our course at once and rode around the hill, along by thickets of wild cherry and plum trees that covered the coulee, in order to fall upon the buffaloes unawares. But the sound of hoofbeats had already warned them. Those that we had seen lying on the grass had sprung to their feet and, with tails aloft, speedily took flight.

We crossed the brook at a mad gallop and followed close upon the fleeing herd. Even the horses shared our eagerness and tried to outdo each other, but I allowed Mackenzie to get ahead so that I could observe him. With his keen eye he had already selected his victim, approached within 2 feet, and fired. His aim was so true that the animal lay dead as I passed on a gallop. It might be truly said that suddenly he fell to earth. He groaned in the grip of death, beat the ground with his hoofs, and rolled over on his side. The ball had pierced his heart so accurately that at first I thought he had fallen from sheer fright.

We went much farther. I had a great desire at least to shoot at a buffalo. Mackenzie bade me follow him. We set out again at a gallop and came up with the herd. He singled out a bison for me and forced the animal apart from its companions. I pursued it over the rolling prairie until I was so close I couldn't miss aim. At my first shot the ball entered just a little too high;

he turned in such a way that my second shot struck his right knee. Then Mackenzie rode forward and in passing the old fellow sent a bullet into his heart. The pouch swung across my shoulder was a great hindrance when I was shooting, because I was forced to keep it in position with my left arm and yet found it difficult to do that and at the same time fire a gun.

While in full chase, drawing nearer and nearer to the fleeing herd, we reloaded our rifles. Mackenzie was laughing all the while at the wounded buffalo, who was trying to run, notwithstanding a bullet in his heart. In truth he was killed! He could go no farther. All at once he stood as still as a block and looked angrily toward us, his nose dripping with blood. I reined in my pacer and took aim, intending to shoot the animal in the head and bring him down. My horse, all in a heat from the swift gallop, could not stand quietly. He snorted, he foamed, he pawed the ground. As a result, my shot went amiss, merely grazing the forehead of the monster.

He hardly moved his head. He began at last to sway, placed his feet wide apart to balance himself, but nothing could help him more. He was obliged to come down, first on a fore knee, then on his side. The beast was too thin to serve me for a model buffalo. We left him lying there and rode back to the first one we had shot. We dismounted, tethered our horses with long halters, and allowed them to graze while I made as exact drawings as I could, showing different views of the fallen bison. As soon as I had finished my sketching, Mackenzie cut out the tongue and other choice bits of meat to take to his wife. Then we galloped home. What joy!

On our way home, Mackenzie pointed out a prairie to me on the left bank of the Yellowstone where several years ago he had caught a wild mare—an adventure that came to a tragic end. He was riding the fleet-footed John at the time and found that he was some distance ahead of the pack horses that were to carry the meat as usual to the fort, as soon as he should have the luck to kill a buffalo. In the distance he saw a drove of dark-colored animals grazing. He directed his course so as to gain the wind and take them by surprise. He made ready his rifle and gave fiery John the reins as soon as he thought the distance favorable. When he got sight of the herd again, he saw that they were not buffaloes at all, but wild horses. As the horses took to flight immediately—for they were just as shy as the former—Mackenzie laid his gun across his lap, seized his lasso of twisted leather, fixed the noose, and pursued the fleeing herd at a riotous gallop.

John soon drew near his wild blood relations, and Mackenzie selected a black mare from among them that was accompanied by a young foal. He rode after her and with his right hand swung the lasso, catching her head in the noose, while, with his left hand, he held fast to the other end of the rope. He drew in the thong, choking the imprisoned animal by a violent jerk backward that forced her to stop, while at the same time he reined in his own horse. The foal turned back and kept near its mother, now brought to a stand by means of the choking noose and thereby subdued.

With the assistance of Spagnole, who happened to be hurrying by, Mackenzie bound the mare's feet together so that he could leave her lying there while he followed the chase; he dared not return home without meat. Unfortunately, he did not find buffaloes as soon as he expected. His return to the place was delayed until the next day, when he found only the colt's head, tail, and feet. The mother, alas, his captured mare, had already fallen prey to wolves.

To have had such a ride and to have made the sketches! As my shot did not bring down the second buffalo, I returned without trophies.

In the afternoon, we delivered Joe Picotte's portrait. Mr. Denig insisted that I demand a flask of whisky in return, and when I refused to bite, because I would rather have had a pair of elk horns, he himself, as a "wink" to Joe, sketched in a whisky bottle at the bottom of the picture. But it was of no avail; there is no longer any whisky to be had at the adobe fort. Joe Picotte offered to give me any Indian curio that I would mention. I would have liked to have asked for the horns, but what would Mr. Denig have said about that? I was thinking only of myself. So we both came away empty-handed.

Bear meat, juicy and tender, was served at supper. Ramsay shot bruin on a headland (projecting point of wooded land) quite nearby. The Dobies' fort is more favorably situated for hunting than ours, because it stands between two densely wooded forests.

September 24—Began a portrait of Mr. Denig—life-sized, knee-length. This work is to be finished before Mr. Culbertson's return from Fort Laramie, for the reason that he may possibly take me with him to Fort Benton.

Bears big with young, if frightened, smoked out, or in any manner driven from their dens during their winter sleep, are said to bring forth their cubs often prematurely. Ducks, when hotly pursued on the water, are said to fix their feet firmly to the grass below the surface and expose only their bills for air, in the hopes of escaping the eye of their pursuers. Indians on a stag hunt disguise themselves by covering the upper part of their body with a wolf's skin, their head with antlers and tufts of wormwood, in order to deceive the animals. Some of them turn somersaults, tumble over themselves, and gesticulate like mad to arouse the curiosity of the antelopes. In order to be successful, they must keep themselves always in lee of the wind. If a buffalo shows an inclination to fight, shakes his head, and threatens pursuit, which is very rare, one is to shoot him in the nose. The shock will stop him for an instant that the hunter must be quick to profit by and get away.

If it so happens that one's gun is not loaded, one is to prop it firmly on the ground, so that, in running, the beast will strike his head against it. This is to be done, however, only at times of extreme danger, because the gun will be broken to pieces by the hurtling of the furious colossus, and one runs the risk of being trampled underfoot.

The Assiniboin were called Assinibuaduk (correctly, Stone Dakota)[7] by the Cree Indians because, it is said, they followed the custom at an earlier period of cooking meat not in the fire but on hot stones. They call Crows Absaroka, i.e., Crow Indians.

In Indian combat, the intensity of the struggle, the most violent fighting, centers upon the dead or wounded, as in the Trojan wars. An Indian's greatest glory is to distinguish himself as a warrior. That is why the various tribes have been in armed conflict among themselves for so long a time that, as a rule, they can no longer recall the first cause of strife. Their real motive springs less frequently from a desire to wage a war of extermination than to gain an opportunity to win distinction as braves. To kill an enemy from a distance bespeaks no courage, is not regarded as the deed of a hero, is not accredited as a "coup." On the other hand, to strike down your foe in hand-to-hand combat requires force, skill, bravery, and cunning.

Inasmuch as some proof is demanded of the victor's having touched his vanquished enemy, if no one is present to bear witness to the fact, he takes off the scalp of the one slain. He cuts off the skin of the head, together with the hair, or only a part of it. To do that requires time, and to expose himself so long to the rage or vengeance of enemies demands courage. In an encounter where many witnesses are at hand, no scalp is required as evidence of valor for which a "coup" may be accredited, but the hero must have touched the fallen enemy either with his hand or with his weapon. This explains the press about the fallen foe. Furthermore, it is regarded the worst ignominy, the utmost disgrace of a band, especially of a chieftain, if the enemy captures the body of one of his men, treats it with insult, cuts off the limbs, delivers them to women for their dance of triumph, and finally throws them to dogs for food—therefore the furious onset in defense of a fallen savage.

Bands of equal strength seldom attack each other unless the war is waged out of plain hate. To expose themselves to a loss without the certainty of gain is not "smart," as the Americans express it, i.e., not crafty, not shrewd. And shrewdness is the better part of valor. If a band of limited members is set upon by a superior force, everyone fights as courageously as a lion, even to the last man—not one attempts to escape.

It is much the practice among Indians to provoke one another by jeering, to challenge one another. It affords them an opportunity to signalize themselves in the presence of their own people. Assiniboin (Dacota, also Nacota, Hoha, or Hohe, called the disloyal by their related tribe, the Sioux) rarely take prisoners. They kill everybody who comes under their tomahawk: the old and gray-haired, women, children, and young girls. All are enemies—have begotten foes or will beget future foes.

Girls from the best Indian families are strictly guarded. Upon going out at night, they are required to be closely muffled, because young "bucks," when in the humor to run the risk of a fray or to expose themselves to the danger of being stabbed, are allowed to try their luck when and where they please. Such practices lure lads of mettle because of the danger involved and afford them, according to their point of view, a sort of preliminary preparation for military exploits that are to be seriously undertaken later on. When once recognized as braves, they no longer stoop to such larks. They are men. They respect themselves as such and act accordingly. As a brave may have wives, as many as he is able to support, he buys (marries) the girl that appeals to him.

I am told that some time ago the daughter of Ours Fou [Crazy Bear], chief of the Assiniboin (now with Mr. Culbertson at Fort Laramie), hanged herself, because—notwithstanding that she was so closely muffled and so strictly watched—one of these young fellows succeeded in taking advantage of her. He made a boast of this and, from chagrin, she hanged herself. Whether she was driven to the rash act by his ill-mannered boastings or by his bold misconduct, the story does not make clear. In consequence of her death, the boy was forced to go away and join another band for a year, and his relatives had to give horses and other presents by way of atonement for his wrongdoing.

Accidental injury or death to a member of a tribe demands the same vengeance or propitiation as death or injury inflicted purposely. The only exculpation held to be valid is the wounding or killing of a man in the disguise of an animal skin that Indians adopt to decoy stags or antelopes. Such an accident is pardonable, because one must shoot on the instant one is aware of the slightest indication of an animal being near. For the further reason, also, that there is the possibility of an enemy concealing himself under that disguise in order to play the spy.

Assiniboin, Cree, Crows, Blackfeet, Flatheads—none of them have any idea of the great number of people that make up the white population, or the least notion of the power of the United States government. Indians look upon the few white fur traders and the people employed by them as poor men who find no means of earning a living at home. Even though one of the chiefs makes a visit to the States to inform himself, none of his tribe believes what he tells on his return. They are unable to comprehend the marvels he reports. A son-in-law of our bourgeois was murdered for no other reason than his refusal to allow himself to be called a liar.[8] Consequently, he shot down the offender at once; then he was killed by the vengeful tribesmen. These are facts I have picked up during Mr. Denig's sittings for his portrait.

September 25—The portrait is finished. The old man is perfectly delighted that he possesses something new to excite the wonder of the Indians. "Who is that? Do you know him?" he asks Indian women and children. As everyone recognizes the likeness as his own, he is very much pleased. Redskins do not understand how a picture of a man can be painted exactly like a given person whom they know. That cannot be done by any natural means, so the spectacles must surely have had something to do with it; for not one of all the other whites is able to paint, much less wear spectacles.

They comprehend quite clearly that the human figure can be represented with a special sort of clothes; they themselves have practice in such hieroglyphics. In their drawings, they designate a man by representing the figure with legs; a woman by a long skirt: in other words, a figure without legs. To paint a face that every child knows for Minnehasga (Long Knife, the Indian name for the bourgeois, or Americans), that is most extraordinary.

The picture of Natoh was amazing, but now, a very man! What pleases Mr. Denig especially is the remark of his wives, that stand wherever they may in the room or walk wherever they will, the picture constantly looks at them. *"Ehah, waken!"* What witchcraft is this!

Since his portrait has proved such a success, Mr. Denig takes much more interest in my ideas concerning a collection of pictures representing Indian life. He is now convinced that I have sufficient ability to execute them in the proper way. He approves of my plan: six landscapes (forest, prairie, river, coulee, a view in perspective, crags); six animal pieces (buffalo, bear, elk, stag, antelope, horse); six scenes from Indian life (the dance, sport, combat, family, hunt, a group about the council fire). "Only they must be large, very large," he said. "Small pictures produce no effect."

We had great fun this evening with our grizzly. He broke loose from his chain and had to be caught again. Mac and Spagnole threw their lassos but their efforts were in vain, for bruin was prompted to ward them off with his paw. Between the two, they finally succeeded in holding him fast between the nooses. While we drew in the lassos to confine the sly and supple bear securely, the old cowherd stood behind him and seized his ears in order to keep his head still while his collar was put on. The old man then ran out of the way, and our prisoner amused us with the clever manner in which he nipped off the nooses.

Natoh, the dog, nipped him several times on the back but was wary enough never to attack him in front. Natoh knows the effect of a blow from bruin's paw, or a bite with his sharp teeth. Three such dogs would cause a 2-year-old bear little concern.

September 26—During the winter season, the Assiniboin and other tribes construct so-called parks or enclosures in the neighborhood of their villages, into which they entice buffaloes and kill them in droves in order to provision the settlement with meat for a long period. Such occasions afford the spectacle of a hunt more vast than one can conceive and accompanied with much tumult and noise. On ground suitably chosen for their purpose, they throw up a wide-spreading circular enclosure of heavy logs and dry boughs. They leave a small opening through which the park is entered. They then set up two rows of stakes that diverge from either side of this entrance and thus form, when completed, a passageway of sufficient width for a herd to pass through.

As soon as the hunters are aware of a nearby herd, one of them, disguised as a buffalo, goes out to meet it. By imitating the cry of a calf, by bellowing, by shaking his buffalo robe and resorting to all sorts of motions, he endeavors to attract the attention of the animal nearest him and then approaches the entrance to the park by slow degrees.

If the decoy can but excite the curiosity of the buffaloes in front and set them in motion toward him as their ringleader, the others follow of themselves. The members of a herd always follow their leaders en masse, kept together by the timidity of the cows, their solicitude for their calves, and the jealousy of the bulls. The crafty hunter moves slowly, never hurries. If he makes but one bungling movement he may betray himself, startle the animals, cause them to take flight, spoil the hunt, expose himself to ridicule, and lose his reputation as a skilled and practiced huntsman to whom only this most difficult undertaking might be entrusted. Not everyone possesses that exact knowledge of the ways and habits of buffaloes, the exceeding cleverness in imitating them, or the craft and courage to expose himself to their horns and hoofs, which ensures success in ensnaring a herd.

As soon as the foremost bison have come near enough to the narrow opening into the enclosure to bring the entire drove between the two barriers, then hunters on horseback, as well as swift runners, reveal themselves in the rear to cut off retreat. By their presence, they keep the animals moving forward. Not until the disguised hunter has reached the "medicine pole" in the center of the park, has presented his buffalo hide as an offering, and has suspended it there along with other decorations and painted objects does the commotion and noise begin.

The decoy rushes out of the enclosure by an opening on the other side and the bison, attempting to follow, are driven in with wild outcries and renewed tumult until the enclosed space is entirely filled. Then, for fear that the ensnared beasts might attempt to break out, all noise is hushed and the entrance is barred. Standing around the enclosure, huntsmen either shoot their captives or kill them by hurling spears. When they have slaughtered the herd to the last beast, Indian women enter with knives, wash themselves in the gore of their victims, grub into the moist carcasses, dexterously cut off the twitching limbs, drink warm blood, and if very hungry, eat the raw flesh.

When on a general hunt—"*mikawua cerne*"—the hunters shoot in full gallop. They count only the arrows or balls that miss their mark. Women follow close behind them, fall upon their first victim, and carefully rip off the hide, which is all that the hunters require. The meat belongs to those who cut it up and haul it to the settlement on travois drawn by horses or dogs.

Indians of both sexes are passionately fond of games, particularly of those that still survive from their age-old free and independent life. In social intercourse they have no important subjects for discussion, such as political or financial matters, religious questions, or their own history, past and present, as compared to that of other remote nations or of other peoples varying widely in civilization.

Their isolated, lonely existence in tent or village offers few subjects for conversation. Because they are daily employed in war or hunting, their interest in these adventures is already dulled by too-frequent repetitions. Their language, utterly lacking in flexibility and grace, is not favorable to the cultivation of wit. Consequently, they turn to games as the only excitement that their quiet way of life provides. They strive eagerly, enthusiastically, to gain their object in view, no matter how trivial or insignificant, but never contentiously. They have no games that offer opportunities for cheating. They indulge in no strife in their play. I have never seen or heard anything of the sort.

The Iowa are fond of card games. On many occasions I have seen two young people sit down on the ground opposite each other, take off their moccasins, and place all four in a row between them. Then one of the players thrusts his hands into each shoe, leaving in one of them his finger ring or some other small object. His opponent now has to guess in which shoe it is to be found. He is allowed only one chance; accordingly as he guesses right or wrong he wins or loses the game.

At the Omaha village I saw Indian youths hurling lightweight spears through revolving rings—a very difficult feat but one that affords superb exercise for the body, because throughout the game the plays run continually up and down the course. At the same time, they bring their muscles into further action by practicing the swift hurling of a lance at a mark in constant motion.

Herantsa are fond of the so-called billiard game, which, when weather permits, they practice in and around their village. They play the game with a billiard wand that they throw with full strength toward a hoop rolling along the ground. This wand or cue has four markings indicated with leather, and at the end a pad made of leather strips, scraps of cloth, or for want of something better, even bunches of grass.

The winner starts the hoop. Both players run along beside it and throw their wands, whose flight is retarded by the pads—called "*idi*" by the Herantsa—so that they do not take too wide a range over the smooth course. The ground is not as smooth as a floor; it is uneven but cleared of pebbles and filth. They reckon the game according to that mark on the cue or wand on which the falling hoop rests. Oftentimes the players throw their wands so uniformly that they fall one upon the other, making it impossible for the contestants themselves to decide which wins. Without wrangling or the least suggestion of contention, they appeal at once to the older spectators, whose decision is accepted.

Although they always put up some small or trifling object at the beginning of the game, the stakes are steadily increased in value until not infrequently they mount quite high; for instance, from bows, arrows, knives, moccasins, to buffalo robes, ornamented leggings, mitasses [leggings], richly adorned leather shirts, tobacco pipes, guns, horses, tents, and it sometimes happens that the players even venture their elder wives. Some members of the Herantsa tribe devote themselves exclusively to this game—they never take part in the hunt.

The "boss" (Meitzer, Schutz, bourgeois) has told me quite a little about games that are enjoyed among the Crows and the Assiniboin. The former are said to be much given to cheating and swindling; the latter are reputed to be generous by nature and good-tempered. They take a shallow wooden plate, put some beans or seeds of corn in it that have been burned black on one side, and add a magpie's claw, one talon of which is distinguished from the others by a white line drawn from the root to the tip. If they have them, they also put in some brass nail heads, then quickly turn the plate upside down.

According as the black or bright side of the seeds lies upward, but especially as to the position taken by the white tip of the magpie's claw, they reckon the count. If the loser is obstinate or his means considerable, the game is sometimes continued for several days without interruption. He is ashamed to withdraw, so long as he has something still to stake. In such a case, for the sake of giving the loser further chance to continue the play, and also to prolong the sport, the following rule is observed: The winning player puts up a stake in opposition to the one that has been advanced by the loser twice the value of all that he has won. When the excitement of play is at its height, they stake tents made of skins, women, nay, sometimes their own lives.

When one loses everything and no longer possesses a dwelling or a family, he may well be ashamed to live longer. His life is never taken, but he becomes the servant of the player who won, i.e., he must serve as hunter. Values range as follows: two knives equal in value a pair of leggings; two knives and leggings, a blanket; two knives, leggings, and blanket are equivalent in value to a rifle; two knives, leggings, blanket, and gun, to the price of a horse; all of those objects taken together equal in value a tent made of skins; and finally, all the last-named group in combination are reckoned to be worth as much as a woman.

A handful is quickly separated from a bundle of peeled sticks about 2 feet long, even while the player passes them from one hand to the other. His opponent must guess the number taken out.

Mr. Denig declares that the Indians dress themselves much better now than in earlier days. When he became acquainted with them first, they were either nude or else clothed in soiled, shabby, ragged skins. Only very seldom, upon special occasions, were they rigged out in their finery. Nowadays they are more cleanly, bedeck themselves with beads and blankets, own horses, and, according to their own fancy or needs, make saddles that are beautiful as well as practical. In short, along with much that might be spared, Indians have received a very great deal from the fur traders that is beneficial to them.

I have not yet decided whether I shall include the modern Indian in my gallery or limit my productions to representations of the primitive savage. If I adopt the latter plan I lose too much that is picturesque—the majestic folds of the woolen blanket, the war horse with his splendid, impetuous rider. To represent Indian life truly, I would better mingle the ancient and modern, thus representing in my pictures life among Indians as it reveals itself today. That affords more variation, more action and character.

All redskins who live along rivers or lake shores are always clean, because they are not only admirable swimmers but all of them—men, women, and children—are passionately fond of that exercise. Herantsa and Arikara go in bathing every day, preferably twice a day than not at all. Even during the influenza epidemic, they took one another into the water despite high fevers, depleted strength, and coughs. The mother bathes herself and her newborn babe in cold water, so long as the water is not cold enough to freeze. It is owing to the lack of such opportunities and due to conditions only that prairie Indians are ever uncleanly. They have no liking for dirt and filth. Such a disposition is not in keeping with their fondness for personal adornment or their excessive desire to please.

There is another question I have discussed at some length with Mr. Denig, that is, whether the American Indians are a happier people since their association with the white race. That depends, he says, upon the conclusions arrived at by modern philosophical thinkers. If human happiness consists in ease of mind, in contentment, then the Indian is no longer as happy as he was in former days.

Now that he is acquainted with articles made of steel, such as knives, axes, rifles, etc., with tinder boxes, the hewing of logs, with horses, blankets, all sorts of materials for clothing and ornamentation, and with the taste of coffee, sugar, etc., he regards these things as indispensable to his needs. He is no longer content with his former implements, but regards ours as incomparably more profitable to him. His life of contentment in the old days deteriorated into a humdrum, lazy existence, yet was the direct result of a mind satisfied. Now he enjoys that kind of happiness no more.

September 27—This afternoon, about 50 Cree Indians, men, women, and boys, came from a nearby village to pay us a visit. These are the first Cree I have seen. They came to beg rather than to barter—their real purpose is to try to find out at which fort they can get the best price for their skins and furs. They have to be attracted with gifts and much liberality, else they trade with the Hudson Bay Company. No Indians are admitted to trading posts in the charge of English fur traders; only what they have to sell is received there. England's commercial policy is revealed here in its true light—the spread of civilization affords a fine pretext under which to advance trade interests.

September 28—Nearly all of the Cree have left. They wore their ancient and original dress almost entire, garments made of dressed skins, and buffalo robes. These people thought Mr. Denig's parrot a great curiosity. They found it hard to part with him. Old and young, chiefs, braves of rank, and men of low degree were constantly laughing at the bird's remarks, though they could not understand his English "How do you do?" "Pretty Polly," etc.; the fact that he had spoken was sufficiently amusing.

A bird that talks must be a miraculous bird—"great medicine." His crying, laughing, coughing, scolding, carried them out of themselves; they could not help laughing aloud. That Indians are invariably stoical is an erroneous idea pretty generally accepted: for instance, when torture is inflicted. Furthermore, in their deliberations, no interruption when one is speaking would be endured. But in their social life, they laugh and talk as we do. I think it is perfectly proper that an esteemed brave respects himself and guards against doing injury to his own dignity by unbecoming behavior, such as overloud talking and inquisitiveness, boyish laughter and chaffing. That is neither stoicism nor the assumption of an official mien but simply shows respect for his own worth, his inherent dignity, his noble pride.

Cree are said to be most valiant warriors, excellent marksmen with the rifle, but very cautious and pertinacious in trade. Assiniboin excel in shooting with bow and arrow, but it must be taken into consideration that they get fewer good rifles from Americans than the former receive from the English.

Indians at this post place little value on us whites, says Denig the bourgeois. They maintain that we are capable of doing anything, just for the sake of getting buffalo robes—we lie, we cheat, we work in the dirt just as their wives do. We are poor people who could not exist without them, because we must have buffalo robes or we should perish from cold. To impress them, therefore, on our part, we think it best to assume a proud, reserved attitude, to act as though we take no notice of them and refuse to imitate them either in dress or in manner. The instant we should seek them, treat them in an intimate, free-handed manner, they would only believe that we were courting their friendship for the sake of protection, and this accordingly would give them a more exalted idea of their importance and a more significant proof of our own helplessness. In that event, we should have to pay dearly for their friendship and their so-called defense, for there would be no limit to their demands.

Among themselves, Indians value liberality, "largesse," very highly as a virtue; in consequence, every gift is designated, even as a coup, on the buffalo robe. But generosity on the part of a paleface wins neither their friendship nor their respect. They do not look upon a white person as one of themselves or as a recognized friend. His liberality shows his dependence; he seeks protection. The paleface owns no land. He is obliged to get permission to found his fort, to trade with the native race, and he is required to pay formal tribute for the privilege. Accordingly, if one presented an Indian with a gift every day of the year—this morning, a horse; tomorrow, a gun; the day after tomorrow, a blanket; the next day, a knife; and so on until the last day in the year—and then might forget or simply neglect to give him anything at all on the 365th day, he would be all the more angry on account of the omission.

The same is true of an Indian woman. The more one gives her to win her goodwill, all the more convinced is she that the donor is in her power. She does not respect him, much less love him, but only treats him kindly for the sake of the gift. An Indian woman must fear her husband; she then esteems him for his manliness. She desires a warrior, no good-natured pantaloon. Therefore, several sound lashings or other rough treatment is necessary from time to time to keep alive her respect and affection. Besides, an Indian woman loves her white husband only for what he possesses—because she works less hard, eats better food, is allowed to dress and adorn herself in a better way—of real love there is no question. After the third and fourth child, when they are getting too old for their Indian dandies, they begin to devote themselves entirely to the father of their children. If an Indian woman runs away, one is not to pay the least attention to her nor to show the least grief; one is to forget her. It is beneath the dignity of a brave to go after her, to beg her to return. It is not considered to be worthwhile. The Sioux, especially, regard it a very great honor to cast off as many wives or sweethearts as possible, in other words, to break off marriages. I think, however, that as this is an old-age custom, the "little wife," for her own part, takes the matter not too much to heart—perhaps is glad of a change.

The brave regards his wife as a purchased commodity that he may throw aside when he chooses, that he may keep in as large numbers as he can afford to buy and support by his hunting. The better a huntsman he is, the more wild beasts he kills and the greater number of hides he brings home. Buffalo hides when tanned constitute his wealth, by means of which he provides himself with all that he needs. The more excellent the huntsman, the more wives he finds necessary. Women are most skillful and quick in the preparing of skins for sale and the buffalo meat they can use for food. It is not strictly true that he refuses to look at a woman unless she be young or beautiful. To be sure, he aims to have always apart a dainty one for his own private pleasure, but the others are for the most part working women—old maids or widows—who are glad to belong to a family. Owing to constant warfare, it all too frequently happens that children lose their fathers and women lose their husbands. Polygamy among Indians is no indication of sensuality but simply shows their system of labor. I have known many Indians who had only one wife and had never had any other.

If a man marries the eldest daughter of a family, he has also a priority claim on her younger sisters. If he presents one of them with a blanket or some other more valuable gift, she regards herself at once as bound to her brother-in-law; she belongs to him. He may surrender her to someone else, but she is not allowed of her own accord to listen to any other man. On the other hand, if he bestows no gifts upon her, she is free when she reaches a marriageable age. The more sisters a man has for wives, the more successful the marriage is supposed to be. They will not fight one another because they are not acquainted with such a thing as jealousy.

Men in charge of trading posts like to marry into prominent Indian families when they are able to do so. By such a connection they increase their adherents, their patronage is extended, and they make correspondingly larger profits. Their Indian relatives remain loyal and trade with no other company. They have the further advantage of being constantly informed through their association with the former as to the demands of trade and the village or even the tent where they can immediately find buffalo robes stored away. A woman of rank is too expensive for a clerk and brings him no advantage, for the reason that he is employed at a fixed salary and receives no further profit. If he falls into debt, he is brought under obligation to the company.

Today I saw a Cree woman with the upper part of her body entirely uncovered, a sign, they say, of mourning for the loss of a child. She was walking and wore a buffalo robe. The Cree woman's garb is like that of the Sauteurs woman, i.e., shoulders and arms bare, skirt held up by means of bands or straps. When the weather is cold, they put on sleeves that are knotted together in the back at the nape of the neck and on the breast. Assiniboin women frequently wear only one sleeve, leaving the right arm free. They wear shirtlike skirts that instead of being held in place by special straps are made to extend over the shoulders.

September 30—Have been hard at work. From a medal, I had to paint the portrait of Pierre Chouteau, Jr., in the gable over the house gallery. All day long I had to work in a most uncomfortable position on an unsafe scaffold. Pierre Chouteau, Jr., is one of the oldest and wealthiest shareholders in the great American Furtrading Company to whom Fort Union belongs.

Indians think cedars and firs the shrewdest of plants because they keep their foliage for the winter. Not bad reasoning. A shrewd and intelligent manager of a house, for instance, would have a green sprig of a fir tree as his emblem. Heretofore, in our interpretation of the flower language, only feelings, not intellectual gifts, have been represented.

Mr. Denig asked me whether I do not consider that Indians, in destroying all reminders of a deceased relative, in never again speaking of him by name but as "the one whom you know," show more delicacy than we do when we preserve remembrances everlastingly, perpetually talk of grief, and nourish sorrow, taking satisfaction in such indulgences and thereby wasting much precious time in wailing that should be turned to better account.

I think, really, that his instances are not well taken, for Indians not only wail and howl for a long time while by the grave of one whom they esteemed but, as everybody knows, they carry the departed one's bones along with them for memorial. Furthermore, only those among us who have nothing better or more worthwhile to do waste their time in lamentations.

I found even less delicacy of feeling shown in a newly married couple's custom of keeping in hiding from their parents-in-law. For instance, if a son-in-law would talk with his wife's father and mother, he must always speak through a closed door or else transmit his message through a third person. He is not ever allowed to look them in the face. In passing them he must conceal his countenance with his hands or his blanket. If he comes unawares into their presence, he is immediately reminded of his mistake. To some degree, the same thing is required of the daughter-in-law, but only in relation to her husband's parents. She has nothing to conceal from her own father and mother. Furthermore, it is required only during the time before she takes up her abode with her parents-in-law or in her husband's tent. It is very seldom that she leaves her own home during her early married life. A son-in-law often lives with his wife's parents, hunts for them, and helps to support them.

Such cloaking and hiding I find ridiculous, and only indicative of false modesty. It would show much more delicacy if the newly wedded pair conducted themselves in a perfectly natural manner and allowed no allusion whatever to their change of state. And such observances among Indians!

FIVE

October 1851

October 1—This morning I put the finishing touches on the portrait of Pierre Chouteau, Jr. This afternoon I was free to do what I liked, so I took my double-barreled gun under my arm and went for a walk on the hill to enjoy the far-reaching view beyond the Yellowstone. I strolled around a bit with the intention of finding out what I could about this vicinity. As I was getting to the top of a hill covered with loose stones, I noticed a bright spot in motion on another height.

I lay down at once to observe the animal more closely with my telescope. I found it to be a fat *cabri* [antelope] buck that evidently had caught wind of me already, though he could not see me. Hoping to get nearer to him, I slipped backward down the hill and approached through a dell. I soon came in sight of a herd of antelopes that, having been given the alarm by the buck, were peering intently about them, trotting back and forth with eager glance, stamping their feet, blowing through their nostrils. Then they started off, one behind the other, turned around again, and finally took to flight, the buck in the rear. What an elegant picture! How quickly lost to view! There was no use in my attempting to pursue those shy creatures on foot, so swift in flight. I turned from the *mauvaises terres* [badlands] and followed the well-beaten path that Assiniboin take to the fort.

When I was forcing my way through the garden coulee (the deep bed of a dried-up stream thickly overgrown with coppices and bushes, over against which lies our potato garden), hoping to start or find other game, I thought that this would be an extraordinarily favorable place for concealment for a lurking enemy. Prying sharply into the thick shrubbery on all sides, I sprang across the now-insignificant brook and was proceeding toward the horse pasture with rapid strides when I heard a rustling of dry leaves behind me;

someone laughed. Turning around, I saw two young Assiniboin leaping out from behind some bushes. I stopped and cocked my gun. The elder, still laughing, offered his hand and gave me a hearty handshake.

From their natural, friendly manner, as well as from their clean and expensive clothing, I knew they were not warriors, still less enemies, though they were doubly armed with bows, arrows, and guns, which weapons they carried at their backs in leathern cases swung over the shoulders. The elder drew these off over his head and gave them into my keeping, with the remark that he would like to examine my gun. I thought that most courteous; he dared not expect that I would suffer an exchange of weapons or expose myself to the danger of being unarmed. That he perceived this at once and acted accordingly predisposed me in his favor.

As I was walking along between the two brothers (their resemblance was striking), the younger gave me to understand, by means of signs, that they had been watching my approach from a distance and had immediately concealed themselves to startle me, just to see how I would stare. On the impulse, I had a good mind to give them a peppering, but I reconsidered. If they had been hostile, I should have had ere then two arrows in my body without anybody's having seen the murder or, perhaps, ever finding it out. Notwithstanding that I returned safe from this adventure, I decided it would not be amiss to avoid in future such dangerous places. Upon arriving at the fort, I learned that the lads were brothers of Mr. Denig's younger wife.

During our evening meal, I was warned against the peril of lonely rambles—all the more dangerous, they say, because I was not a hunter and therefore did not recognize signs that would betray the possibility of an enemy lurking near. Only this spring, I was told, a woman of the Cree tribe set out on the longer route from this fort to that of the opposition. Hardly a half-mile from here, she was slain with arrows by Blackfeet and then scalped. The enemies had concealed themselves so effectually in high grass that even this keen-eyed Indian woman herself did not notice them, though she was only a few paces distant.

Later in the evening, Carafel related to me an adventure he had with the Sioux, as a result of which he is still lame in one foot. Two years ago, he was told to go on horseback with Ramsay (now with the "Dobies"), to a settlement of Assiniboin.

As they were traveling through some rough ground five miles from here, they met, quite suddenly, about fifteen Sioux who came over a hill just at the moment they themselves arrived at the spot. The Sioux fired, wounding Carafel, who was riding ahead, from head to foot, and killed his horse. Ramsay ran off at full speed. As Carafel's horse fell to the ground, his gun went under the brute's body and he was unable to pull it out; consequently, he was without any weapon to repel his assailants.

Notwithstanding his severe wounds, he fled also. While running at full speed, his feet caught in a shrub or a tangle of tall grass and he fell. He sprang to his feet again, for his pursuers had already overtaken him. One of them was in the act of discharging a gun in his face, but Carafel still had sufficient strength to seize the barrel and turn it aside until some blows with the butt end of the rifle dashed him to the ground. He felt then that all was lost. Just as he was passing into unconsciousness, he said in Assiniboin, "Sioux, it takes a great many of you warriors to kill one white man."

All at once his murderers fled from the spot. He collapsed. He recovered consciousness after a time and crawled to the adobe fort, the nearest place of refuge. He is said to have made a pitiable appearance; a bullet had grazed his foot, cutting some ligaments to shreds.

That flight of the Sioux warriors seemed most extraordinary to me. Mr. Denig, who had told me of the adventure earlier, explained their behavior by taking for granted that they had supposed the two riders to be Chippewa half-breeds, their deadly enemies, and first became aware of their mistake when they were near enough to see Carafel's blond curly hair and blue eyes. Invariably, every half-breed has black, straight hair and dark brown eyes. They left Carafel prostrate and without assistance, notwithstanding their friendship—nay, blood relationship—to the Assiniboin, because they thought he was dead and feared they might draw vengeance upon themselves if they were known to have done the deed. Ramsay is a *metif*, or half-breed.[1]

Indians believe in spirits, and though they have never yet had any visible evidence of such things, they talk with them and take counsel. They think that spirits follow them about 2 feet above the ground.

Mr. Denig says to me frequently: "When you go to the Blackfeet territory," etc. Dare I hope that I shall go so far, that Mr. Culbertson will take me with him?

October 2—After dinner Mr. Denig came to my room and asked me to accompany him on a cabri hunt. From the gate, he had just seen seven of those antelopes grazing on a hill in one herd. To be sure, what he saw were only high spots moving about, but Mr. Denig is keen-sighted and well practiced in interpreting signs on the prairie. He takes much pride in the fact that even his wives have not as good eyesight as he.

He conducted me to the garden coulee that we might get out of the wind, which was blowing over the hill from the west. We hurried along up the brook bed, but with the utmost caution, in order to get around on the other side of the hill where the antelopes were feeding. Having arrived there, the bourgeois took off his coat and hat, examined his priming pan, and crept up the hill, but not without first giving me instructions to remain perfectly still, not to spoil his sport by noise due to overhaste.

In my eagerness to see something, and maybe to get a chance to take a shot also, I crawled to the nearer entrance to the little coulee, took my hat off, and lay down in the grass. Some of the animals were quietly grazing; others lay unconcerned on the ground. Unluckily, Mr. Denig was obliged to content himself with killing a female antelope that was in a position that left her flank exposed. At the report of the gun, all the rest took flight, unfortunately, to the other side of the valley.

I was much astonished to see no horns among the female antelopes that I have had the opportunity to observe at Fort Pierre. I was all the more surprised at this for the reason that both Bodmer and Catlin represent their antelopes (cabris) with horns alike, which in itself seems unnatural. I have seen positively no female cabris with horns. Are there two different species, or are the artists in error? They made the mistake of representing buffalo herds consisting only of bulls—no cows. I must admit, however, that one does see small droves of bulls only, but this does not apply to the cabri bucks. Neither did Audubon know of female cabris without horns. Nevertheless, I am absolutely sure that neither the doe that was killed nor her companions showed any signs of growing horns.

The cabri that had been shot made two desperate leaps and fell dead. The buck lingered to muster in the remaining doe, but Mr. Denig got to his feet, allowing himself to be seen and not reloading his gun. The shy buck took to flight. We hurried over to our quarry; the bullet had pierced her heart—had gone directly through her breast. I bound her dainty feet together and took her on my shoulders, completely encircling my neck, and carried her to my room. I felt her warm blood soak through my clothes and flow down my back.

Upon reaching the fort, I laid her out on the floor and immediately set about painting my first antelope. Mr. Denig's wives were waiting around, most impatient to prepare the little animal for food, but I had not brought it a distance of three miles for the purpose of satisfying myself with an incomplete study.

October 3—Just before dinner, Packinaud was brought home in a cart, wounded. He and Mackenzie rode out yesterday on a buffalo hunt but found nothing until early this morning. As both of these men are ambitious to be thought the best buffalo hunter, they galloped full tilt into the herd. Packinaud, who was riding John, had the advantage of the better mount, for John is an excellent and enduring traveler, only too unruly for some riders. The instant he is given the reins, he is in full gallop—never needs to be urged on, never gradually relaxes speed; his first spring measures all of 21 feet.

When the two hunters neared the buffalo herd, John tore off, neighing for joy. Andre, though himself a good runner, is not so spirited, and therefore more easily guided. Because he is not so impetuous and powerful, his rider is much more sure of hitting the object aimed at, of securing his victim. In his mad rush, John carried Packinaud into the midst of the herd and crowded him so closely between two buffalo bulls that he could not get his gun in a position to fire. At the same time, one of the bulls turned aside, but the other tossed his head with a jerk, made a pass with one horn through his pursuer's left shinbone, and stuck the other into the horse's breast, bringing him to a halt.

Meanwhile, Mackenzie had already killed a cow and was following closely behind Packinaud when the latter was stopped, passed him, and fired on the bull, which immediately tumbled over. Our wounded man called Mackenzie to his assistance. Mackenzie sent the Spaniard immediately to the fort to bring a cart. They think P.'s shinbone is broken.

After dinner, nothing to do. Weather ideal, temperature mild. Who could restrain himself from taking a walk? Danger? Well, anyone who stands in fear has no need to come into these wilds. All the more necessary, being here, that one carefully explore the whole region—know the ground. What I lack in keen-sightedness and acute hearing, I shall endeavor to offset with courage.

If I only had better eyesight, how I should enjoy this life. I would not desire a better lot than to roam around, now on foot, now on horseback, with sketchbook and gun. Just now, when I have overcome the most difficult hindrance and my life purpose is so near fulfillment, it is impossible for me to think that my life should be in peril.

The image of the graceful cabri buck hovered ever before my eyes. I was much inclined to go in search of him again. As I had seen the little band several times already in the neighborhood of that brackish stream, I turned my steps thither, stumbled upon several wolves, but in the end came across fresh tracks in the sandy soil—they had been made by antelopes! Following them, I mounted the hill. As I was not expecting to meet the animals so near at hand, I was too incautious and showed myself to them really before I was aware of their presence. To be sure, I ducked instantly to the ground, but away they went over mountain and vale, and all was over with my cabri hunt. I reproached myself severely for my carelessness, my inconvenient habit of indulging in dreams, inopportune musings.

After deciding to hunt antelopes and then giving my exclusive attention to their tracks, successfully approaching and meeting with the animals, even my very habits as painter caused me to frighten them by showing myself too soon and to lose my chance to study the habits and postures of these beasts of the chase. In vain I searched for them with my telescope. I could not find them anymore. I did get sight of a herd of buffalo grazing several miles off, and I enjoyed watching them. Now, I said to myself, if I am unable to steal up on them, that is convincing proof that I have no talent for hunting.

I hurried through the many dells and tiny valleys and around the hill to the buffaloes. Concealed in grass or shrubs of wormwood, I peered this way and that over a hillcrest, fearing that the animals had already run away. With beating heart, I finally crept up the last steep incline of a ridge, crawled on my belly to the edge of the plateau, and saw the herd hardly 30 feet distant from me. There were thirteen bulls and one calf. Several birds, about the size of a dove with white bodies and blue-gray wings (magpies?), were sitting on the animals' humps in the midst of the thick, shaggy hair, picking off vermin.

One of the bulls pleased me immensely with his odd appearance; he was almost totally black and much more shaggy than the others. Tufts of hair on his forelegs, above his forehead, and under his chin dangled about with his slightest movement. When viewed from the rear, the front part of him—all overgrown with bushy hair that rose high above his hump—seemed to have nothing at all in common with his hinder parts. It seemed not to belong to the same beast.

For a long while I lay stretched at full length in the grass, completely absorbed in a detailed study of those beasts. In my pleasure as painter I forgot entirely the role of hunter, though I might have had an excellent chance to shoot the black imp through the heart. After a time, they went on farther, sliding down a steep descent to a narrow path on the other side that led through a defile. Then I was eager to fire upon them. To forgo such an opportunity would show lack of skill, indeed.

Knowing that buffaloes go uphill not nearly so rapidly as they go down, I made a detour over ground covered with rocks and boulders, through deep hollows, brambles, and thorns, in order to reach the pass and take them in the flank. As the sun was already low and I was a considerable distance from home, I had no time to lose. I concealed myself behind a great rock just at the point where the defile opens upon the prairie, the place where Mackenzie shot the first buffalo on the day he went hunting with me.

The black fellow was one of the last to pass me. I fired. He turned aside and ran off at a gallop, the others with him. Expecting to see the wounded buffalo fall, I remained where I was, neglecting to discharge my second barrel upon him. He refused to do me the favor of falling dead. He continued to run—perhaps he is still in flight. I reloaded and hurried around the Butte de Mackenzie (as the old cowherd named this hill and the nearby pass in memory of Mackenzie's father, who used to be manager at Fort Union) to the road leading to our trading post.

There I saw a rider who was waving his cap to me. I waved mine in return, and then I recognized Mackenzie. Ah! I thought, they have also caught sight of the herd from the fort, have mounted at once, and have sent the pack horses ahead. It was evidently true. Other horsemen came into view, followed by the riderless pack horses. Mackenzie, whose chase I had spoiled, caught a glimpse of still another queer old fellow taking his ease alone on the prairie. Better fresh meat, though a little tough, than none at all, he said, and gave

Andre the reins. There was a tendril of up-curling smoke, and the buffalo fell to the ground.

I had now been discovered by Joe Dolores, our horse guard, who sprang down from his nag, fastened the long halter to one of the pack horse's forefeet in order to force him to stand, and called out to me to mount and follow. Not a bad idea. To be sure, a pack saddle is far from being a comfortable seat, a lariat a sorry bridle, but walking alone over a wide prairie at night is still less agreeable. I swung myself upon the horse and he galloped forward of his own accord, to join his comrades.

Upon coming up with the others, I found that they had already stripped off the buffalo's hide on one side, had cut off the hind legs, had bound together the tendons and thrown them across a pack horse, had distributed the choice bits in accordance with hunters' prerogatives, and were ready to start back to the fort. Night fell. Mackenzie and I hurried forward. The Spaniard took advantage of the darkness to filch a tanned white calfskin from a neighboring hill that had been hung there by an Indian as a votive offering to the sun. He came up with us again at a full gallop before we rode into our courtyard.

Mr. Denig was much relieved in mind to see me again. He feared that I might have lost my way, might have got bewildered in the rough, trackless wilds, or else had met with an accident. With the hope of directing my attention to the location of the fort, he had given orders that guns be fired several times. His two young brothers-in-law expressed the intention of going in search of me at daybreak, if in the meantime I should not have returned. For excuse, I offered him my irresistible delight in being in the buffalo region, where I could make a thorough study quite comfortably of those wild beasts.

"That is the way with all you people with your hobbies and favorite occupations," he replied. "In your eager zeal you discard prudence altogether. Then when an accident happens, we have to bear the blame. A report is immediately spread abroad in the States that the dead man was rich, that he was killed for his money, or if he was poor, that his death was due to jealousy or some such motive."

October 4—The Blackfeet tribe on this side of the Rocky Mountains is estimated to have 1,500 tents and approximately 4,000 warriors; Crows, 440 tents and 1,200 braves; Assiniboin in this vicinity, 420 tents and as many as 1,050 braves; those farther north on Winnipeg Lake, from 200 to 300 tents. Cree, or Knistenaux, who trade here occupy 150 tents, but the entire tribe is said to amount to 800 tents. Arikara are reckoned to have 600 warriors in 300 tents; Chippewa, 3,000 tents; and Sioux, 4,000. Pawnee and Arikara, and Assiniboin and Sioux are not from the same parent stock. Pawnee and Arikara belong to Caddoan stock; Assiniboin and Sioux belong to Siouan stock. Mandan, above Fort Clarke, have 16 tents (lodges), only 7 of which are occupied. Together with those who live with the Grand Mandan, among the Herantsa tribe, they numbered 45 men before the recent cholera epidemic.

Mr. Denig came upon me while I was working on a sketch of my feminine beau ideal. He was extraordinarily pleased with the form and wished to have it painted at once, so that he might hang the picture on the wall in the reception room. He could not forbear his bad jest concerning my hard task in attempting to portray a naked human figure so divine, so exalted, that it would make no appeal to the sensual. He made me feel sick. I was not too willing to expose my ideal to further remark. But I know that I must accustom myself to this conclusion: There will always be ordinary people who see only physical attraction in a nude body, not spirit.

October 5—After Mr. Denig and I had washed and dressed Packinaud's wound, he brought the conversation round to the name of a Herantsa woman who is called "Fifty." On her account, fifty men suffered the penalty, an evident euphemism, because she ran away from her husband twice, all on the same evening. For like misdoing, fifteen paid the penalty on account of an Assiniboin woman. Carafel happened to be in the camp at the time and had been invited to join them, but declined (briefly, a rape en masse). The latter woman, from indulgence in the practice for such a long time, lost the use of her legs. In Belle Vue, I saw a Pawnee woman who had been taken prisoner on the prairie by thirty Omaha braves, and so abused by all thirty of them that she remained a cripple for life.

It was there also that I heard the story of fifty Comanche having abused a white prisoner in like manner and then left her in such a wretched condition that she was found maimed and insane by her people. I think that Indian women do not so easily lose their reason, at least from such causes, because they are less afraid and defy pain.

Now and then Indians give what is properly called a glutton feast. Everyone invited is served with an unusually large portion of meat. To the incessant tattoo of the drum, they devour what is placed before them. The one who first swallows his portion is victor; the one who fails to do so is required to get rid of what is left by paying a forfeit, i.e., by presenting a gift.

Whether from excess of joy over their triumph or from hate, Indians bite into the flesh of slain enemies, but this occurs only in their rage immediately following a battle. They do not go as far as the Aztecs and eat their victims.

Mr. Denig came again to see the sketch of my ideal human figure, repeated his obscene remarks, and expressed again his desire to possess a painting of it. When he received a curt refusal, he found only faults in my conception of feminine loveliness—she looked ugly, was much too thin, etc. I replied that I would much rather hear him find fault with the sketch than to listen to such coarse remarks. It was beneath my dignity to paint a nude figure merely for the sake of appealing to his carnal passions and those of other men. I was entirely at his service for the painting of other objects, but I would not paint this.

October 7—For a moment there arose such unusual noise made by Indian women and children at the rear gate that everyone rushed down to the riverbank with the expectation of witnessing Mr. Culbertson's arrival. The excitement was occasioned, however, by the sight of an Indian with his wife getting ready to swim with their two horses across the Missouri. One of our Assiniboin swam to the sandbank and demanded to know who he was. As we supposed, he was Herantsa, not Absaroka.

With the aid of my telescope, I was able to watch his interesting preparations. He accomplished the crossing of the river in a similar manner to that described by me earlier when I swam across the Papillon. By means of a dried buffalo hide they formed a sort of flatboat on which they placed the saddle and their personal belongings, and to which they fastened a long cord. While he was carrying the skin boat and leading his horse into the water, his woman, screened by her own nag, stripped herself naked and, driving the horse before her to the river's brink, gave over her clothes to her husband, who thrust them underneath their goods and chattels. Then with powerful strokes, he started over, holding his horse's leather lariat between his teeth, and the long cord with which he pulled the boat after him. His wife followed, guiding her nag in the same manner. They reached the shore on this side without the least trouble.

For the sake of keeping on good terms with my bourgeois, I began to paint another female figure, but this one not entirely in the nude.

October 8—Today an Assiniboin brought the first news I have received from Fort Berthold since I left. He says the Arikara are still dying like flies under frost. The survivors are in a fury. They have razed the blockhouses of the opposition and stolen their goods. Dorson found it necessary to bring his great guns into action (4-pound cannons) in order to protect himself from the same fate. If this be true, Dorson has no further prospect of trading with the Arikara. Nothing is left for him to do but ship his goods to Fort Pierre. No further illness is reported among the Herantsa.

Indians do not value time at all; among them the idea that time is money does not prevail. They estimate the price for the work they do, irrespective of the time they take in the accomplishment of it. Besides, they must be doing something, otherwise they would find the days entirely too long and tedious. Consequently, they work rather to kill time than to derive profit from it. They live at random, generally speaking, without purpose in life, so they do not have to regard time as capital. On the contrary, they find it more frequently a burden. I go forward leisurely with my pictures. There is no haste. The more easily I appear to paint, the less my work is valued.

What costs little is regarded as of little worth. We had proof of that not long ago. An Assiniboin came to get medicine for eye trouble. He expected the charge to be nothing less than a buffalo robe, or perhaps a horse, just as he would have been required to pay to their jongleurs, or doctors. As it happened, he received the remedy as a gift. He uttered no thanks, nor would he use the eye water; he no longer had any confidence in its healing power.

Situated on the steep bank of a river on the open prairie, and exposed to every wind that blows from any point of the compass, Fort Union is said to be the coldest place of all the posts belonging to this company, even as cold as those situated on Hudson Bay.

October 9—Sitting before a jolly open fire by the side of the wounded Packinaud, while a cold, strong wind howled in the courtyard, I listened to amusing adventures related by Carafel, who was today in fine humor. One of his stories interested me more than the others because I know most of the people concerned. The hero is that sly dog Vilandre (Carafel, a born

Canadian, always says "Vilandra"). He is equally well known as a tip-top trapper, trader, and hunter, and as a reckless spendthrift not overscrupulous about honesty.

One day, Old Gre and his comrade hired Vilandre to go along with them and trap beavers in the vicinity of Blackfeet (Pieds Noirs) territory. On the way, his two masters quarreled all the time, never agreed with each other about anything, and finally brought matters to such a pass that our hero could stand it no longer. He said to them, "Now, here, this won't do. You two never agree. After this fashion we shall accomplish nothing. Two masters for one hired man is a bad arrangement. It is better for me to employ both of you. Sell me your horses and traps, and I will pay you later on in beaver skins."

They traded. They realized an unusually large profit from the hunt; it was, you see, in the good old days. They brought back between 400 and 500 bundles of ten skins each.

Colonel [David] Mitchell, the present U.S. agent of the Indian Department in St. Louis, was then bourgeois at Fort Union. When he saw the three trappers approaching, he went forward to meet the two old traders, paying no attention to Vilandre, who was leading the way with two heavily laden horses. Mitchell knew nothing of the later agreement and intended, of course, to make himself agreeable to those who went out in charge of affairs, congratulate them upon their successful hunt, and invite them in. Vilandre passed on by the employees of the company who were standing beside the gate, curiously looking on, while waiting to receive the packets. He carried his head as high as did the bourgeois himself. And imagine the astonishment of the latter when he saw Vilandre haughtily pass the gate!

"What! You will not trade with me?" he asked the old "grumblers."

"The beaver skins belong to Vilandre, not to us."

The expression of certain faces immediately changed—business took a different turn altogether. Mr. Denig, clerk at that time, was dispatched at once to present his compliments to Vilandre and to ask him to unload his pelts here. In the end, he relented. As he rode up to the gate, he caught sight of a splendid girl, the daughter of old Garion by an Indian woman. He was much pleased with her and said to himself, "This night you shall be mine."

He sold his furs, which were bringing high prices at that time, paid his quasi-employers forthwith, clothed himself throughout in new apparel, assumed the arrogance of the devil, and bought a great number of articles for gifts. When the horses were brought in from the pasture in the evening and corralled (put in an open stall), he took his best runner and, leading him to Garion, said brusquely, "Take him. He is yours!"

Garion demurred, suspecting Vilandre's purpose at once.

"Holy virgin," shouted Vilandre, "am I such a poor man that I can't afford to give away a horse? Haven't I still my little gray?" Thereupon he stroked the gray horse caressingly, without bestowing even a glance upon the beautiful girl near him. But he sent a friend a little later to Garion asking his daughter in marriage.

Her father consented, on the condition that a marriage contract be drawn up in writing and signed. Well and good. Vilandre went at once to Moncrevier[2] (now with the Pawnee), requesting the draft of an agreement that, when read aloud, would contain all the usual expressions and requirements, but with this difference: A provision was to be inserted permitting him to leave the bride whenever he chose.

Moncrevier, a sort of wag, found much pleasure in anticipation of the impending wedding feast and made all things ready. Garion was satisfied; his daughter, who received many presents, was content; and Vilandre, on the same night after his return to the fort, was in possession of his beautiful bride.

How long do you think he kept her? One entire winter. When he determined to send her away, he set her on a good horse and presented her with abundant apparel, as well as provisions.

"Holy virgin," he cried, "when I bid farewell to my wife, whom I am casting off, I will not take the shirt from her back. I put her on a horse and supply her with goods. I don't mind the loss of a beaker of coffee." A beaker—a mug, cup, tin drinking cup—was also used for measuring sugar, coffee, and meal. It holds a pint. Coffee struck off level with the top, sugar or meal heaped up, is reckoned a pound.

I have finished the picture I was painting. While working on it, I was often set laughing by Mr. Denig's remarks. At every stroke of the brush he found fault, just as with the other one. I let him chatter, because his judgment is in no sense authoritative so far as I am concerned. I strive to please him in other matters.

Finally, when the meaning of the picture began to be apparent, he began to understand and became then just as much concerned for fear I might spoil what I had done well. "Don't touch it again. You will certainly ruin it. Stop! Stop!" And so on.

Indian words for "friend": *taro* (Iowa), *digahau* (Omaha), *kondah* (Sioux), *kuna* (Assiniboin), *marequa* (Crow and Herantsa), *nitschuwa* (Cree), *sihuan* (Arikara), *manuka* (Mandan). *Koki* in Pawnee means "stone"; *gaggi* in Arikara means "bad."

October 10—Have cleared up everything. The bourgeois now has all that he desires from me as a painter. Mr. Culbertson is to decide upon his arrival whether I go with him or remain here, and what, on the whole, my occupation shall be in future.

To give me an idea of the easygoing manner in which Indians frequently count a coup, Mr. Denig told how once upon a time when Sioux and Assiniboin were at war with each other, a band of sixty warriors marched up to the gate before he was able to get it closed. Luckily, aside from the married women, there was only one Assiniboin here, a boy whom he confined under lock and key in a small room just above the one I now occupy. The secret was soon found out; a woman divulged it to one of the braves, who came to Mr. Denig forthwith and offered both his gun and his richly decorated robe if in return he might only shake the boy's hand.

He would take no weapon at all with him and even desired Mr. Denig's presence. But the latter refused, saying to the Indian brave, "If you wish to count coup, you are to seek the occasion in battle."

Mr. Denig spent his first year in this business at Fort Pierre, under Mr. Ludlow.[3] One summer he had to go out on the prairie with several Sioux to hunt in order to get meat. As soon as they came near the buffaloes, they pitched their tents, one for him and his wife, a second for their relatives, a third for the remainder of the company. All the men except himself left the tents and went out at once to hunt buffaloes. As they stayed away longer than was expected, he took a walk about the settlement to find out where the hunters were.

Soon he discovered several buffalo bulls rushing directly upon the camp. He hurried into his tent to get his rifle. Meanwhile, his mother-in-law had gone in there and was standing nearest him when he entered and called in haste for the gun, which the old woman handed to him. He killed two bulls. For several weeks afterwards, he was the butt of all jokes, because he had spoken directly to his mother-in-law. He should have called to her from without the tent but was in such haste that he did not for a moment realize that he was not speaking to his wife. Jokes are rare among Indians and survive so much the longer. They lose nothing here, even from constant repetition.

Once during a war between the Herantsa and Assiniboin tribes, sixteen Herantsa braves on a visit to the Crows passed here that they might be put across the Missouri as good customers of the big company [American Fur Company]. They had hardly seated themselves in the office when a band of Assiniboin arrived. Mr. Denig was greatly disquieted for fear of conflict when the two hostile bands stood face to face. He required both chiefs to promise him at once that they would regard the fort as neutral ground. When the most distinguished of the Assiniboin entered the office, he offered the pipe.

The chief of the Herantsa refused to smoke the pipe, notwithstanding that he was surrounded by the enemy in superior numbers. Mr. Denig threatened to show him the door: "He should make the effort." After the hostile parties had grimly surveyed one another as long as they liked, the Herantsa walked proudly but quietly out to the gate, with a challenge to the others to follow them.

Many times, fur traders for the same company are brought into strangely complicated relations. Indians look upon fur traders who have an established post and carry on business with them as one of themselves. They regard more or less as a foe, a fur trader to the same company who is established in the domain of their enemy. Even the most intelligent among them, such as Four Bears (Quatre Ours), cannot understand why white people who go from here to the Arikara or Blackfeet—enemies of the Assiniboin—should not be treated by them as enemies: For instance, why Charbonneau at Fort Berthold was unjustified in firing upon the same Sioux who came from Fort Pierre; why one is not permitted here to fire upon members of the Blackfeet tribe merely because they carry on trade with palefaces at another fort, yet do not hesitate to rob any white person whom they might find traveling alone from this fort.

Fur traders are not liked but merely endured, because they barter things necessary to supply the Indians' wants. They are required by every tribe that grants them the right and the ground for a fort to furnish protection and assistance in any conflict with enemies (inside the fort only). Fur traders are to regard the foes of Indians with whom they deal as their own foes. Only those carrying on trade on their own account, not for a company doing an extensive business, would find it possible to agree to such terms; nor would those independent traders be allowed to deal with any other than that especial tribe and their friends. After all, it is easy to understand that no tribe likes to see the same company with whom they deal sell arms and ammunition to their enemies.

On a recent journey from Fort Benton to this post, Mackenzie met a warlike band of Blackfeet on the lookout for Assiniboin. He was alone, but fortunately he was riding John, famous among the tribes of this section for the swift pace at which he can travel. As Mackenzie thought he had nothing to fear from the approaching Blackfeet, he did not evade the warriors. They surrounded him, asked him all sorts of questions, and, declaring him to be an Assiniboin, demanded his horse, his gun, and his knife. He did not acquiesce to those demands, of course, but sought to get rid of them by cunning, and then give John his head.

He protested to the Blackfeet that the company's steamboat was nearby on the river, and he had been sent to meet the steamer and deliver important tidings. Now they wished to see the boat. They rode forward a mile to a neighboring hill, from the summit of which they could get a view of the Missouri. Meanwhile, Mackenzie made them a present of some tobacco. At the first favorable moment, he put spurs to John, who, with a frightful bound, galloped off and away. Mackenzie knew that the braves would neither overtake him on their saddle horses nor make any attempt on his life.

When two Indians who are not hostile meet on their wanderings, they usually stop several paces apart and question each other as to whence they come, what news they bring, whether anything unusual was noticed along the path, and whether they met anybody. If either reports news of significance, they sit down together and, if possible, smoke a pipe. As a rule, the younger offers the pipe to the older and concedes to him also the privilege of beginning the cross-questioning. If one of them has the way before him along which the other has come, he is warned concerning every trace, every significant indication of danger near at hand. If he has found no sign of anything to fear, the other goes on all the more unconcerned.

Indians never greet each other with handshake or nod; neither do they wish one another "Good day" or "Good morning." If they are well acquainted but still have nothing further to say, they give their watchword, "*Hou!*"

A stranger who approaches an Indian settlement or village where strangers are rarely seen has not long to wait before he knows in what direction his course lies. As he can never come unexpectedly into a village without having been discovered beforehand by either the busy or the idle inhabitants, a soldier is immediately on hand to receive him and conduct him to the soldiers' or assembly lodge. This is the largest hut in the settlement and serves as the meeting place for their deliberative assembly or council, as well as for the soldiers' guardroom. All important news is discussed there, and decisions arrived at concerning the chase, war, and wanderings. The stranger will be received there, then questioned concerning his purpose in coming and the information he is able to give. No woman is allowed to enter the lodge.

In every case, a soldier is a brave who has already distinguished himself by counting several coups. He is always more or less tattooed. Figures, lines, or points are made with a needle on his skin and then rubbed over with powder or coal dust, so that the tattoo marks assume a blue-black color. Indians in this region are not tattooed over the entire body but usually on the throat and breastbone, or over the chest and shoulders, sometimes on the shoulders and arms or merely on the forearms or on the shin. The latter is decorated only with large dots, hoofprints, or spearheads. They never tattoo their backs, for a warrior does not manifest by his hinder parts that he is a brave.

Women and girls wear tattoo marks by means of which they make known the nation to which they belong. For example, many Iowa girls have a large dot between their eyebrows. Frequently they decorate themselves with two dots, one above the other. One point is said to signify that the person in question has given away ten horses; two points, that she has given away twenty. That may have been the custom originally, but many of these girls so marked would have been glad to own, once in her lifetime, one good, sound horse.

But what did they signify at an earlier period, when Indians did not possess horses? It is certain that pricking or tattooing the skin was practiced in primitive times. Tattooing was the naked primitive man's first means of decoration, of distinguishing himself. His artist was well paid for the work, sometimes receiving even an ordinary horse. When people began to wear clothes, tattoo marks became not so much the vogue.

Huawepine was the only girl whom I knew among the Iowa tribe having tattoo marks on the breast—a trapeze extending from the base of the throat to the pit of the stomach. Sauteurs women branded themselves by means of one, two, or three lines diverging from the corners of the mouth toward the chin.

Soldiers are recognized by their tattoo marks, but also by their bearing, their dignified demeanor, and their especial manner of wearing the buffalo robe or blanket. They throw the latter about the body in such a way that the right shoulder, breast, and arm remain free. That part of the robe which is supposed to cover the right shoulder they draw under the right arm and hold in place with the left hand. Thus they form a drapery that falls in natural, majestic, and graceful folds, the most beautiful drapery for the human body that I know.

In addition to their passion for ornamentation, Indians are adept in giving the blankets a graceful swing with their small hands. They have this art at their fingertips. In this, as in other things, practice makes perfect. They take not the slightest pains to produce an effect and rarely arrange their blankets from any motive other than their own comfort. They only wear their ornamented buffalo robes to make a show. The Indians' blankets are never clumsy or unwieldy. Whether they hang freely from the shoulders, are drawn up over the head so as to wrap the body closely, or are allowed to drag on the ground, they are always soft and pliable.

All well-proved braves are soldiers. They serve as police force and as advisory council for their camp. Their regulations for maintaining order are strictly observed. They have due respect for their own law. They devise the method of punishing the refractory—may inflict beatings or even the death penalty. Their decisions are proclaimed by a crier. For instance, suppose that buffaloes are discovered in the vicinity? If one individual hunter should set out after them, he would drive them away before the other huntsmen arrived, and lessen their chances for means of livelihood.

Consequently, individual Indians are not permitted to go on a chase from a settlement or camp, except in pursuit of animals found singly, never in pursuit of a herd. As soon as the news of approaching wild beasts is received, the soldiers assemble at once for deliberation as to the time and the manner in which the hunt is to be conducted. It frequently happens that most of the soldiers are on the warpath, but some of the older ones always remain at home, the number depending upon the size of the camp.

After their decision has been publicly made known, every huntsman—the most distinguished as well as the poorest—gets himself ready, and they enclose the herd in a circle. Woe be unto the man who, in overhaste, attacks inopportunely and upsets the plan. His horse will be shot dead from under him, or his weapons will be broken in splinters.

Every fur trader selects several of the most highly esteemed soldiers, upon whom he bestows rich gifts for the sake of having their protection both for himself and for his goods. As a rule, each fur trader lives in the tent of one of his protectors.

When we stopped on the *St. Ange* at Fort Pierre, it happened that a band of Teton Sioux was encamped near the fort. A group of a dozen soldiers in grand array greeted us first with a salvo, then came on board to welcome their acquaintances, and finally kept watch over the cargo that had been put ashore. What a welcome prize they were for me! A dog was shot instantly though the heart because he was in the act of lifting his leg against the piles of goods. Women and children were standing in a group apart, curiously scrutinizing the white strangers.

Every year upon the steamer's arrival, those soldiers are there in their military garb to welcome representatives of the company with whom they do business. Yanktonai were awaiting us on a bluff, where they had raised the United States flag. We found it difficult to land there but were obliged to accomplish it, for politeness' sake. Those Yanktonnais, in full array, made the most original group I ever saw. Carrying a tobacco pipe in his hand, the chief stood on a crest of the bluff that had been washed smooth like a high pedestal. His braves in various postures stood round about him at the river's edge. After the warriors' welcoming scene was over, the women were allowed to descend first and come aboard.

As a matter of course, every warrior has a family, of which he is chief. He loves his children extraordinarily. His word of admonition must suffice, for he never inflicts corporal punishment upon them. He sets a good example for his sons in conduct as a future brave. He impresses upon his daughters the virtues of modesty and chastity but leaves the training under their mother's care. For the sake of household peace and order, it frequently happens that a soldier gives his quarreling wives a beating. In his own tent, he assigns a place to sleep and a place at the fireside to each member of the family, just as he does for visitors and guests.

As head of a family, he plays no tricks in his own tent, especially with his small children. For that sort of thing a soldier's hut is chosen, where neither women nor children come. There he seeks his recreation, laughs, sings, smokes, dances, and thoroughly enjoys himself, so long as there is no matter under consideration before the council. In that event, decorum is strictly required.

When the man of the house—father or brother—has slain the wild beasts and brought them home, his duty is done. Women take off the skins and dry them, prepare the flesh for food, get the fire ready, take care of their children, make the clothes. All women's duties and pleasures are distinctly designated for them.

No woman has any voice in the council, is ever listened to, or has her advice followed, not even one who has made herself conspicuous for bravery, as often happens when a village is taken by surprise. Women spend their hours of recreation in looking after their children, visiting, chatting with one another, singing, dancing, making clothes, painting and adorning themselves, and with affairs of love. They have a share in the dressed skins, which they exchange for clothes, ornaments, and dainty tidbits. Their sweethearts' gifts are usually dainties and handsome pelts from the hunt.

Sisters have a claim on everything that a brother or brother-in-law possesses. For instance, an Indian comes riding into camp and meets a sister (sister-in-law and brother-in-law are called sister and brother, just as uncle and aunt are called father and mother). She expresses a wish for the horse he is riding. He springs down forthwith and gives her the beast, even though it might be his best racer. Such a proceeding, however, is held to be contrary to right and justice. For the most part, girls prefer a dappled horse to those of any other color, because they strike the eye and are easily distinguishable from all others.

Men's employments are confined to keeping their weapons in order, making ornaments for the hair, taking care of their horses, hunting, and waging war. The following facts prove that they have bettered their lot by contact with the fur traders: For one buffalo robe, they receive 60 loads of powder and shot; for 6–10 robes, a gun, which may or may not be a good one but is always fit for use. For one robe he gets in return a sufficient number of shots to kill at least fifty of the larger or smaller fur-bearing animals. He would require three days to grind and polish one arrowhead from flint rock, a longer time than an Indian woman needs to prepare a buffalo hide. The arrow has this advantage: It can be discharged without noise and can be used any number of times. At a distance of more than fifty feet, the hunter is no longer sure of hitting a small object. Among Indians of the Upper Missouri I did not see the leather band worn around their left wrist as a protection against the rebound of the bowstring, as they are used by the Iowa, Fox, and Omaha Indians. Indians on the Upper Missouri are more well-to-do tribes and generally are provided with rifles.

Mr. Denig declares that drinking whisky does the Indians no harm whatsoever. To be sure, here as elsewhere, brawls and murders not infrequently occur as a result of drinking, but wild Indians think nothing of such things as that. On the other hand, they were more reliable, were more industrious, and cared more for their personal appearance at the time when Uncle Sam allowed them to barter for whisky than at present, for the simple reason, universally accepted as true, that people work more diligently for their pleasures than for the necessities of life. In whisky, they find a keen incentive to work, Mr. Denig says. In order to enjoy a drink, the man went on the chase more frequently; his wife dressed a larger number of hides. Since that time, they have brought in fewer skins for exchange, not for the reason that the buffaloes have decreased in number, but that Indians—so long as they have meat, the food they prefer—will not exert themselves at all for bread and coffee. For whisky, they are willing to suffer hunger, cold, and most strenuous exertions for days together.

This is all doubtless very true, but let us consider also the other side of the question. The fur trader's principal reasons for wishing whisky back again as a commodity for trade with the Indians—notwithstanding the peril to their own lives—is the enormous profit they derive from the sale of it, a profit all out of proportion to the one now realized.

They made a gain earlier ranging from 200 to 400 percent; their gain today is not more than 80 percent. Fur traders form their judgments and carry on business as such. They regard civilization of the Indians with detestation, because that means the end of their traffic. They know that when Indians begin to cultivate their land, they will become independent. They will no longer follow the chase as their chief occupation; consequently, there will no longer be a supply of furs and skins, the present sources of the fur traders' ready money. Anyone who investigates the history of the dispossessed

Indians will find fur traders always among them, warning the tribes against the whites, their own countrymen, and yet at the same time abetting the plunderers.

What has the Hudson Bay Company ever done to benefit the Indians since they have had the chartered rights of English fur traders in North America? Nothing! What evidences do we find here of the Englishman's love of mankind? English philanthropists give themselves tremendous airs where trade is not adversely affected. So do American fur trading gentlemen in all matters that do not affect their financial interests.

They are not concerned about the Indians' morality or advance to civilization, because that state of things would interfere with their trade. As long as there are buffaloes to kill, fur traders are going to take a resolute stand against the civilization of Indians, not openly, to be sure, but in secret. Americans will see to it that this vast trade is not allowed to be ruined at the expense of the redskins. Unless they begin with cultivating the soil as their principal work, even missionaries do not prosper with their missions in the neighborhood of fur traders.

Missionaries of different faiths all agree that it is impossible to convert Indian tribes where the tribesmen have whisky in their possession. Their faith, their prayers, and their teachings are powerless against the might of that inspiriting drink. Yet there are some tribes that, wholly apart from any interference on the part of missionaries, will not endure the sight of whisky among them, for example, the Cree, whom experience has made wise.

The warmth of this open fire exerts its expansive influence upon body and soul. I am inspired with an uncommon desire to write. Any day I may leave this place (may or must?). I had better preserve on paper whatever facts worth remembering are now floating about in my head.

An Indian orator speaking before an assembly addresses the audience according to the relation he bears to his hearers: for example, my people, my friends, my kinsmen, my comrades. If the orator finds it necessary to employ an interpreter, he divides his speech into several parts, stops at the end of each section, and has his interpreter translate what he has said. He counts off each section interpreted on his fingers and continues until all the divisions or points have been brought forward and transmitted.

As are all the other larger tribes, the Assiniboin are grouped into bands, each of which has its own chief or leader. The more numerous a chief's adherents, the higher his rank; he is valued according to the number of warriors he can summon. However excellent, valiant, or shrewd a warrior may be, he will never become chief unless he has followers, or extended relationships.

The five bands of the Assiniboin that severally owe allegiance to no supreme chief are Band of the Left Handed Chief (Gaucher); Band of the Maidens; Band of the Canots; Band of the Bluffs; Band from the North. At an earlier time, Gaucher was the most powerful, celebrated chief. Like the infamous Omaha chief Black Bird (Waschinga-Schaba), he seems to have removed his most dangerous rival from power by means of arsenic. The Assiniboin were then at war with the whole world—with the Blackfeet tribe, the Crows, Arikara, Herantsa, and even the Sioux, but there is no fighting against great odds. In the end, they were compelled to conclude a peace with the Sioux, Herantsa, and Absaroka.

Mr. Denig says Indians have the only system of education that makes men out of boys and wives out of girls. They educate children for a definite purpose in life: The boy is brought up to be a good huntsman, a brave warrior, a wise father; the girl, an industrious, faithful, and discreet mother. In the training of youth, they have no further object in view. In such training as this, a good example accomplishes more than instruction, high-sounding phrases, and the inculcation of principles one never lives up to. The duty of a father is to prepare his children for happiness under any conditions; to train them to know how to submit to misfortune with shrewdness, with long-suffering endurance and fearlessness at times of assault, or to bear up against them; to give his son occupations adapted to his native gifts and inclinations, in order that he might sustain himself thereby.

According to Mr. Denig, there are three dangerous shoals on which young people so frequently run aground: idleness, love of drink, and card playing. Sexual instincts, he says, lead to no peril. "Love—damn the word!—is a madness in the brain, a contagious disease like smallpox or measles," he says. "I would much rather take a dose of Epsom Salts than recall the folly of first love, pure love. If it is not stopped, that lunacy makes one ridiculous, childish, ashamed of himself." There is always something true and worthwhile in what he says, only he expresses himself in strong language.

So pass the long winter evenings in this wilderness.

October 11—This afternoon, the sky was so clear and the sun shone so delightfully warm that I could not resist taking my gun and going to the hills once more in search of antelope. If the buck would only once allow me to approach near enough to see his horns, I would not thirst for his blood. I had my usual luck: saw nothing that engaged my attention particularly, began to indulge in daydreams, and walked straight ahead. A man sees such a great number of bright yellow spots scattered over these hills that unless he is keen-sighted and pays close attention, it is difficult to tell whether the objects are rocks or antelope.

The man at the fort who possesses the keenest, quickest eyesight is a 70-year-old Spaniard, our cattle herder—the most illiterate man among us. Precisely for the reason that his head is empty of ideas, and his wits so blunted, he occupies himself with nothing but the herding of cattle. For the sake of finding something to interest him while engaged in those duties, his eyes stray continually to the distance. He talks aloud to himself incessantly about what he sees. His undivided attention is given to this region that he has known for so many years. He knows by heart every blade of grass, every stone, every shrub, every tree, every elevation or depression of the ground, every hill and brook. The slightest variation in the landscape attracts his attention. Our other Spaniard, who guards the horses, is less noted for keen sight. Women and the laying of traps share his thoughts and frequently distract his attention.

Packinaud glories in stalking deer as only few Indians can. The other hunters, who are equally successful as bookkeepers and tradespeople, grant him this claim to the "excellence of the Indian" but tell him at the same time that he is also as ignorant as an Indian, for he can neither read, write, nor reckon, although he was brought up in Canada. I lack keen eyesight altogether. In the first place, I am not quick-sighted; furthermore, I am so intensely absorbed with other ideas, studies, and dreams: matters that are not only unnecessary, but in the highest degree prejudicial to the huntsman.

Today, as before, I allowed myself to be seen by the antelopes long before I knew whether the objects in front of me were rocks or animals. It was only when I became aware of yellow and white spots moving through the dry grass that I took out my telescope and saw how the frolicking antelopes were making fun of me, playing with one another under my nose until they were chased from the hilltop by the buck. They vanished into the valley, appeared again in full speed on a distant height, darted with leaps and bounds across, and gave me the last glimpse of their shining bodies. I followed their tracks in vain, but I did see a wolf whose head and neck looked singularly blue. He was running down to the brackish stream but found no water to his taste.

Wolves are a common enough sight here, but they are not seen in packs, except when one finds a wounded animal, which howls to bring others to his aid. When they see or get the scent of people, they scurry away and lie down in some sheltered place to find out whether they are pursued.

As they are never reduced to such straits for food in this region as in settled countries, they are not so wild or so dangerous. For instance, I was reading in a St. Louis newspaper that in the region about Dubuque (which is not thickly populated), an Indian returning home in winter with a load of meat was set upon by wolves with such fury that he could barely save his life, though he threw out all the meat to them. In this region, there has been no record of a man having lost his life from an attack of wolves.

Indian tribes are separated into smaller camps for the sake of moving from place to place with more rapidity and of feeling more secure about provisions; these bands are also subdivided into special groups, each of which claims a certain rank. Young men, braves, girls, and older woman have their own bands, to which they pay rather large sums in time, if they have the means. Each of these groups has its own distinctive name, decoration, and dance.

Its purpose is purely social, offering the members a variation from their usual diversions. The band of highest rank is made up of the most celebrated warriors—The Band that Never Saves Itself. Others have the names of favorite animals, but never the so-called medicine birds and beasts, the flesh of which they do not eat, the skins of which they refuse to prepare for sale. Such birds and beasts are not identical in any of the tribes. They exclude as such eagles, bears, beavers, and wolves. On the other hand, they accept buffaloes, dogs, foxes, pheasants, turtles, elks, etc. At these dances, eunuchs wear no clothing at all except moccasins, not even the breechcloth. They fasten an eagle feather on their limbs.

Because of the limited supply, eagle feathers are very high in price. For designating a coup, only tail feathers are worn, and an eagle has only twelve of those. They are a dingy white, with black ends. Here, an eagle's tail costs as much as a horse or six buffalo robes. Indians take great pains to catch war eagles; they rarely, if ever, shoot them. At the fort, we have an eagle in a cage. Once a week, he is given a large piece of meat. He has never once drunk water since he has been here.

To ensnare the birds, two Indians go out into a wild region and dig a hole in the ground deep enough to conceal one of them, who gets in, is supplied with food, and is then covered over with boughs and twigs by his companion. Care is taken to leave spaces between the boughs through which he can see. His companion then lays some carrion on top of the covered pit and leaves the scene. The hunter often has to remain several days in his lurking place but is happy even then if he accomplishes anything—moreover, if a bear does not fall foul of him.

When an eagle swoops down upon the carrion, the concealed hunter seizes him by the legs and pulls him down through the boughs, and plunges a knife in his heart. Woe to the Indian if the eagle attacks him with beak and talons, for those birds inflict terrible wounds. In their sharp-pointed claws they possess greater strength than a bear. With their crooked beaks they tear away flesh, leaving great hollows in a person's face.

Later on, Morgan and I had a rather severe struggle with our eagle. On account of the cold weather, the eagle and the bear were put in a small out-house. One day, I found a frozen pig near the palisades and wished to give it to the bear. When I entered, I saw the eagle's cage turned upside down, the eagle squatting on top of it. The bear presumably had picked a quarrel with the bird between the wooden slats of his box.

I called Morgan to assist me. He took an old buffalo robe and I took my wide riding cloak, with which to cover the eagle and secure him without exposing ourselves to sharp beak and frightful talons. As Morgan approached him, he flew away. I threw my cloak in his direction in such a way as to catch him in it. We bound him at once with leather thongs and carried him into my room.

We had no more time at the moment to give to him. We had hardly gone back to our duties in the store when someone shouted that the eagle was walking about in my room. To prevent his escape through the window, it was necessary to catch him right away. I found my cloak torn to pieces by his powerful claws. This time he turned upon us in a frightful manner and inflicted several severe cuts with his feet on Morgan's arm. But for Morgan's good fortune in having on leather clothes, the talons would have made a deep wound. As it was, that arm pained him a long while.

I was inquiring today whether a pipe of peace was ever put to a wrong use, in order to foil a friend by treachery and bring about his overthrow, or whether it was always regarded as sacred. Among Absaroka and Herantsa, the sanctity of the peace pipe is held to be inviolable; among other nations, it depends. If the end in view is only to get rid of an enemy, all means are justified. So it was, they say, at the time when Crows and Assiniboin were still at enmity with each other. They were beginning to be weary of war and to question whether their feud was due to any well-defined cause or was merely a heritage from their forefathers that no longer justified real feelings of hatred as a motive to continued hostilities.

During that time, in spite of warnings from the whites, four Absaroka insisted upon coming with their families to their relations, the Herantsa, at this fort for the purpose of bartering for corn: in other words, to beg. The Crows came upon a camp of Assiniboin. Knife, Spotted Horn, Celui Qui Suit le Chemin (Pathfinder), and other chiefs proffered them the pipe in the tent. Unsuspecting, the Crows laid aside their weapons and smoked. The Assiniboin rushed upon them and murdered them. Their motive seems to have been to get possession of the Crows' good horses rather than their scalps, for they sent the women and children back on foot.

When it came to a division of their four-footed prizes, Spotted Horn had a quarrel with the son of Pathfinder, whereupon the former let fly an arrow that struck the latter in the back and killed him. As a penalty, Spotted Horn was deprived of his share of the booty and made to sweat for other gifts besides, in expiation of the crime.

On the occasion of another such peace proposal, twenty-eight braves of the Herantsa tribe were murdered by the Yanktonai. Later the Yanktonai concluded a peace, with the motive being to overreach the Herantsa and make victory over them all the more certain. As it was the custom for the Herantsa to leave their village at Fort Berthold in winter and move to the region of the Knife River to hunt, the Yanktonai thought they would find large quantities of corn at the abandoned village. A group of them sneaked up. Luckily, the Herantsa had got wind of that villainy and were lying in ambush in front of them and in their rear. Not one escaped; all were slain.

Crows are noted for the good order maintained in their villages. We may assume this has reference more particularly to good conduct on the part of men than of women. In that tribe, women take the liberty of going to the deliberative council, where they enter the discussions and make the braves listen to reason, a proceeding never heard of in any other Indian nation. Among the Iroquois, this is a right of the women and the women chiefs.

The women of the Crow tribe are known more for their industry and skilled work than for beauty of face and form. Young Crows are as wild and unrestrained as wolves.

Among the Absaroka, old Sapsucker was a soldier of first rank in his earlier years who became their most famous chief. After the harvest season once, they made ready, as usual, to visit the Herantsa to barter, or rather to beg for maize. Owing to their feud with the Assiniboin, they realized the danger of the venture, for detached parties were always attacked. Old Sapsucker assembled his forces as usual and came over the Missouri to Fort Union. His object was to find out whether the Assiniboin would pounce upon him at the head of his army. He first sent forward twenty braves mounted on picked horses as a vanguard to feel their way. It was known that the combined Assiniboin bands were in camp between the two forts and that their warriors were on the watch. He gave orders to his vanguard to avoid any encounter but to find out where their foes were and keep clear of them. They brought the news here that in a few days, their entire set-tlement would desire to cross the river. Flatboats are also kept on the river at this place for the convenience of people at the fort, and their customers. The Dobies below us are situated at the mouth of the Yellowstone and use no ferryboats.

As soon as they had taken some rest and had gained the information required, they proceeded farther along their way. Two days later, sixty braves came riding along to support the vanguard and to dispatch couriers here, there, and everywhere. Finally Sapsucker arrived in command of a hundred soldiers, the *gros d'armée*. The other members of the tribe, including women and children, followed on foot, convoyed by four squads of braves. In this manner, the shrewd leader reached the village of the Herantsa unperceived and, while conducting his affairs with them, kept his spies on the alert around the enemy's settlement. His return, in reverse order, was accomplished with equal success.

When outlying pickets discover the enemy, they give the following signal to their forces in the rear: They gallop up and down and then crosswise the line. If they come upon buffaloes, they ride slowly up and down in a straight line, often throwing dust in the air.

October 12—Saw today some other attractions that afford motifs for pictures. In the morning, two lovely girls were bringing water from the river. After we had eaten, I went with Mr. Denig on a hunt for antelope. Saw first an Indian sitting beside his horse, musing on the surrounding scene. He then mounted and rode away singing, a somber figure sharply outlined against the horizon.

Next we saw a red fox that Mr. Denig might have shot, if he and I had not been absorbed in conversation. We found our herd of antelopes again at their accustomed grazing place near the brackish stream. They were obviously on their guard; instead of grazing, they were constantly peering around, sniffing the air, giving every evidence of unrest. Mr. Denig crept up the hill where they were tripping about, and beckoned me to come out of my excellent hiding place, where I should have had the best chance in the world to shoot the buck. He reproached me for a blunderer who had again let myself be seen unnecessarily or else had made a noise. On the contrary, I had been as still as a mouse. The instant my companion fired, the beasts fled with amazing leaps, arching their flexible backs in the manner of cats. We discharged our rifles at once upon the fleeing herd, but to no purpose.

We had hardly lost sight of our escaping quarry when we were startled by the unexpected report of a gun nearby. Friend or foe—that was now the question. We reloaded our rifles with care and set forward in the direction from which the sound had come. On the trail leading to the fort, we soon met a group of Indians we did not know. There were four men and two women accompanied by several dogs laden with packs of dried meat. At the sight of us, two of the latter ran off with their travois, and their companions followed them to a considerable distance.

Mr. Denig took the redskins for Cree. By means of signs, he invited them to come with him to the fort. They laughed and remained standing where they were. Well, he thought, they are customers of the opposition, going to the Dobies. They wanted whisky; we had none to offer them. After all, they decided to follow us along the characteristic Indian trail with its three parallel paths.

At once, Mr. Denig remarked to me that it would be hard to bring them over to our side, yet it would be to his discredit if his attempt failed. To be sure, they had nothing with them of any value, but they would make a great deal of fun at his expense when they arrived at the Dobie fort and gave their own account of all the things he had promised them. When we came to the parting of the ways and he saw them turning off, he made signs that he would give them as much meat and coffee as their stomachs could hold. "*Hou!*" They followed us. They were Chippewa, who in their speech constantly reminded me of Potawatomi.

October 13—While we were weighing the meat and hanging it up to prevent mold, and also to keep it out of the way of hordes of mice (there are no rats in the fort any more than at Fort Berthold), there arrived a great band of Assiniboin, including many women, laden horses, and dogs. As these caravans afford me my only chance to observe different groups of Indians in this region, they are always welcome as further means of detailed study, especially their method of laying on the loads and, during the sale of their commodities, of unloading their packs. There is no evidence of festive array on these occasions.

October 14—While we were getting together the goods for Carafel's winter quarters and packing them into uniform bales weighing an average of 70 pounds each, eight half-breeds from the Upper Red River came to the fort seeking employment for the winter. (This is not to be confused with the Red River in Arkansas and Texas.) They gave an account of a recent attack on their people by the Sioux. These Chippewa half-breeds have severed themselves from English sovereignty and have come under the Star-Spangled Banner of the United States. From their share of Chippewa domain, they have chosen the delta between the Pembina and the St. Peters River.

These metifs have intermarried with both full-blooded and half-breed Indians. They are descendants from Lord Selkirk's colony. Among those colonists were also some Swiss from English regiments of the time, who after the war with France served in Canada and were discharged there.

Their land is not particularly productive. They still prefer the products of the chase to agriculture, for which tendencies their Indian and French blood is chiefly responsible. They have time for the summer hunt while their crops are growing; after the harvest, for hunting in the fall. In the winter season, the men try to earn money as engagés, scouts, and interpreters in the service of various fur traders.

On these hunting expeditions, the metifs take dried meat, hides, tents, and cooking utensils around with them on two-wheeled carts. Each band chooses its own leader to direct the hunt and to take measures for defense, in the event that they are set upon by enemies. When such caravans are crossing the prairie, they are accustomed to require that carts be driven in a certain order and, upon halting, to form a ring or square about the men and brutes as a means of defense. They push the poles or shafts under the foremost carts.

According to their story, the other day sixty metifs were on a buffalo hunt with their families. During the chase, three of them were captured by a greater number of Sioux. The latter counted some 800 tents, hence about 2,500 warriors. Another camp numbering 600 tents was pitched farther back. Conscious of their superior strength, the Sioux were most insolent, and yet cowardly. In spite of their power, they attempted to trick the metifs and take them unawares. They made the three prisoners believe that their intention was to conduct them back to their carts, shake hands with the other half-breeds, and smoke the pipe.

Accompanied by a strong guard of soldiers, the captives were taken in the direction of their barricade. Neither the three metifs held by the enemy nor those behind the clustered carts put any confidence at all in good intentions on the part of the Sioux. Meanwhile, those in camp had driven in and confined their cattle and horses. They had further strengthened their defense by filling in open spaces between the carts with heaps of dried meat, rawhide, and saddles.

The prisoners—who were riding one behind the other in the foremost file, where they could be seen by their friends—decided among themselves that if it was possible, they were going to take flight as soon as they came within shooting distance of their own people. The one in the rear was mounted on a horse of slow gait, so he had poor prospects of escape, but he did what he could to enable his comrades to avenge his death. The instant the two foremost captives put spurs to their horses, he shot the Sioux nearest him; the same bullet brought down three braves. He himself was felled on the spot, but his fellow prisoners escaped.

The metifs behind the carts shot a number of the Sioux, and the enemy then surrounded their barricade. For two days they galloped hither and yon in their attempts to fire upon the cattle, but no hand-to-hand combat took place; they dared not make an attack. The men said that in the metif's camp, a Chippewa woman was beside herself to do battle. She was constantly trying to rush out and fight at close quarters with the Sioux and became extremely angry when her relatives restrained her. Finally, she took off all her clothes and, standing naked, waved her skirt at the enemy with jeering words. She sang and whooped at such a rate that three other women were induced to make similar demonstrations.

The Sioux lost 80 men and 65 horses, and many more were wounded. The metifs' rifles kept the enemy at such a distance that their balls fell short of the carts. The Sioux were too far removed to use arrows at all. The half-breeds' loss amounted to twelve horses and four oxen. They kept swift horses saddled, ready to make an attempt the instant the opportunity was offered. Fifteen foolhardy fellows even rode out once and fired a volley with the hope of enticing the enemy to come at least within range of their archers, but in vain. Attracted by the repeated shooting of guns, a larger group of metifs drew near, whereupon the valiant Sioux took to flight. This is the metifs' story. Sioux, in their turn, will give a different account.

Then the wounded Packinaud told his story to prove that he had at least seen combat. As he does not appear to be a hero in the action, one is inclined to believe his narrative. Ten Dakota were on the warpath near the Herantsa settlement. They were discovered in a thicket back of the upper cornfields, where mosquitoes swarm in thick multitudes. Frenzied by the pests, six of them dug holes with their knives in which to cover their bodies, and the other four ran off. The Herantsa were not overeager to seek out the hidden enemy and attack. They had to be foolish rather than valiant to expose themselves unnecessarily to certain death. Suddenly a Cree came galloping along and shouted, "Where is the enemy?"

He was shown the small wood where the Dakota were suspected to be lurking. He galloped thither, and the Herantsa, ashamed, followed him. Five bullets pierced the skull of the brave Cree, blowing out his brains, and the sixth shot hit the Herantsa next to him. From the powder smoke, the attacking party knew then where the Dakota were concealed but had to tread down willow plats before they got sight of them. Many a brave met his death there. When one of the Herantsa shot to death the first Sioux, he called out at once that he had slain a foe, whereupon his companions rushed upon the others and instantly brought down four. The sixth plunged into a bog and sank. A Herantsa was in the act of pushing him down when he, a young boy, begged to be shot rather than drowned. With a thrust of the knife, the Herantsa sent him into the other world.

At that moment, Packinaud came upon the scene of action just at the right time to witness the amputation of limbs for trophies. With increasing heat, he brought his narrative to its conclusion, accompanying his words with Indian signs. He sat down in a greatly excited state. He really looked as if it was all over with him.

A decrepit woman who hobbles about this place with the aid of a walking stick has lived in a tent before the gate for four generations. She is the widow of that renowned chief of the Assiniboin, L'Armure de Fer (Iron Arrow Point), better known as Le Gros Français (The Great Frenchman). He was the leader of the Gens des Roches (People of the Rocks) whom Lewis and Clark met on their expedition.[4] She must be more than one hundred years old. She hobbles about, bent double with age.

When they can no longer be of use, old people have anything but a pleasant life among the Indians. They must be fed when there is a lack of food; they must be carried along when the band is moving in haste. As a consequence, one finds all too frequently that on their wanderings, Indians abandon old members of the band to a wretched fate, without shelter and without means of support. They are given only a stick with which to dig the pomme blanche. This is the prairie turnip, Psoralea esculenta Pursh, or the pomme de prairie of the voyageurs.

Such an aged woman, supported by Mr. Denig, lived a long while just outside this fort. She put together a heap of twigs for a shelter under which to abide; snow kept her warm. Two young blades from the band to which she belonged took counsel together, as to whether to build her a more comfortable hut or to do away with her. Since she was of no service whatever, they argued, she was not worth so much trouble. They decided upon the latter alternative and cudgeled her until she was dead. When the old Spaniard went next morning to take her what was left from the morning meal, he found the aged woman with head split open. The two young Indians who were sitting near told him lightly that she was better dead than alive.

I do not deliberately pass over in silence such cruel acts. Apart from my sympathy and friendship for the Indians, I have a just comprehension of their feelings. I assert boldly that in proportion to mental and moral training, these so-called savages are guilty of fewer acts of inhumanity and cruelty than are citizens of self-styled Christian nations. Not a day passes that the newspapers, both in Europe and in the United States, do not publish the most bloodcurdling, shameful deeds. I think the Indians' barbarity during the wars of extermination was perfectly natural; their fury and wrath were aroused to an extreme degree. Were the people on the borders less savage? Did they not scalp with equal zeal?

Only the other day, a feeble Indian woman came to the fort, after she had been left 14 days on the prairie to starve. She carried only a few pommes blanches that she had got for her scanty fare.

Generally speaking, women age more rapidly than men, for the reason— so it is said—that they smoke less. Yet the Indians' habit of inhaling tobacco smoke and exhaling through the nose results in a serious injury to chest and head. Consequently, though they smoke a blended tobacco, mild and sweet-smelling, they suffer quite frequently from lung trouble. They smoke a brand of American manufacture, the only tobacco they can get, mixed with dried leaves or bark they procure for themselves. I have now become accustomed to using this Indian blend but do not exhale through the nose. I never smoke that sort of tobacco anywhere else. I find the aroma very agreeable. To offer a well-filled pipe to the visitor is in strict accord with Indian etiquette. I am duty-bound to acknowledge the courtesy, particularly since I do not understand their speech.

October 15—Walked with Carafel to his winter quarters, mainly to assist him in getting things arranged. His principal lading of goods will come later. Afterwards, I helped him hang up the rest of his cured meat and put the store in order.

The father of our new trader, Battiste Lafontaine, was the best-mounted buffalo hunter ever known in this region. Once he ran buffaloes with others in the Yellowstone to see which of them could kill the greater number at full gallop. He covered 1 English mile in 6 minutes and shot 12 cows— that is, two every minute—notwithstanding that cows run much faster than bulls. Lafontaine weighed 230 pounds but sat his horse so lightly and comfortably that the beast was not sensible of his weight.

Owen Mackenzie can load and shoot 14 times in 1 mile but does not invariably hit the object at which he aims. Still, I do not doubt that

Mackenzie has the skill to shoot 12 cows in 1 mile, if his runner should come up with that number. Last year Mackenzie ran a race with Clark from Fort Benton on a wager and broke his collarbone during the adventure. He was just getting a start to his goal when his runner stepped in a hole and fell. Mackenzie went hurtling over the horse's head and came down on one shoulder. He won the race nevertheless, in respect to both his horse's speed and the rapidity of his shots.

When running buffaloes, the hunters do not use rifle-patches but take along several balls in their mouths. The projectile thus moistened sticks to the powder when put into the gun. In the first place, on buffalo hunts, they do not carry rifles, for the reason that they think the care required in loading them takes too much time unnecessarily when shooting at close range; furthermore, they find rifle balls too small. The hunter chases buffaloes at full gallop, discharges his gun, and reloads without slackening speed.

To accomplish this, he holds the weapon close within the bend of his left arm. Taking the powder horn in his right hand, with his teeth he draws out the stopper, which is fastened to the horn to prevent its being lost. He shakes the requisite amount of powder into his left palm and closes the powder horn. He grasps the gun with his right hand, holding it in a vertical position, pours the powder down the barrel, and gives the gun a sidelong thrust with the left hand, in order to shake the powder well through the priming hole into the touch pan (hunters at this place discard percussion caps as not practical).

Now he takes a bullet from his mouth and with his left hand puts it into the barrel, where, having been moistened by spittle, it adheres to the powder. He dares not hold his weapon horizontal—in the position taken when firing—for fear that the ball may stick fast in its course, allowing sufficient air to intervene between powder and lead to cause an explosion and splinter the barrel. There is no danger so long as the ball rolls down freely. Hunters approach the buffaloes so closely that they do not take aim but, lifting the gun lightly with both hands, point in the direction of the animal's heart and fire. They are very often wounded in the hands and face by the bursting gun barrels, which—especially when the weather is extremely cold—shatter as easily as glass.

The hunters always aim at the heart of the larger beasts of the chase, the surest and simplest method, since the heart is an inevitably vulnerable part.

When hunting wolves, foxes, and beavers, they aim at the head, so that they may not do damage to the small, costly skins by perforating them with bullets. Buffalo chasers must not only have the enduring qualities of swift riders, but they must also be accustomed to the habits of the animals. A buffalo runner must be faultless in pressing close upon his quarry, and at the same time being alert to spring aside if a buffalo tosses his head. Otherwise, if he is only a passable horseman, he will immediately find himself upon the ground and may count himself happy if he is not trodden underfoot.

The metifs cannot find words with which to praise highly enough the magnificence of a buffalo hunt, when from 500 to 600 horsemen attack, encircle, pursue, and slay an entire herd, even to the last cow and calf. On such occasions, only the hunter who fires the shot that kills has any claim on the slain animal. Therefore, each of them has some sign by which he designates his booty; either the arrows are marked, or a certain number of buckshot are mixed among the bullets, or else the hunters throw something from their wearing apparel upon the expiring beasts. As in any case, not everyone in such a large number gets a shot—oftentimes many of them are not well mounted—but the successful hunters have some portions of meat to spare. They always keep the hides for themselves. Among the Indians, the flesh of the animals is equally distributed.

This evening, two old acquaintances from Fort Berthold arrived here: Le Nez d'Ours [Bear's Nose] and l'Estomac de Corbeau [Raven's Stomach], the proudest and most powerful soldiers of the village. On the way to the Absaroka, they left their companions behind at the opposition fort. They say that three hundred Arikara died from cholera. That whole story about Dorson's being compelled to bring his cannons into action was an invention, related just for the purpose of having some story to tell and to get something to eat.

In reality, the Arikara killed only one white person, an old man coming from the timber yard. The Herantsa lost 20 braves, among which number 6 Mandan are included. Women and children were not counted. There is no longer any sign of epidemic, so the Indians returned to the settlement at the last new moon. Mr. Kipp is reported to have provided 14 braves with clothes of European make, which act denotes the measure of his fear. Bellangé, they say, arrived safe, boasting much of his excellent marksmanship.

Most of the Herantsa are well disposed toward me; merely a few customers of the opposition talk violently against me. They say Jeff Smith has egged them on to bad feeling, less from real dislike on his own part than from self-interest. This Jeff is said to have gone out beaver hunting with a German once, and after great success with their traps, he murdered the latter for the sake of stealing his horse and beaver skins. Smith is now bourgeois at the opposition fort.

Le Nez d'Ours told me how he had come upon 30 Assiniboin from the Gens des Filles. At the sight of him, everyone began to howl and scream, because owing to the present peace, many Assiniboin scalps remain unavenged. Four Herantsa were supplied with guns as an inducement not to show the captured scalps again. Their leader is Le Loup Court Queue, who once shared my room with me.

During this conversation, several of the company spoke of rudeness and bungling on the part of Pierre Gareau. He repels all young men. He refuses to associate with any but the most prominent men, yet those same young fellows will later on be the most distinguished among their tribe. Bad speculation.

One of the aged women was calling her dog: "Kadosch! Kadosch!" As they usually entice the brutes with "*Suk! Suk!*" I asked Mr. Denig whether Indians name their dogs. "Only as illustrated in this instance," he replied. "*Kadosch* means son-in-law." Yes, it is a fact that they treat dogs as members of the family. I dare say many people, unfortunately, have chosen life partners no more faithful than a four-legged beast.

October 16—About 10 o'clock, Mr. Denig sent me to find out from Joe Picotte when he expects to take up his winter quarters on the Lower Bourbeuse. He and Joe have agreed not to be rivals in trade, inasmuch as such competition is of no profit to either of them but only incurs greater expense in the matter of gifts and disturbs pleasant relations. On the way, I met the Herantsa who had been left behind at Fort Adobe [Fort William] and were now, on horse and afoot, in search of their companions at our post.

I was first spied by a woman who was walking ahead. Instantly she cried out, "*Ista uwatse! Ista uwatse!*" ("iron eyes"—spectacles). That was the name I was immediately given by those Indians, because spectacles on a person were such an amazing characteristic to them. Iowa called me "Ista Mantu-gra," which has the same meaning as the above, but the Assiniboin designated me "Ista Topa" (Four Eyes). Remarkable that in so many languages, "*ista*" means "eyes."

I had to shake hands with them all. Le Loup Court Queue was friendly and wished to know how soon I would return to Fort Union. He would await me with Nez d'Ours. Under the impression that he would be able to see as well through my spectacles as with the telescope, he was eager to get possession of them. To convince him of his wrong idea, I put them on his nose. With his keen eyes he was unable to see anything at all through the spectacles, of course, and became all the more wonderstruck. As this is the only pair I have with me, I could not surrender the inartistic—for me, I am sorry to say—but indispensable decoration. What would I not give for a pair of Indian eyes!

Perhaps it is much better that my eyesight incapacitates me for the chase. With my passion for horses and for wandering, and my inclination toward romantic adventure, I might become an Indian myself, especially since the difficulties in the way of providing an adequate income in the overpopulated, civilized States has deprived me of the desire to return. At the same time, I cannot tarry here always for the purpose of fulfilling my plans. I have to go back whether I will or no.

What sly dogs these Indians are. How well they know the way to put the fur traders' teaching to their own use. Now, why did Le Loup Court Queue (Short-tailed Wolf), a customer of our company, sleep all night at the opposition fort and allow himself to be entertained there? Joe Picotte says the Arikara destroyed Dorson's fort and left his intact because they prefer the opposition to the big company, particularly since the latter no longer grants favors or courtesies to anyone. But the Arikara in this region plundered both posts alike. Why was that? No, these Indians simply wish to be accommodated with board and lodging at both trading posts.

One cannot rely on stories like Joe's, but I do not credit such lies to Nez d'Ours and l'Estomac de Corbeau (Raven's Stomach); braves with such pride as theirs would not stoop to falsehoods. Besides, they conducted themselves as befit loyal customers and came directly here without allowing themselves to be seen at the opposition fort. L'Estomac de Corbeau was most affable toward me. He sat with me beside the open fire almost the whole of yesterday and today, smoked, talked now and then, watched me curiously when I was writing or painting. I understand that their object in making this visit to the Crows is to procure horses for themselves and to induce the latter to take maize from them, for they have such an abundant crop this year that they are at a loss to know what to do with it.

I have never witnessed among Indians anywhere such laughter, such chattering and pranks as these Herantsa carried on at Packinaud's sickbed. Packinaud lived 9 years among the Herantsa. In fact, he is connected with many of them through his Herantsa wife, speaks their language well, and can outdo them in singing and howling. Perhaps the Indians are companionable with him for the reason that they have lived so much together. Or is it that wanderers are more unrestrained, more crude, more unthinking, so to speak? Perhaps they were expressing their joy at seeing him again. Packinaud came here for the first time on the *St. Ange* to be employed as either hunter or interpreter among the Crows.

Thinking he would greatly please the Herantsa, Mr. Denig told them how highly he respected their chief, Four Bears. However, his flattery did not commend him to their favor, for every soldier among them regards himself as worthy of quite as much respect as a chief. Le Loup Court Queue replied that he and "Raven Stomach" bring far more robes than the chief brings. They said the chiefs are old-fashioned personages, severe, taciturn, unable to see a joke, quick to lay low any young man who opposes them; hence, they are not so well understood or loved as they might be. Mr. Denig assured them that he knew well they were all gallant warriors, but their chief was a man of more understanding, was less superstitious, and had better judgment in conducting the affairs of a nation.

"Now I will see what they think of the portrait," he remarked aside to me.

They recognized Mr. Denig's picture immediately upon entering the office, strode up to it, and offered to shake hands. They were extraordinarily astonished when they found no response whatsoever on the part of the image. They placed their fingers on their lips in token of their amazement. No living person was standing there; the image was not reflected in a mirror; they found the solution to this mystery beyond them.

They also recognized Natoh's picture instantly but could not comprehend why one would pay such honor to a dog. As they had seen the parrot before on board the *St. Ange,* they did not find Polly such a curiosity as did the Cree. Polly came on the same boat with me from St. Louis. After they had inspected the white lady on the wall in the reception room, examining her from every side, even from heels to head, Mr. Denig asked them whether they believed that he or his dog must inevitably die on account of this.

Without saying a word, they drew their blankets over their heads and went out of the room.

Later on, they expressed a desire to see my quarters also. They found so many things there that they wanted and began to beg so, first for one thing and then another—my knife, tobacco, pipe, matches, comb, mirror, even the clothes on my back—I soon had enough of them. As I am no longer living among the Herantsa, I refused to give them anything. I shall bestow nothing else for the sake of their goodwill. If I were to give them presents, they would most likely think that I was actuated by fear. L'Estomac de Corbeau was the only one who conducted himself differently. He seemed to scorn his noisy tribesmen and to prefer the quiet in my room.

Mr. Denig is constantly talking to me about the worthlessness and incapacity of engagés, not an interesting subject. Though what he says is more or less true, such conversations are not agreeable. He complains about them so much that I used to think that he felt it necessary to justify his severe treatment of the "hands," according to the saying, "The dog struck gives a yelp." I observe now that he wishes me to understand how I am to demean myself—what attitude he expects me to take as clerk. He knows how engagés find fault with him from one year's end to the other, have complained about him already in St. Louis so much that employees invariably say, "Only not to Fort Union," as though the place were a convict prison. Why is he in such bad repute? Merely for the reason that he makes them work. He does not allow them to be idle the livelong day, except when they are feeding. They are paid well and promptly for their labor, receiving as a rule goods from the store to the amount of their wages before they have earned them. If they are allowed to fall deeply in debt, if credit is given them for their year's pay, they abscond and enter the employ of the opposition. Not less than 12 newly employed engagés of the big company went over to the opposition in the following May at St. Louis, after each of them had received, besides spending money, blankets and clothes charged to their account.

They exert themselves only to escape work by subterfuges and to fill their stomachs. They are idle by nature, and this trait is intensified by dislike of their employer. They are lazy because they know there is nobody in this part of the world to take their place. They are boastful and insatiable. Mr. Denig expects the clerks to support him in every emergency, whether brought about by dangers from the outside or within the fort; to shoot down any person who attempts to lay hands on him; to take part in the affairs of the workmen; to never yield a point with them; and to treat them like dogs.

Mackenzie told me how the engagés in the lumber yard fled at the sight of him when he and the horse guard came near them on their return from the recent hunt. Although they were expecting him to bring them meat, upon seeing him and his pack horses in the distance, they took for granted that they were looking at Indians. Having abandoned guns and axes, they ran to Morgan in extreme fear, crying "Indians! Indians!" Morgan instantly recognized the supposed Indians, called his gallant band together, and gave them a scolding. Mackenzie left them a full lading of meat—as much as one horse could carry—and they devoured it all in 2 days. He left a load of meat weighing 250 pounds, which, divided among 6 men, makes 20 pounds per day for each laborer. If one deducts about 5 pounds for bones, there remains still a goodly portion of meat. They are most extraordinary eaters.

Morgan, their foreman, does not dare wander about with his gun but must give his attention exclusively to the men, otherwise they will do no work.

October 17—Slept little last night. First, the Herantsa sang their war song. As I was getting to bed, they began another chant in the interpreter's room and accompanied their singing with the drum. Of course I could not fall asleep. After tossing from one side to the other for ever so long, I lost all patience. Throwing my cloak about me, I went to find out just what the hubbub was about. Dimly lighted by the open fire and one candle, the room was crowded with performers and onlookers made up of redskins, white people, and half-breeds. According to Indian custom, eight Herantsa and seven Assiniboin sat opposite one another on the floor, encircled about with a pile of bows, quivers, knives, calico, etc., and were playing a game.

Two Assiniboin were making motions in every direction with their closed hands, swiftly passing a bullet ball from one hand to the other, while the other members of their party sang, "*e, e, e, eh, e, e, e, ah,*" keeping time by beating a tattoo with sticks on washbasins and boiler tops. In an excited state of eager expectation, both singers and players swayed their bodies continually from the hips.

One of the Herantsa who had laid the stake in opposition to the two Assiniboin had to guess in which of the two players' fists the bullet was to be found. When he felt sure that he knew, he made a quick thrust with his left arm in the direction of the fist in which he supposed the ball to be, struck violently on his breast with his right hand, and with a cry, designated the fist mentioned. If he failed to guess the right one, the winners whooped for joy and gathered in their stakes. Then they smoked reciprocally from the same pipe as a mark of continued friendship.

Other contestants began the game over again. One of the Herantsa wished to make himself particularly conspicuous. Sitting nearest the fireplace, he raked out all the ashes in front of him and concealed the bullet there, or rather, he tried to make his opponents think that he did. He moved his fists among the ashes in imitation of a buffalo working his way through mud and mire or rolling over in the dust. He grumbled and bellowed all the while like an angry bull, threw ashes all over himself and around him, pawed and groaned like one possessed. His mimicry was unequaled. As a rule, hunters are particularly clever in imitating the movements and sounds made by beasts of the chase. They certainly have opportunities enough to study them, and they make use of such in their dances and sports. After an Assiniboin had won almost every stake the Herantsa had put up, they stopped the game.

The Herantsa took their leave after breakfast this morning. They were to be put across the river near the timber yard because that is the place where the boats are kept. To prevent our valiant engagés from taking flight upon the approach of the Indians, Mackenzie mounted John, his favorite runner, and rode on ahead to see that the boats were in readiness. While Mr. Denig was tarrying below the gate for Owen Mackenzie's return, he saw a large herd of antelopes bounding out of a wooded coulee and onto the prairie. At once, he called me from my room. There were at least forty of them, sweeping along one behind the other, and a horseman was close behind them. We took the rider to be an Indian, but when we saw him in a mad gallop constantly gaining on the cabris, we doubted whether any Indian's horse would be able to overtake those swiftest of all wild beasts on the prairie. Indians' runners are too insufficiently nourished; therefore they lack brawn, endurance, and wind.

With the aid of my telescope, I recognized Mackenzie just as he was turning his course from pursuit of the herd, which had escaped in hollows and dells among the hills. As he turned his horse's head in our direction, my heart leaped to see John so full of fire and energy. Mackenzie could hardly restrain him. He had to make him gallop sidewise, which he succeeded in doing, with the utmost grace and skill.

If Owen had had his gun, several antelopes would have fallen victim to his skill. He is now provided with half of his supply of goods for his winter quarters on the Lower Bourbeuse. While assisting in getting his wares together, I was led to reflect on how much more simple a matter it is for the bourgeois to say, "Bring that keg of bullets from the power magazine at the rear of the warehouse," a distance of at least a hundred paces, than it is for me to do it. To carry 300 pounds in one's arms is no simple matter.

After sunset, three fat hinds came out of a nearby thicket and took a walk on the prairie. I watched them a long while, and with much interest.

October 18—According to La Bombarde, Indian words in most common use here are all from the Chippewa speech or from the related Cree language: *moccasin,* shoe; *ihqua,* wife; *musqua,* my wife; *wigwam,* tent; *apischimo,* saddle blanket; *mikawne,* bivouac of a hunting party; *papuchs,* child; *mitass,* leggings; *wuasch,* sink hole; *sumite,* pemmican.

This morning, four Cree came galloping to the fort from the hollow below our garden to announce the approach of a band and to get tobacco to welcome the newcomers. They said that while they were concealed behind shrubbery in the sunken streambed, they noticed three strange Indians whom they took to be enemies. As soon as they received the tobacco, the four Cree hastened to greet their friends and conduct them to the fort. Joe Picotte, who had already sent them 45 plugs of tobacco and 6 pounds of vermilion to entice these customers from us, won only two to his side. It is really to the Indians' interest to deal with the opposition; if it weren't for that post, they would have to pay twice as much for the goods they buy.

The two disloyal Cree did not fare so well, because they did not have as much cured meat for barter as Joe's gift was worth. Joe gave them a piece of his mind when, after having received all of his tobacco and vermilion— which was a high price to pay for the small amount of meat they brought— the two families also desired to be fed and lodged at his post.

The two leaders of this band of Cree, Rassade au Cou (Bead for the Neck) and Bras Casse (Broken or Crushed Arm), now told how they had driven those three suspected Indians from their hiding place and had spoken to them but did not understand their dialect. They were on foot and had ropes bound about their bodies: horse thieves. Since all Indians have the same sign language, they are always able to make themselves understood, no matter who they may be or whence they come. Mr. Denig supposed them to be Cree from some other band whom these chiefs would not betray.

Morgan came down the river this evening with his two rafts and the flatboat.

October 19—This morning Le Tout Piqué (Fully Tattooed) brought in another crowd of Cree, including women and children. Some time ago, I had painted a flat pipestem white and sky blue in alternating fields, and in the four fields I had painted a buffalo, a wolf, an owl, and a bear. I presented this pipe to Piqué. The smoking of this pipe for the first time was to be celebrated with great ceremony in the office, i.e., an address on the part of Le Tout Piqué and the smoking of the pipe on the part of all braves in company with the bourgeois. Mr. Denig had the kindness to invite me to be present. In return, Mr. Denig was permitted to pass himself off as the painter of the pipestem. He entreated me not to laugh when I witnessed a scene which would seem no doubt perfectly nonsensical to me. But it was only his own air of official gravity, when clothed in the buffalo robe, that I could have found ridiculous.

I found Battiste sitting in the middle of the room as interpreter. A beautiful buffalo robe lay on the floor beside him. Braves of both bands squatted in close rows against the walls. Rassade au Cou, Bras Casse, and one other were seated on a sofa. Le Tout Piqué stood in front of them and directly opposite Mr. Denig. When I entered and modestly took my seat in a corner, Piqué asked Mr. Denig, through the interpreter, who I was. "A trader from below," replied the bourgeois. I had to sit behind Mr. Denig. A common engagé is no part of a soldier and not worthy of notice.

With much dignity, Piqué now came forward, put the handsome buffalo robe about Mr. Denig's shoulders, and, holding the new peace pipe in his right hand, offered us his left in greeting. Grasping his robe with his right hand, he took two steps backward and began his speech. He said he had been brought up a patron of this fort, was a loyal adherent, never brought even one skin to the opposition. He had left 50 tents of his band at home; they were waiting news of his reception here and wished to know whether he was treated well. The chief delivered his address in sections, and at the end of each, Battiste interpreted what had been said. Battiste did not use English, but only French, which he spoke not by any means well, repeating

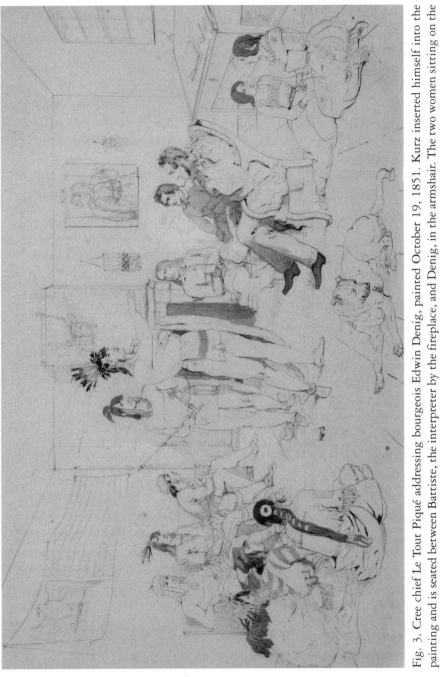

Fig. 3. Cree chief Le Tout Piqué addressing bourgeois Edwin Denig, painted October 19, 1851. Kurz inserted himself into the painting and is seated between Battiste, the interpreter by the fireplace, and Denig, in the armchair. The two women sitting on the floor beside the bourgeois are probably Denig's two wives. (From the collection of Gilcrease Museum, Tulsa, Oklahoma)

his words continually and altogether making a bungling effort that was out of keeping with so solemn a ceremony.

In his reply, Mr. Denig promised friendship and fair prices, whereupon a distinguished brave lighted the pipe and gravely extended it toward the bourgeois. Each of us took several whiffs with becoming seriousness, and then the soldier proffered it to his chief, who had remained standing erect and dignified in the same place where he had stood while addressing the assemblage. He took the peace pipe in his hands, held it aloft, and then lowered it, pointing with the tip of the stem toward the earth, toward sunrise and sunset, smoked, and returned the pipe to the master of ceremonies. Luckily, the interpreter was the last of us three to smoke, for, being acquainted already with their manner of conducting this ceremony, he drew so vigorously as to rekindle the tobacco. Otherwise, while Piqué was propitiating the heavens (good spirits), earth, and sun, the pipe might have gone out, which would have been regarded as a bad omen.

The pipe bearer next invited the assembled braves to smoke, each according to his rank, a ticklish business. Then the guests were served baked meats and sweetened coffee, which they were invited to distribute themselves, so that no one might think he was slighted or neglected by a white man.

Every time a band of Indians annoys Mr. Denig with their begging, he flees to me and unburdens his heart by calling them names. At such times he bestows much praise on other Indians who are not here but who get their share of abuse at some future time. He is always in the best humor with Indians when none are around. He longs for them in matters of trade; he then prefers them to all other people, his own countrymen not excepted. Today the red men who were at the fort stood high in his esteem, but since they have shown that his many courtesies only encouraged them to beg, to expect presents, he thinks them good for nothing, not worthy to unloose the shoe latches of Indians who inhabit the eastern domain. They would rather see enemies of their own race go to ruin than to combine with them against the whites. They are more given to superstition than Indians in the East, he declares, less intelligent, not so brave, and, so far as he knows, they have nowhere a regularly constituted leader, etc.

One must consider that the tribes of the eastern domain had their wits sharpened through many years of warfare. They received their instruction by constant intercourse with white people of various nations. They became more wise by contemplation of unending losses. How often have hostile tribes of redskins in the East combined against the common foe, and for how long a time? One may also consider the small number of distinguished leaders and counselors among them within a hundred years. In proportion to their superior knowledge, the white race has produced even fewer.

Mr. Denig assures me that I should count myself happy that, owing to my nearsightedness, I was prevented from entering fully upon the Indian mode of life. Unless a white man were rich, he became the sport of savages when he went about naked and wore long hair reaching to his shoulders, as was the practice with some men at Fort Alexander on the Yellowstone. Indians esteem a white person only when he gives evidence of talents that they do not themselves possess. They would never respect any white man more highly than themselves as hunter or soldier. So far as Mr. Denig is concerned, he would never desire to adopt the life of an Indian unless, by large means, he could establish important connections through many marriages and win their veneration with the aid of chemistry, medicine, or the art of jongleury [sorcery].

What he affirms in this regard has been proved in the case of [Robert] Meldrum, bourgeois at Fort Alexander, that trading post among the Absaroka. Though Meldrum is a soldier of note, his scalps and his trophies from the hunt have not won him influence among the Absaroka. He is esteemed for his prodigal liberality, on account of which he has fallen into debt instead of accumulating money. He is said to be an efficient gunsmith but not an especially shrewd businessman. If, through ambition or vanity, he aspires to take the lead in establishing a widely extended family connection, certain Crows of consequence become immediately jealous and go to the opposition, or come here to barter their buffalo robes.

October 22—As Morgan has been sent with a complete assortment of goods to Vice de Carafel's winter quarters, I am going to have at least 2 days' peace. He is rarely at the fort, so he has no regular bed but always takes up quarters in my room. I admit he is a most civil, well-educated Scot, but he is incessantly on the move, constantly opening and shutting the door, his three dogs following behind. Anyone who supposes he can concentrate his attention on writing or drawing under such circumstances, I say only, let him try it. Last Monday I found a pair of fat Virginia deer on the riverbank. Upon the occasion of our first snowfall at this place yesterday, I had to carry a letter to Fort William in the face of a biting west wind.

After our midday meal, I helped to bury two papooses that were brought here by some Assiniboin. An old mourner made a speech at the grave expressing gratitude, which is said to have shown him to be a man of much intelligence. In the evening, Smith and Cadotte, the two hunters, arrived, bringing some horses taken from the Blackfeet. Their Indian women have longed for their return. On the way, expecting no thievery by our supposed friends the Assiniboin, they did not guard the drove. In consequence, they were robbed of ten horses, including some of their most excellent runners.

They also brought news of seven Assiniboin who, three months ago, were out on the warpath against the Blackfeet tribe to win renown for themselves; all were killed, as was to be expected. At the same time, they had already taken eight scalps from the Blackfeet and had wounded some 20 more of the enemy in the neighborhood of a village. Then one of the chiefs called his people together and rebuked them for their disgrace in permitting such a small hostile force to approach near enough to do so much mischief. At the head of 200 horsemen, he overcame the concealed Assiniboin and destroyed them all.

Today, Nai [Owen Mackenzie] and his wife and crew of assistants set out for his winter quarters on the Lower Bourbeuse, traveling in a keelboat loaded with commodities. They made an attractive picture: Nai was standing at the helm, his young wife was sitting on the covered bale of goods in front of him holding his gun, three men were at the oars, an old woman was leaning against the bales. On shore, two beautiful Assiniboin girls were harnessing a black wolfhound to a travois. Other girls were picking berries among the autumn shrubs.

Cadotte, who arrived yesterday from the Blackfeet territory, is regarded as the best stag hunter in this region. As they express themselves here, "He even beats Packinaud shucks." He is a genuine Mountaineer, possessing to a marked degree both their good and their less favorable qualities. He is unrivaled in the skill of starting, pursuing, approaching, shooting, and carving a deer. In other respects, he is heedless, wasteful, and foolhardy—half Canadian, half Cree.

Dauphen, another of the same sort, lives an isolated life on the prairie with his two wives. He left the opposition in debt and now hunts on his own account. Assiniboin look with disfavor on such independent characters who are without friends and have no business connections anywhere. If by chance he once spoils a hunt which they have arranged, he can jolly well count on a good drubbing and the loss of all that he owns. But for the relatives of his wives, he would have been driven away long ago. Although he was formerly a trapper and followed the related business of trader, he can no longer find employment with either of the companies, on account of his questionable character; he has defrauded both of them.

Once, when Mr. Denig was journeying across the prairie with Dorion the drinker, who was serving him as interpreter, they wandered into a company of hot-brained Sioux. Dorion owned a strong-limbed, bad-tempered pack horse that was being urged on with the entire gang. This animal gave an Indian boy such a kick on his forehead that for quite a while he was thought to be dead. Of Iowa blood himself, Dorion knew at once what he had to do to get himself out of the pickle. He was aware of the fact that Indians do not excuse such accidents any more than they pardon the unintentional killing of a relative.

With no more ado, he seized the nag's halter and gave the beast to the boy's father. Dorion was not to blame for the misadventure, but he was certain that in the event of intense suffering or the death of that boy, the father would first of all slay the horse, and it depended upon circumstances whether he would exercise his vengefulness upon the animal's owner as well. In order to forestall any such unpleasantness, he also presented his own riding horse, which appeased the father and saved himself from the consequence of present or future wrath. In the event that the father sought revenge, a white man would have raised a quarrel, or else he would have killed the Indian. Dorion conformed to the custom of the people among whom he lived.

I was making inquiry concerning the story Charles Martin told me when I met him at Council Bluffs with his Mackinaw boats, about his friend Lambert's having pursued an American from Missouri all the way to Fort Hall in Oregon to kill him, because the latter ran away with "his old woman." Mr. Denig holds a totally different opinion concerning that so-called heroic deed. Not that he calls into question the daring of the man, but Denig declares that in doing what he did, he turned his ability as soldier, hunter— or in other words, as Indian—to the wrong use. No Indian brave dares take his wife's elopement to heart; at least he dares not manifest his feeling by any outward act. He would be made a laughingstock if he took one step toward bringing her back. Accordingly, if a white man adopts the Indian life and customs, he is to take braves of prominence for his models, not young bucks. Mr. Denig maintains that even from the standpoint of a white man, Lambert acted unwisely. Notwithstanding the fact that his having brought back his runaway wife and having got the better of her abductor speaks of courage, perseverance, and shrewdness on his part, his act did not bring back happiness to either of them.

So the bourgeois thinks it much better for a man to treat the matter lightly when an unfaithful wife runs off, and buy himself another at once. Lambert's chase all alone to Oregon was a daring exploit, but what did he gain by going in pursuit of an erring wife, only in the end to take her life? As the story goes, after following his "blonde," whom he very truly loved, across a wide tract of wild country, through the domain of several hostile Indian tribes, at last Lambert came upon the fugitives at Fort Hall. His wife tried to offer excuses and to appease him by flattery. She enticed him out on the prairie, where his enemy the American came to meet him. By the advice of her lover, the woman removed the bullet from Lambert's gun. Fortunately, he discovered that treachery before it was too late. Having replaced the ball, he shot down his enemy, to the great amazement and grief of his "blonde." In his rage over her deceit, he brought her down also. He took his vengeance—a twofold vengeance.

Mr. Denig also confirms the report that Indian mothers now and then forcibly bring about miscarriages, either by taking a strong drink or by means of the stick with which they grub for pommes blanches (prairie turnip, the *teep-se-nah* of the Assiniboin). This stick is pointed at one end and provided with a knob at the other, upon which the body's weight can be thrown in such a way as to drive the point under the roots with little exertion. They use this for killing their infants by pressing the pointed end below the heart at the time of delivery, or else by pressing the lower part of the body violently upon the knob.

Sometimes they throw their newborn babes into the river and drown them. Why do they commit these crimes? They have no love for their children? On the contrary, their maternal affection is strong except when, on account of a child, they lose the love of their husbands. A pregnant wife is repugnant to an Indian; he turns to another. That vexes the loving wife in her turn, for her husband constantly ignores her on account of her being with child. She tries to shorten the period of pregnancy in order to be loved again.

What we call children born out of wedlock had often such a fate as I have described. They are proof of a mother's loss of virtue in an earlier love affair. Having been deserted, such mothers in their bitterness of heart put their little daughters to death, feeling that they are better out of the world than exposed to the harsh experiences of this life. Owing to this same repugnance on the part of their husbands, mothers suckle their children until the fourth or fifth year. It always impressed me as so droll to see boys with bows and arrows in their hands nursing like babes at their mother's breasts.

Tomorrow we begin our domestic plan for only two meals a day: late breakfast, early supper. Days are so short that meals come too near together. Makes the cook surly, Mr. Denig told me, as if he felt obliged to offer some excuse. As if his evident purpose were not to have us eat less. "In cold weather, one's appetite is keener," I replied.

October 23—Mr. Denig gave me a buffalo horn that some time ago had been polished by Owen Mackenzie for a powder horn. It is very large and lustrous black. Cow [buffalo] horns are too small; those of fully matured bulls are broken into splinters by their fighting.

Morgan is back again. While he was away, I had to do his work both as clerk and as foreman. Packinaud is still confined to his bed; he cannot stand on his broken shank. I have to look after him. Having been the only clerk besides, I have had a great deal of work to do for two days. But I would rather make myself useful than be bored.

October 24—We buried another Assiniboin papoose. Afterwards, when Mr. Denig wished to smoke with the mourning relatives, he could not find any of the small leaves that Indians in this region mix with the commonly known American tobacco. He sent me to a nearby copse to cut some twigs of the upland willow, so that he might show me what sort of tobacco mixture is used by the Sioux. I hurried out and, with my scalp knife, cut off just above the root an armful of young shrubs about the size of a man's finger. I brought them back, and with a knife, we first carefully removed the outer red bark and threw it away. Then we beat off the bast [fiber], dried it at the fire, cut it up fine, and mixed it with the American tobacco. This willow bast fiber is said not to dry out so well as that earlier used, nor is the smell of it so aromatic.

At midday, Morgan and I were treated with a splendid cold breakfast or lunch. Mr. Denig served crackers and butter, pickles, sardines, cheese, and excellent hardtack—real luxuries in this part of the world. Then we cut another load of osier shrubs, brought them in, stripped off the bast, and dried it. As smoking in Indian ceremonies is a strict requirement according to Indian etiquette, this mixture must be just as scrupulously provided as food. Morgan occupied Carafel's bed. There was war in my room when he and his dogs met Mr. Denig and his doggie. Hoka is particularly jealous and vicious.

Mr. Denig had to admonish Packinaud again this evening to wash his wounded leg himself in order to make our work less disagreeable. For 21 days, mornings and evenings, I have washed and salved his wound, a service that he or his stupid wife might just as easily perform. He never seems to have once thought of keeping the wound clean, though we have often told him the flesh was as black as a Negro's.

October 25—With the remains of a lap dog, we entrapped our first wolf. In laying the snare, they dig a hole 3 inches deep so that the trap lies even with the ground, and then they cover it with earth, grass, buffalo chips, etc.

Attracted by carrion, a wolf or a fox steps unaware upon the springs and his leg is caught. To prevent his running off with the trap, the latter is fastened by means of an attached chain to a heavy log or tree trunk. For fear of unnecessarily piercing his pelt, an animal caught this way is never shot but is killed by a blow on the head with a bludgeon.

I spent almost the entire evening discussing religion with Mr. Denig. Though both of us are Protestants, we are agreed that the Catholic religion is better suited to the civilizing of barbarous people than our own Protestant faith. We know that uneducated tribes with their limited understanding find it impossible to grasp purely abstract teaching; therefore, such appeals make no impression upon them whatsoever. First of all, savages must be inspired with awe by means of visible, mystic symbols, and influenced through their feelings. They cannot be expected to have a grasp of the considerable knowledge of history and geography necessary for even a slight understanding of our religion.

I was here interrupted by Morgan, who wished me to accompany him to his traps. This time we found a gray fox that I struck dead and brought home to paint for him. These animals are full of fleas.

Earlier, Père Point, a Jesuit, lived here and tried to inculcate strict morality. They let him preach without any opposition until he began to reproach

Mr. Denig with a plurality of wives. The bourgeois replied that his older wife was sickly, but he still kept her for their daughter's sake and for the reason that she had always conducted herself well. He was not one of those who think that man was given strong passions by Nature merely to be continually tormented, merely to crucify the flesh without ceasing because, owing to circumstances, he might not have a wife, or if the first wife was incapacitated, he might not get a second helpmate. In the States, a man in his situation would have sufficient grounds for divorce, but he refused to cast off a good woman who was not to blame for her condition. Said he, "You join together Indian women and dissolute men with your holy rites, not a word of which the women understand, and just as little the men regard. Since they do not know what they promise in the ceremony, they make false vows from which you are again quite ready to release them, upon presentation of a gift. Are not such things done in the name of religion? Do you not thereby give licentiousness the semblance of your sanction?"

When we went again to look after our traps, we found that the carcass had been dragged quite a distance away by wolves. Our Spanish horse guard told us in his Spanish-French-English jargon: *"Jamme* wolf *dragge de carcasse* way from *de trappe. No seen una pareilla chose. Ni* now *putte* horse's *snoute* on *de pickette, de* wolf no more carry awaye."

Night scenes here are decidedly picturesque. Armed with guns and hunting knives and provided with lanterns, we moved across the dusky prairie that seems to have neither beginning nor end, but to melt into the wide heaven from which it can only be distinguished by scattered stars. The captured animals are struggling about us and gnashing their teeth, the dead just removed from the traps. While the traps are being set once more, the concentrated glow of lanterns, the hunters' original attire, and the dark background all combine to form a picture at once suggestive of animated life and awe.

October 26—At daybreak, we found two gray foxes in the traps. Painted a picture of one of them. In the study of hairy beasts, watercolors are of little advantage, pointed brushes still less. For reproducing the curl of hair, broad oil brushes are best. By adroit manipulation of the latter, the effect is achieved; with pointed brushes, one has to draw hair for hair.

As evening came on I was reading Alison's *Essays* when Mr. Denig entered, much surprised that I was not on the riverbank. Herantsa were there to be put across. Morgan had already left some time ago to fetch them.

On their way to visit the Crows, three Assiniboin, together with the *berdache* (hermaphrodites are frequent), were slain by Blackfeet.

"And you are sitting so quietly here by the fire, while all the rest of us are in spasms of curiosity. Man, you are not keeping up with the times!"

Out I went, taking my telescope with me, but I was unable to recognize any Herantsa. There were too many women.

There were also white people, who kept their horses separate from the others. An Assiniboin woman came down to the sandy shore crying aloud and struck the ground three times with her buffalo robe as a sign that she had lost three of her people. The other Indians were no less distinguished visitors than the noted chief of the Absaroka and his most celebrated braves. Chief Rottentail is their leader on this side of the mountains; on the other side, Big Robert is chief. As Packinaud speaks the Herantsa language fluently and has the distinction, therefore, of being our one and only interpreter for Absaroka, these great celebrities had to be conducted to his room.

Rottentail's resemblance to Louis Philippe of blessed memory struck me at once: the same capable expression of *citoyen*, the same shrewd look of merchant, the same official mien.[5] I was sorry that he did not wear the Indian style of dress rather than the American. His suit of clothes was fashioned from a blue blanket. He wore gray leggings but no shirt, no vest, neither neckcloth nor hat.

As soon as the Crow women had brought in their heavy bundles and everything was in order, Rottentail produced a superb military headdress, which he put on the bourgeois' head, and hung a handsome buffalo robe on his shoulders. Denig looked comical enough, but no one dared laugh. The pipe was lighted and offered by Packinaud to the chief. Each smoked in his turn.

Rottentail began to relate how the Herantsa endeavored to deter them from coming here, saying that we were afflicted with dangerous diseases: His life and the lives of his followers would be snuffed out. However, his heart was strong and his friendship for Mr. Denig not to be shaken. Conscious of their double dealing, the Herantsa took another route in their return home (but the scoundrels had been well treated). While Rottentail was speaking, the name "Ista Uwatse" did not escape me; neither did his obvious reference to myself. Packinaud does not interpret word for word but only what seems to him worthwhile. Mr. Denig asked that his thanks be conveyed for assurances of friendship and good faith on the part of the chief, and said he should be convinced that nobody at Fort Union was sick.

While the Absaroka were being served meats, crackers, and sweetened tea in the office, I dressed the wound on Packinaud's leg. I asked him what had been said about me. Nothing. But I was too well acquainted with the Indian sign language to believe that nothing had been said concerning me. I saw Rottentail indicate me two different times with his finger, then make the sign for writing or drawing, then of becoming ill and dying. Moreover, when I went with the horse guard to examine the traps, he said to me: "Crows tell me Gros Ventres say you bringue de cholera up, and make all you painte die—heap die!" So that was it: lies and false reports.

October 27—Caught a wolf. Brought him in to serve as the model for a study. There are wolves here of great size, and also prairie wolves, which are much smaller—the latter appear to be half fox. There are many different colors of the larger species, varying according to age and season of the year: black, brown, yellow, gray mixed, snow white. To set more than two traps with one carcass is useless, for the noise made by the captured animals drives others away. When the dog used for baiting the trap is consumed, one has to strew small pieces of meat over the concealed trap and all around in order to ensnare the animals.

Bear's Head, the chief in command of the soldiers, is a warrior of great ability and power. He gave Packinaud a long account of their journeyings and dangers, their experiences on the chase, their battles, and the hunger they endured since last winter. They suffer terribly from hunger every time they are obliged to take the far journey over barren plains and wild mountain ranges to purchase horses from the Flathead. As Bear's Head spoke just as distinctly by means of signs as by words, I understood everything. He took much pleasure in seeing me so attentive. The portraits also pleased him, I am sure, but upon looking at them, he shook his head. When these braves heard the parrot coughing, one of them said at once that Polly had the same disease from which they themselves had suffered last winter, and they might catch influenza again.

Because Rottentail was given a piece of painted cloth—very large and diaphanous—by Mr. Denig last winter, the latter was blamed for causing that epidemic, just as I am censured now. Yet Rottentail related with evident pleasure how he had made use of the picture to cover his pillow, on which he always laid his head when he went to sleep, and invariably beheld Mr. Denig in his dreams. He ascribes the goodly number of scalps (32) which he and his braves took from the Blackfeet to that painting. Lucky for Mr. Denig; otherwise he would not only have forfeited their esteem but would have lost their patronage and brought injury to himself besides. Bear's Head wished very much to possess the banner with the painted eagle.

The six white men from Fort Alexander did not come over the river in our boats, because they are deserters from this fort. They belong now to the opposition. Joe Picotte sent them over in long boats made of buffalo hides.

We received news from Bruyère, a trader in these parts. He brought some commodities in a keelboat to Fort Alexander, where he must wait for Mr. Culbertson at Meldrum's. In the afternoon, the famous Absaroka Amazon arrived. Mr. Denig called me to his office that I might have the opportunity to see her. She looked neither savage nor warlike. On the contrary, as I entered the room, she sat with her hands folded in her lap, as when one prays. She is about 45 years old and appears modest in manner and good natured, rather than quick to quarrel.

She gave Mr. Denig a genuine Blackfeet scalp which she had captured herself. How amazed as well as overjoyed was I afterwards when Mr. Denig presented the long black scalp to me! A scalp is an Indian curio of rare worth, for the reason that a brave so very seldom parts with those trophies. After long pleadings and promises on my part, my former father-in-law Kirutsche had brought me a piece of leather once on which was found some short black hair; he would have had me believe it was a piece of skin from a human head. I took it to be a piece of black bear's hide. Our human scalp is very thick, to be sure, and difficult to distinguish from an animal's skin, but the short, thick hair is not.

Relatives of the three Assiniboin who were slain have planted a pole and fastened thereon two leather pouches that belonged to the dead. There for a long time they wailed and made blood offerings by cutting their arms, cheeks, heads, and legs until blood flowed. One of the dead men is that Assiniboin who won the high stakes from a Herantsa. He was a son of the Assiniboin chief L'Ours Fou (Crazy Bear). The other was called L'Homme de Nord [Man of the North], the same who some time ago was relieved from eye trouble by Mr. Denig and repaid him with most annoying barefaced begging afterwards. The third was Good Tobacco, a woman. She was taken by surprise while asleep in her tent. The boy, son of L'Ours Fou, was attacked first. He received eight wounds at the first onset and his hips were broken, but he did not die until several days later in the Crow village. He was not scalped.

Some lads who were not in the tent, but had gone most likely to the Crows' settlement with the berdache (hermaphrodite), saved their skins. Absaroka in the vicinity heard the firing, mounted their horses at once, and put the Blackfeet to flight. They followed a long distance in pursuit; when they at last came in sight of the enemy, found them entrenched on a hill, having concealed themselves in a hole they had dug. The Crows did not risk smoking them out of their improvised redoubt. The Blackfeet were able to get away during the night.

October 28—Absaroka are continually here. Despite their assurances of loyalty, they go from one fort to another and allow themselves to be lodged, fed, and presented with gifts. They seek the place where they can trade to their best advantage, for they are exceedingly shrewd in business matters, a match for our traders. When Rottentail returned from the opposition, he said Joe Picotte himself—not Bonaparte, his Crow interpreter, but the person in control of the fort—had assured him repeatedly that I with my drawing and painting spread the deadly infections, diseases; that I was to blame for death among the Herantsa, who drove me away from their settlement; that if he, Rottentail, and his braves should tarry long in our neighborhood, they would be blown to the moon. If that is not carrying trade rivalry to the limit, I am no judge of such matters. The miserable wretch would put my life at stake for the sake of a few buffalo robes!

What would one naturally expect of such a liar, but that he would sacrifice everything to his own selfish interest. I did not know why he should have anything against me; or was it for that reason that he had cheated me in St. Joseph? Envy of the big company is not his motive; furthermore, he had the commodities for these Crows sent to Fort Alexander. Now that they are coming here, he has not a sufficient stock of goods to furnish a continual supply to Assiniboin, Crows, and Cree. Joe would like to have the Absaroka go home, and I am to be used as a scarecrow to frighten them away. Crows have no such idea that I shall bring death upon them with my painting, but they might probably think I could do so by other means. Their minds have been too diligently worked upon by our competitors and they are too much dominated by superstition not to be affected in the end by such influences. All this is especially annoying to me, because I shall be the occasion, sooner or later, of injury to this company, to whom—up to the present—I am indebted for much kindness. If it comes to that, I may not remain here unless I give up my art, and I will not do that. Now that I am so near the accomplishment of my aim, as far as my studies are concerned, I will not renounce the realization of my dreams!

Though the Crows do not know from experience about the devastating epidemics, as do the Arikara, the Mandan, and the Herantsa, they have heard about them. The coming of the first artist was coincident with the breakout of smallpox. Though the plague of cholera was without any such coincidence, how can one get these Indians to believe that? This is the third time things have so happened. Isn't that sufficient proof for superstitious people? And each time it was either a portrait painter or a landscape painter that brought the deadly disease. The painter of animals (Audubon) did not oppress them with pestilence.

What did Crows say last winter when influenza was so dangerously prevalent among them? That Mr. Denig had avenged the theft of 10 horses by inflicting aching chests, bursting heads, and swift death. They were confirmed in that fear by the fact that already 150 were dead, counting among them some of their most prominent tribesmen, while in the nearby Assiniboin camp there was not a sick person to be found. The Assiniboin were laughing about it. The Crows swore revenge, came here and defied Mr. Denig to his face. He was troubled in mind but fearless in manner, though he really regarded himself as a lost man. To prevent further spread of the disease, however, the Indians brought back nine of the stolen horses. Mr. Denig then delivered a forceful speech, assuring them that he was too good a friend to inflict such a revenge upon them for the loss of a few horses. Nay, he was here for the purpose of bartering buffalo robes. If he should cause so many Crows to die, would that help him to get robes?

But there was one Crow too wrathful, too much enraged by the loss of his best beloved relatives to be appeased. Mr. Denig saw at once what the man had in mind. He walked up to him, looked him sternly but calmly in the face, and shouted, "Shoot, if you dare!" The Indian fired his gun in the air.

A redskin thinks twice before he murders his trader. He is aware of his dependence on the fur traders and of the reciprocal interests that unite them.

On the death of their friends, the tribes get beside themselves sometimes; if such bereavements follow swiftly, one upon the other, they excite themselves further by wailings and complaints.

An Assiniboin brought news today that the mother of L'Ours Fou's boy had hanged herself with a rope because while at the burial of her grandchild, she heard of the death of her son, the father of the little corpse lying before her. The shock proved too great for the poor woman! Besides, she felt uneasy about her husband the chief, who was in constant insecurity among the palefaces at Fort Laramie.

October 29—Absaroka withdrew as soon as they saw there was nothing more to be had by begging. Summer and autumn are the dullest seasons in trade hereabouts. Hides are not yet available, therefore Indians have no medium of exchange. They must make preparations then for the winter hunting, yet they have no equipment and seldom have credit. They keep a supply of cured meat, but that brings in only less important things such as knives, beads, calico, powder, and lead, not guns, blankets, or horses.

They beg. They promise patronage. The trader must assist them in turn, else business at his trading post will be dull. He must attract customers. If he does not, the opposition will, and as a result, Indians will not come near him. They do not look upon the trader as indispensable, except for articles that they regard as luxuries and that they come to the post to get more frequently than provisions and clothing. Oftentimes a trader feels compelled to lend an Indian a gun during the hunting season, though he knows that he is virtually making a present—entailing a loss. If he presses the redskin for payment, the latter transfers his patronage to the opposition. Ah, it is the opposition that keeps the Indian on his feet. But for the competition, he is bound to one trader, enchained, so to speak, to one man's prices. Yet there is also proof here that too-liberal credit makes no friends.

For some time past, I have been thinking that my diary will be sufficiently interesting to publish someday in connection with my drawings. At first I wrote down ideas, accounts of my own experiences, and some historical facts for myself alone, more as an aid to my recollection than for any other reason. As my notes to the present time contribute much that will give closer acquaintance with the fur trade, the life of the Mountaineers, and Indians as it is no longer found anywhere, the publication of my journal can do no harm.

An Assiniboin shot at Morgan and me as we were going around the cattle stall (old fort) on our way to the wolf traps. Talking together, we passed quite near a small encampment. An Indian heard us, did not understand the language, failed to recognize the speakers, and sent a bullet over our heads. Morgan called out to him that we were *waschitscho* [white men].

I attempted to write the war song according to its rendering by one of these Assiniboin. He sang without words merely for his own encouragement. Apart from the words, the melody has little variation and no significance. The "e" is like our "la" in the practice of song. The first syllable of every verse is a high note, shouted from a full throat. The tones then become softer, lower, until they are a hardly distinguishable murmur, then suddenly the loud note of a new verse rings out again. When heard in these solitudes at the darkness of night, those abrupt loud cries, in contrast to the slow movement of the verse and gradual softening of the tones, produce a most singular effect, like savage exultation combined with lamentation and words of counsel.

The well-known, much dreaded war cry—*Ju, ju, he, haha*—sounds like the neighing of a horse, yet is often given a tremolo sound by the motion of the hand before the mouth. The modulation varies according to the nation.

October 30—After he had sent ahead three messengers to announce his coming, Knife, brother of L'Ours Fou, arrived this afternoon with the corpse of his sister (sister-in-law), brought on a travois drawn by a horse. He wishes her to be buried beside her daughter, the daughter who hanged herself because a buck boasted that he had taken indecent liberties with her. Mother and grandchild lie beside each other enveloped in their blankets, then wrapped in a buffalo robe. The bodies were brought here because no wood can be found on the prairie with which to erect a scaffold, nor have the Indians picks and shovels to dig graves sufficiently deep.

Inasmuch as the mourners brought four packs of buffalo hides—that is, 40 robes—with them, the bourgeois had a meal served them consisting of boiled meat and corn, sweetened coffee, and beugnies [beignets: doughnuts], all of which the aged women and the children ate with great relish. They could hardly restrain themselves from looking glad in spite of their grief. With great avidity they cleaned the dishes with their fingers and licked them with craving tongues. As usual, the distribution of the food was left to one of their soldiers, because the task is rather a difficult one to so apportion the same quantity to each that nobody has cause for complaint. Men were served first, then women. Children were counted with their mothers.

A coffin was readied during this feast. The family took charge of the body and laid it in the rude box. As a gift, Mr. Denig spread a new blanket over it, the top was nailed down, and six of us carried it to our God's acre, lowered it ourselves into the already prepared grave, and then covered it over. Knife made us a speech expressing gratitude. We withdrew, leaving the relatives of the dead to their howling and lamentation. On this occasion there was no need to employ aged women to mourn, for sorrow was sincere and heartfelt, as one could readily believe. Four members of one family dead within two weeks is cause enough for grief. When the first outburst was over, Knife ordered a meal prepared at his expense for his relatives. This was eaten at the grave, after the deceased had been served her portion. The lamentation began anew, accompanied by the cutting of their flesh and offering up their blood without feigning or dissimulation. It was a moving sight, indeed.

Indians look upon suicide not as a crime or cause for shame, but as something natural and right. No one who is conscious of joy in life and hopes for better things in the future ever kills himself purposely. As soon as hope is gone, the allurement of life is at an end; doubt, disgust, and weariness set in. The equal balance between sensibility and reason is disturbed, and a disordered mind is the result. Momentary insanity—morally or spiritually— renders such a person irresponsible, not accountable. Therefore, his deed is no crime or disgrace.

October 31—The unexpected often happens. Mr. Culbertson has arrived at last this evening from Fort Laramie. We heard the glad news this afternoon from Ours Fou, who had hurried on in advance to mourn with his family. "Uncle Sam" has appointed Ours Fou chief of the Assiniboin. During his absence, fate has robbed him of his wife—his only wife—his son, and two grandchildren. Anyone who saw this grief-stricken chief would never speak of an Indian's lack of feeling. They love, hate, experience sorrow and joy just as we do. Only in the face of the enemy are they too proud to show the pain they feel. Ours Fou was grieved to the soul, most profoundly affected. Gazing before him in a kind of stupor, he wept silently. His hair and his body were besmeared in token of his sorrow. Morgan felt that he must conceal the chief's weapons for fear he, too, might be seized with too great a longing for those he loved best.

SIX

November 1851

November 2—The news from Fort Laramie fails utterly to justify expectations. No treaties were negotiated, much less concluded.[1] Uncle Sam made no display of military power to impress the Indians.

Colonel Mitchell, the United States agent, is said to have been befuddled most of the time from too much drink, to have made great promises to the Indians, to have appointed several braves to the rank of supreme chief without the approval of the respective nations, to have made gifts, such as stores of meal, blankets, etc. Quatre Ours, Bonaparte, and their associates say they were expecting a grand military display in which soldiers of many nations would take part in all their war regalia, rather than an adjournment of the conference. Nevertheless, the instant they were told by the Sioux—representatives from Fort Pierre—about the outbreak of cholera among the Herantsa, the Mandan, and the Arikara, they were off bag and baggage to their homes.

Mr. Culbertson says I should be glad I did not go. Though I should have seen more than 2,000 warriors decked out in martial array, I should have witnessed no dancing, because no dancing was permitted or anything else that might incite hostile tribes and disturb the harmony of the occasion. Neither should I have seen a single wild animal, nor any hunting.

Mr. Denig says Mr. Culbertson has been named a colonel by his friend Mitchell, the United States agent, and from now on, we are to address him by that title. Colonel of what? Here we have neither regular army nor militia. Oh, the passion for titles among these republican Americans!

Our new colonel gave a ball last night. His Indian wife in her ball gown, fringed and valanced according to European mode, looked extraordinarily well. She has much presence, grace, and animation for a full-blooded Indian.

One or more tragicomic intermezzos were not wanting—results of liquor drinking. Joe Picotte had to be put to bed after he came near to having a fight with our Indians.

Spent the entire day stripping off willow bast, drying it, and mixing it with tobacco. As long as this visitation continues, I could employ myself day after day preparing the mixture.

November 3—Late last night Mr. Denig waked me up to keep Mr. Culbertson company. Now and then we took a little whisky, smoked a great deal, talking in a desultory way about God, man's destiny, etc., until finally the conversation was directed to the principal subject in view: where I was to be, and what I was to do in the future.

Mr. Denig wished to know precisely in what way he was to employ me; whether he might be allowed to order me to paint any picture he desired. I had expressed my opinion once to Mackenzie that I was not employed as painter to execute just any picture.

"Now, here is our master. Tell me, have I the right to order you to paint a picture?" Mr. Denig demanded.

"No, sir," I replied. "Not after that agreement with our Mr. Picotte. I refused to paint only one of my compositions for you. You know why. The other pictures I painted because I take delight in such work, and besides, I wished to show my goodwill and my willingness to be of service in any way I could. Before the traders went away to their winter quarters, I was altogether superfluous here. I was glad to make myself agreeable and useful."

Mr. Culbertson remarked that the portraits I had painted pleased him so much that he would like to possess one of himself and another of his wife. In addition, I was to execute a replica of the dog Natoh's picture, so that he could take the original to his post in Blackfeet territory. He said further that Mr. Denig will have need of me, so I remain here as clerk. In summer, when Mr. Picotte senior [Honoré] comes up on the steamer, I shall certainly be satisfactorily remunerated. Such a statement I found brief and to my liking.

So I am to remain here. I am satisfied. I wonder how long my remark to Mackenzie had stuck in Mr. Denig's throat. A small glass of gin emboldened him to be relieved of it.

Bruyère, who brought Mr. Culbertson's horse on while the colonel himself came down the Yellowstone by boat, is now the only clerk besides Morgan. Packinaud is still in bed. When Morgan is busy as foreman and Bruyère at his trading post on the Upper Bourbeuse, I shall find enough with which to employ my time this winter. I am now an employee, not a visitor.

November 4—Those Assiniboin who came to visit their chief were hardly gone when twenty other tents were pitched below the fort. There is no end to smoking and feasting. Even as I was closing the gate—one of the duties belonging to my new position—I heard a noise out on the prairie like the creaking wheels of old carts. There were nine two-wheeled vehicles brought by metifs from the Red River who come to trade, to get work, or else to seek shelter as independent hunters in this region.

Since I have taken charge of the keys of the fort, various and sundry duties devolve upon me. Early in the morning I must open the gates; in the evening I have to close them. At night, I must open them again, if anyone without wishes to come in. If strangers are there, I must report the fact.

I must keep my eye on the two bastions and their contents; have charge of the press room where robes and furs are stored, and of the hides and skins in reserve; have supervision over the meat, both cured and fresh, and the distribution of the same to families entitled to it, and over the vehicles, saddles, implements received, their safekeeping and proper distribution. I must look after the tools, see that they are kept in good condition and properly distributed; must see to repairs; am expected to assist at the saddling and unsaddling of horses, as well as hitching them up and unhitching.

November 5—Began painting Mr. Culbertson today, under the same difficulties due to insufficient colors and the wrong sort of brushes: ceruse, black, vermilion, Prussian blue, yellow ochre, and chrome yellow are the only colors I have, while my brushes are those generally used for the beard and for flat painting. "Art is long" and "Time is fleeting" are old adages, the truth of which are daily put to the test.

This evening there was incessant knocking at the gates. Assiniboin, encamped outside, think they may be constantly coming in and going out the whole night through. Fine idea of order! What excited them so much this evening was the arrival of a runaway Indian woman from the camp below, closely followed by her husband in pursuit. He had exhausted his horse and was himself stiff and sore from the long ride to fetch her back. First came her knock at the gate toward the river. Before I could let her in and conduct her to the Indian women inside the fort, the man was already pounding at the opposite gate. If he makes her eat humble pie, we shall

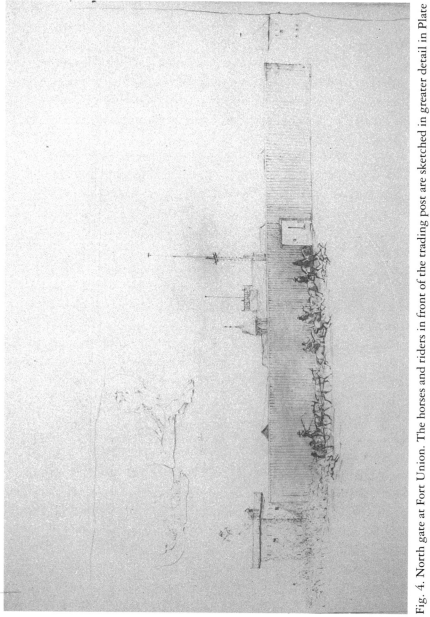

Fig. 4. North gate at Fort Union. The horses and riders in front of the trading post are sketched in greater detail in Plate 11, "Returning from the Dobies' Ball." (From the National Anthropological Archives, Smithsonian Institution Museum Support Center, Suitland, Maryland, accession number 2856-95)

have had only a little drama. If he fails, we may have a tragedy, unless he becomes a laughingstock and the play ends in comedy. As yet he has only been made sport of by a perfectly respectable crowd. The hero, meanwhile, does nothing more than look exasperated; the heroine is in fear of a beating.

It is queer that Indian women never carry their children in their arms, but invariably upon their backs. They swing their papooses over their shoulders, standing all the while with backs bent, until they have drawn the blanket over the child and closely about their bodies.

November 6—If Mr. Culbertson's Indian wife had not received news of her youngest brother's having been shot by Assiniboin, I should have had the chance to study one of the most beautiful Indian women. In token of her grief, she had her long, lustrous black hair cut short.

November 7—Smith brought me a large beaver he caught in a trap. Another study. What an ugly head!

November 11—Last week I was so busy I could find no time for writing. Even if I should have had a leisure moment or two, there was no open fire to make things cheery, for no wood has been procured. All hands were otherwise engaged.

Last Friday I finished the portrait, which was immediately hung on the wall in the reception room, where it was soon damaged by Indian women and children who insisted upon touching it to convince themselves that the figure painted there was really alive. As I had so many other things to do, I was forced to hurry with the painting.

On the same day, the Crow chiefs came again to greet Mr. Culbertson and to enjoy his hospitality and receive gifts.

Saturday, Bruyère rode over to his post on the Upper Bourbeuse, where Carafel is attending to his duties. Both will stay there when the exchange trade becomes brisk pretty soon. Now I am the only clerk. I shall have to procure all things needed and look after everything. The two men in charge think more about their drinks than of giving me directions. Shift for yourself! Do the best you can, only leave me now in peace! This would be the trend of my mind today, if I had time to think my own thoughts. Both complain vehemently of the hypocrisy that characterizes both political and religious life in the United States; they find nothing but strife, deceit, and lies. They laud the way of life among the Indians. Both are Americans, and if sober, neither would utter such plain truths.

Now that I've gotten so mixed up with the fur trade, I wish I had some acquaintance who knows at least one of the dialects spoken in this part of the country. In this Babylonian confusion of languages among the representatives of various nations, it is hard to master one single dialect—Assiniboin, Crow, Herantsa, Cree, Mandan, and even Blackfeet all mingled together, and then again mixed up with English, French, Spanish, and German.

Instead of giving out the meat to all at the same time, one has to wait on each one separately—certain clerks have introduced that order of things— in order to substitute something else to favorites. One woman demands *"tandoj,"* and another *"waschua,"* a third the same thing in another speech. Then a laborer will come and ask for an ox yoke. Another will call it an *"outil,"* a third an *"apischimo."* Then Mr. Culbertson appears to make an inquiry. Mr. Denig follows, bidding me to do something different. After him come Indians asking me this and that and expressing their desire to barter for something or other. Every moment, the language in which the questions are asked varies, yet I am supposed to understand and reply, "It might be done, but it won't do."

Sunday, Mr. Culbertson and his family departed. It is cold weather for a journey to Fort Benton.

Tuesday, yesterday, and today I have been constantly engaged in putting Assiniboin and Crows across the river, a cold, damp business. Had to assist the women in unloading their goods and chattels, as well as in loading again, so that I could make the trip across with more dispatch and regularity. Had frequently much ado with horses and dogs that either refused to go aboard or, when on the boat, would not remain quiet but even sprang into the river. Mr. Denig now begins to take a hand. It is well he finds clerks necessary to back him; otherwise, unless he were more decent to the latter, he would soon have trouble with both engagés and clerks combined.

Mr. Denig would be supremely happy to be put in command of at least 10,000 men and empowered to make them do some sort of work. To command is his greatest pleasure; desire to command, his most characteristic trait. Stood he really so high that he could look down on us, he need not perk up his head so.

I have observed several picturesque snow scenes: Indians pitching their tents or breaking camp; the Indian village in the forest on the opposite river shore seen through mist, smoke, or falling snow; groups of Indians engaged

in loading or unloading their commodities; and the river covered with floating ice. While busy at work one is less sensible to the cold than when at
leisure in a room where there is no fire. Cold, wet weather, weariness: when
one is satisfied in mind, nothing of that sort matters.

November 13—First, I rowed our hunters across to the opposite shore,
then I took several Cree families over. Cree women are more businesslike in
transferring their goods and chattels to the boats than Assiniboin are.
Around the various campfires, men and young lads sit and smoke, or else
stand beside their horses. Boys and girls frolic among their many dogs; children play with puppies as though they were dolls, or carry them like babies
on their backs beneath their blankets. The women employ themselves with
their chattels, their tent poles, and their beasts of burden.

Thirty tents swarming with Indians are there, thrown into relief against
a background of forest, the bare trees of which, blackened by fire or lightning stroke, are now laden with snow. There is a confused din of calling
voices, beating of drums, strokes of an ax, crash of a falling tree, whinny-
ing of horses, shooting of guns, and howling of dogs.

The barren prairie extending behind the fort on this side of the river has
its attractions also. A light fall of snow gleaming through the dried prairie
grass creates a bright surface that appears now dark, now golden, now rose-
hued. This gleaming surface is further brightened by a group of gaily
painted tents with their attendant poles from which are suspended trophies,
such as scalps, buffalo beards, strips of red cloth, etc. The place is enlivened
by human figures: men walking about with majestic mien, some actively
engaged, some idle; youths at their games, girls carrying water, women
trudging in with wood, cleaning and scraping hides; horses saddled for use,
grazing or tethered near their owners' tents; a multitude of dogs eager to
steal something, chasing one another about, scampering away with some
old bone, a piece of leather, or an ill-smelling rag. These dusky forms seem
almost phantomlike, thrown into relief against the glistening snow seen
through smoke or mist. There is no strife; no oaths are ever heard.

The incessant drumbeat, the howling of dogs, the neighing of horses, now
and then a loud call, are the only sounds that come across the sandbank from
that village. There are neither harsh tones of dispute nor conflict, neither
glad notes of song nor yodels. Only the tattoo of the drum resounds, from
beside a sickbed the music of the mountebank, not denoting joy. An Indian's

ideal of enjoyment in the home is a feast. Tobacco smoking is his diversion; dancing, his excess of indulgence in pleasure.

November 14—While we were bringing Mr. Culbertson's boat to land with great difficulty, a beautiful wild goose with straight white neck and green head swam down the river. Not an Indian would lend a hand to assist us with the boat. That would have been far too great a condescension on their part.

November 15—Early this morning, we thought the dog Natoh would die. Several days ago, he had a fight over his Tschakan, during which he must have injured his back. Morgan's dogs, Bull and Badger, had escaped from their master. Badger showed deadly hate toward Natoh and fought him at every opportunity. Though he was younger and weighed less, his fury of attack, his remarkable perseverance and agility more than offset those disadvantages. Besides, Badger has teeth as sharp as those of a wolf, while Natoh's are worn dull from age. Each dog is his master's dearest pet, and they were once set upon each other so that they might determine which master has the most powerful dog in all the land.

Natoh is now afflicted with a great swelling on his left side and has eaten nothing for 3 days, to the serious concern of Mr. Denig's wives. I advised Mr. Denig to open the tumor, so that it could be drained of blood and pus. He did not venture; the dog is much too surly. Today the swelling burst by itself, whereupon Mr. Denig congratulated me, saying that if the brute had died, the Indians would have ascribed its death to the picture I painted.

"Everything will turn out all right if nothing happens to me during your stay," he added. "Otherwise, you'd better look out."

Well, I assume the risk. For the present, I know nothing better to do. It will soon be unsupportable for a painter to stay among these savages. At present, my danger is the result of Catlin's coming here, and Bodmer's, though they themselves are not in any way to blame. I could do nothing to prevent even greater difficulties that, on my account, might befall future artists traveling in this region. The illness of this dog may well serve me as warning to leave nothing neglected that I would like to sketch.

Was told by an Assiniboin, who out of curiosity accompanied his chief to the Platte River (Fort Laramie: the situation [treaty talk] was on Horseshoe Creek), how they were given domestic animals to supply them with food. They refused outright to accept the cattle, so Mr. Culbertson had to take over the beasts and give the Indians corn and biscuits. In the first place, our redskins would not eat pork at all, neither fresh nor cured. This Assiniboin, who for want of a better name we call Platte Man, entertained his friends with various anecdotes; for example, how three United States soldiers were forced, as a punishment, to drag along after them three heavy balls attached to their feet. This he turned rather cleverly to ridicule. He told how some white men were attempting to sell whisky when soldiers broke open the casks and to the great regret of the narrator, let the liquor flow out on the ground, where it did nobody any good.

I also read the treaty which the United States proposes to make with the Indian tribes: again nothing but hypocritical phrases to impose the belief upon a distant public that Uncle Sam takes the Indians' fate much to heart. In reality, it is high time that he did so. In the first place, to appoint supreme chiefs over the nations who are neither chosen nor recognized by the tribes themselves is of no advantage to anybody but only engenders jealousy among rivals.

In the second place, to promise—on condition that Indians no longer make war on one another or do injury to any member of the white population—to distribute $50,000 annually during a period of 50 years according to the poll among the nations west of the Missouri: what does that mean? How many such treaties would be kept with the Indians? What an easy matter to provoke an affront and then to refuse the annual payment. During a period of 50 years! What guaranty have Americans that their Confederation of States will continue for so long a time? Is it not in the power of any new administration to annul this treaty made by their predecessors? [President Andrew] Jackson made himself particularly conspicuous in that respect. He resorted to bayonets in his effort to set aside a treaty made by his predecessor, President [James] Monroe.

As I was rowing Le Plumet Caille [Quail Feather], a chief of the Cree, across the river, he said to me, looking northward and describing with his hand a semicircle from the point of sunrise to that of sunset: *"Tout ça a moi."* He repeated these words several times in the presence of Assiniboin who might well understand his signs. Now, the actual domain of the Assiniboin lies between the Yellowstone and the Missouri; therefore, the latter tribe were most likely driven across the river by Crows and Blackfeet upon land belonging to the Cree. Now I understand also why Cree set the prairie on fire—to drive Assiniboin from Cree hunting grounds and force them back into their own former territory.

November 16—That I might have something to enjoy on Sunday, I took different sorts of saddles that are used in this region and made drawings of them.

November 17—Weather is clear and cold. Have finally decided to order a winter suit made of buckskin from Madame Bombarde. Up to the present time I have worn my summer clothes with a buckskin shirt. I am little sensible to cold, owing to the exercise I take in the performance of my numerous duties, and to my inner satisfaction to be able to paint so many interesting studies each day. They say that newcomers during their first winter endure the low temperatures better than the natives, but the weather is now too severe for my comfort. I feel the cold more today, on account of being unable to get wood for a fire. The oxen made use of Sunday for a distant hike, and by the time they are found, brought back, yoked, and driven to the forest and back again with a load of wood, night will already have fallen. Besides, there will be a great many applicants for that one load.

Mr. Denig feels quite comfortable in his large armchair, smoking his short-stem pipe beside his iron stove that glows with a rousing fire. The instant I come in to attend to something or to ask a question, and incidentally to hold my hands over the delectable base burner which attracted me today like a magnet, the bourgeois invariably finds a new task that takes me into the open air, on the theory, I presume, that the best warmth is obtained by constant bodily exercise.

I am continually required to walk down to the river to find out whether that arrogant Sioux has yet reached the opposite shore, and to row him over at once.

As I pronounce the word "Sioux" according to the French and heretofore have heard no other pronunciation of the word from any American, I was greatly astonished when Mr. Denig made sport of me about it and declared that one said "Suh," not "Siuh." He could bring neither any proof of the word's origin from the Dakota language nor any reason for the pronunciation he claimed. According to Charlevoix, it is said to have been the final syllable of the word *"nadowessioux."*

Mr. Denig also tried to make me appear ridiculous for saying that certain animals could be tamed by means of salt. According to his habit to curry favor, Jim Hawthorn was at once ready with his invented anecdote about a hunter he knew who never went on the chase without a bag of salt with which he could entice any herd of buffalo he might come upon—in fact, some thousands followed him for several days. I simply replied that it was his intention to make me appear absurd; I would give my information somewhere else.

The Sioux imagines himself of tremendous importance because he was a representative at the great assembly on Horseshoe Creek and has received a number of gifts. He is so imbued with self-assumption that he boasts of the number of Assiniboin he has slain in battle. He even brags about having killed the mother of Ours Fou. He is unpardonably tactless, for he intends to live here among his former foes. Besides, he was born an Assiniboin but was taken prisoner while a boy by the Sioux and brought up as one of them. As peace is now established between these related tribes, he wishes to rejoin his kindred.

To give himself airs, he presented two good horses for his wife. He hardly had her with him 4 days when she was taken away by her kinsmen in order to provoke him. Now he wishes to get his horses back. Mr. Denig is very curious to find out whether he will succeed.

Natoh was also a cause of much running around on my part. He went to the woods early today, most probably to breathe his last in solitude and to spare the women the painful sight of his final grapple with death. He is dead.

Knife and his soldiers who trade at our winter posts brought back the horses that were stolen by Assiniboin. For the sake of producing actual evidence of their friendly attitude and of their desire to redeem their honor, these braves bought the horses at their full value from the thieves, who are customers of the opposition. For their trouble, they received gifts at the value of two buffalo robes per horse from the company, which is considerably more than the purchase price of the animals but better than losing [these trading partners] altogether.

When I was sitting beside the open fire so long and earnestly desired, Mr. Denig told me how his chief had the jury in St. Louis decide two questions of much consequence to the engagés. First, whether the company was bound to pay his entire wage to an employee who had fallen ill and make no deduction for time lost. It was decided that the engagé was to be paid

only for the time he worked. He was to be furnished board and lodging but
no medicine. This seems hard on a laborer who, by reason of the service he
renders, falls ill or becomes incapacitated for work. Still, the company pays
an employee his entire wage if they find no cause to complain of him in any
other respect. According to this ruling, Packinaud will have all the medicine he needs during his illness charged against him on his account.

The second question is whether the company is obliged to pay an employee
his full wage when the latter bartered hides and skins from Indians in excess
of the demand, contrary to an agreement entered upon voluntarily not to trade
as private individuals in buffalo robes and furs. The jury rendered this decision: Pay the man in full for his work but have him indemnify the company
for loss incurred, or else give up the hides and pelts. Hint to me: I am not
permitted to barter for any robes or fine furs with the Indians myself, but only
through my chief as agent, in order that he may not lose his profit on the
trade. Furthermore, I am not allowed to possess any more raw hides or pelts
than one sample of each species, or any more buffalo robes than I am in need
of for my own bed.

November 18—Toward evening, Jim Hawthorn arrived from St. Louis on
horseback, accompanied by another man. I hope we shall have some news.

November 20—Yesterday we had another ball. I thought at first that Mr.
Denig had received most satisfactory news from the States. On the contrary, his
prospects of visiting New York next year are smashed to bits. But when the
younger Madame Denig appeared among the dancers wearing a rose-colored
ball gown in the latest fashion, direct from St. Louis, a light dawned upon me.

I was indebted to that new and beautiful frock for the unhoped-for pleasure of beating the tattoo on drum or tambourine. As I cannot dance, I have
to comply with others' wishes by helping with the music. It's a pity that this
ball gown had not been on hand when the reception was given to honor Mr.
Culbertson. How jealously the two beautiful dancers would have looked
askance at each other, just like two beauties of the white race at court.

However, rose color goes not well with a copper-colored skin. To be sure,
the complexion of a pure-blooded Indian woman is no darker than that of an
Italian or Spanish brunette, but rose color is not becoming to them, either.

Before breakfast, I learned several words in the Dakota language from
Ours Fou, who seeks the solitude of my room. Beside the open fire, he can
brood over the loss of his loved ones and meditate upon his future eminence.

The good old chief seems to take heartfelt pleasure in my writing down *"Minnehasga tokia? Tschauda waschteh, Osmie schitsche"* and pronouncing the words after him.

Rowed across the river today for the last time. The stream is so thickly blocked with floating ice that it will soon be entirely frozen over. I brought back the Sioux. He found neither his four days' bride nor the two horses with which he purchased her. To console him, Ours Fou found him another "little wife."

When he started over, a dog belonging to an Assiniboin woman remained behind. For a long time, the woman called, "Kadosch! Kadosch!" Discouraged by the bitterly cold stream, the lean wolfhound ran like one possessed up and down at the river's edge, then, with arched back and dragging tail, began to howl distressingly. The old woman never ceased calling "Kadosch."

Who could long withstand that familiar summons? The dog sprang into the freezing water, worked his way bravely through the floating blocks of ice, now disappeared among them, now was forced to bound upon such a float to prevent his being crushed, now swept along with the yet ductile but half-frozen ice layer that almost entirely surrounded him. A larger, more solid mass, impelled by its own momentum, moved with rapid, whirling motion through that yielding stratum and burst it asunder, bringing the poor brute into the fairway again. Finally, after the gallant fellow had been borne far downstream by the ice-blocked current, for some moments lost entirely to view, he scrambled to shore and was received by the woman with open arms. Had he gone down, the old woman would no doubt have suffered the loss of her last and only friend.

Another dog did not fare so well. He was very hungry. He saw a child sucking a juicy piece of meat and fairly itched to get possession of it. He looked slyly about him to find out whether he was being observed, turned his head this way and that, pricked up his ears. Just then the child pulled the meat out of its mouth. The hound could resist no longer; he snapped hastily for it, but in securing it, he bit the small papoose. He started off with his prize. Hearing the child's scream, its father, whom we call the Platte Man, seized his bow. Quick as a flash, he laid the thief low with an arrow through his heart.

The Arikara are said to have lost 400 souls during the cholera epidemic and to have been terribly enraged against the whites in consequence. They have as yet resorted to no violence.

November 21—When the old Spaniard came in to breakfast this morning, he announced to Mr. Denig that while out guarding his cattle, he saw a pair of white-tailed deer in the near distance. Cadotte was instantly dispatched. In an hour's time, the buck was brought in. Cadotte brought the head all intact with horns for me to paint. My collection of studies increases slowly but surely. Never despair! Today I received my winter suit of calfskin, made metif-fashion with a hood, and sewed throughout with sinew.

November 22—Through misrepresentation and lies, Joe Picotte made another attempt to alienate Assiniboin from the big company by declaring that his competitor would annihilate them with contagious diseases. How stupid! What profit could be derived from the destruction of one's own customers?

Joe is kept in a state of continual provocation because the United States government takes no notice of his company and yet always upholds the greater corporation. Naturally, this is a cause of friction between competitors! Possessing a large amount of capital, the big company has already put many of its competitors out of business altogether and has absorbed others. These Dobies have held their own for an unusually long time but still make inconsiderable profit. Only Campbell, in charge of their drinking house in St. Louis, is making a profit.

Before I knew as much about the fur trade as I know now, I was astonished to find prices so unreasonably high. As I became more and more closely acquainted with the business and attendant expenses, I knew that it could not be otherwise. When commodities are obliged to be transported 9,000 miles, nay, some of them halfway around the world, the outlay must necessarily be considerable.

Wares are shipped here from Leipzig (little bells and mirrors), from Cologne (clay pipes), beads from Italy, merinos, calicos from France, woolen blankets, guns from England, sugar and coffee from New Orleans, clothing and knives from New York, powder and shot, meal, corn, etc., from St. Louis. The company owns factories at home and abroad for the manufacture of their staple goods. Their trade in furs extends throughout the entire Indian domain from the Upper Mississippi to Mexico. Their trading posts are spread along the St. Peters River, the Missouri, Yellowstone, Platte, Arkansas, Gila, Bear River, throughout Oregon, California, Utah, and New Mexico. Trade is distributed through the districts according to the location of navigable streams or some other means of communication: Upper Mississippi Outfit, Lower Mississippi Outfit, Platte Outfit, etc.

Members of the company, P. Chouteau, Jr., [Peter A.] Sarpy, [Bartholemew] Berthold, [Benjamin] O'Fallon, et al., live in St. Louis, where they have their office, an immense storehouse. From there, goods are shipped to the various posts; skins and furs are received in exchange and are sold throughout the world, especially to Russia. In every district there is an agent, employed at a fixed salary ($2,000) and paid in addition certain profits on sales. He has charge of several posts. He orders supplies from the company but is not usually obliged to pay for them in pelts. He is at liberty to dispose of the hides and skins that he takes in exchange in the market where he finds the best prices.

Agents are required to pay a yearly interest on capital advanced, together with the cost of insurance for goods delivered at the factory price, plus the cost of transportation. He knows, therefore, what the approximate cost of his commodities will be and has only to reckon sums necessary to pay the salaries and keep of his employees, and largesse to Indians, in order to maintain his trading post with success.

Mr. Culbertson is agent for the Upper Missouri Outfit and has supervision of three posts: Fort Union, Fort Benton, and Fort Alexander. Mr. H. Picotte is agent for the Lower Missouri Outfit, which includes supervision of Fort Pierre, Fort Lookout, Fort Vermilion, Fort Clarke, and Fort Berthold. Mr. Papin is agent on the Platte, having charge of Fort Hall and Fort Laramie.

A bourgeois or head clerk is stationed at each post. He receives a fixed salary of $1,000 and a stated percentage on sales. He buys goods, just as agents do, at the cost price. The bourgeois keeps his own accounts. He orders what he needs from his agent and delivers to him all that is received in exchange for goods sold. Whether he makes large profits or suffers losses depends on how well he knows how to calculate to advantage, and to regulate his own expenses.

Agents and bourgeois form, so to speak, a company of their own, insofar as they all agree to buy goods from the stockholders at a stipulated price, which includes interest and transportation charges. If skins and furs bring high prices, the agents make a surplus which they divide among themselves and the bourgeois, according to the peltry contributed by each. The stockholders assume responsibility for all damages to commodities in transit. Agents are only required to answer for goods received at the destination to which they are consigned. All shipments are secured from loss by insurance. The premium is quite high for goods sent up the Missouri, because there are such a great number of snags.[2]

The less a bourgeois has to pay for the upkeep of his fort, in salaries for employees, and for skins and furs, the greater will be his profit and that of his agents, who are also bourgeois of a fort. On average, clerks and engagés are paid the wage they receive in the United States, but they are required to buy everything from the trading post where they are employed, and at the price demanded there. Fortunately, they have neither the necessities nor the occasions for spending money that one has in the States, otherwise they would save nothing.

The traders, clerks, interpreters, hunters, workmen, and their helpers employed at the forts, who are content to buy on credit from the company, seldom lay by anything for a rainy day. They marry. Indeed, for the purpose of chaining to the fort, so to speak, those who are capable, those who are indispensable, the bourgeois endeavor to bind them down for the next year by advancing sums to them on credit.

For supplies intended for their own use, the bourgeois pay the same price that they would be required to pay to the stockholders for the same article, but they demand much more from their employees and the Indians. For a medium buffalo robe they charge an employee $4; for one extra good (prime), $8; for a robe enriched with ornamentation, $15, even a higher price than is charged in the United States. For instance, for the usual robe, Indians receive in exchange 2 gallons of shelled corn, from 3 to 4 pounds of sugar, or 2 pounds of coffee. The total expense of preparing a buffalo robe for sale, reckoned as one sum, would not exceed $1 gross. In St. Louis, these robes are sold at wholesale for at least $2. The agents and bourgeois can easily realize 100 percent profit, if they know the trade. It is not true in every case, however, that a bourgeois is an expert trader. Those managers are chosen from among clerks who have been trained in this part of the country. Many of them who become efficient clerks under good and careful management are not in every respect competent to conduct a business to the best advantage.

A craftsman or workman receives $250 a year; a workman's assistant is never paid more than $120. A hunter receives $400, together with the hides and horns of the animals he kills. An interpreter without other employment—which is seldom—gets $500. Clerks and traders who have mastered the court language—the speech of those Indians for whose special advantage the trading posts are established—may demand from $800 to $1,000 without interest.

All employees are furnished board and lodging free of charge. That means engagés are provided with nothing but meat, a place to sleep, and one raw buffalo hide. Hunters and workmen eat at the second table: meat, biscuit, and black coffee with sugar. Clerks are served with the bourgeois at the first table, which is, on average, a well-furnished table for this part of the country. We have meat (well selected), bread, and frequently soup and pie on Sundays. Everyone must furnish his bedclothes; however, one may borrow two buffalo robes from the storehouse.

If an employee has a mind to save, he can almost put aside his entire income, under certain conditions. In that case, he must have a supply of clothing on hand and must be content with the fare at the fort, indulge in no dainties or feasting, and never allow himself to come within 10 feet of the Indian women.

As these employees are not stimulated to greater exertions by increases in pay or percentage, it is hardly to be expected that they will work harder or make sacrifices for a company that is accumulating great wealth, and charging them such extortionate prices at the same time. Independently of the equal salaries they receive, head clerks have advantages over traders that inspire them to greater zeal and more willing sacrifices. Both at the fort and at their winter quarters, clerks and traders are continually beset by begging customers of the company they serve. They are in no sense obligated to give away their small earnings merely for the purpose of procuring a greater number of buffalo robes for their agents. Bourgeois not only like for them to be generous with the customers but, on the other hand, either directly or indirectly require it of them.

A few years ago, Mr. Denig came near to getting a sound beating because of some such unreasonable demand that he made of one of his clerks. He fled to his bedroom! One must consider that in this part of the world there are no courts. One must first catch the criminal, whether guilty or merely accused. In an entire year, there are but one or two opportunities to dispatch the prisoner and witnesses the great distance from here to St. Louis. Even then, the finding of the court is uncertain—nobody knows what the verdict will be.

One can easily understand why people in these wilds rarely resort to process of law. Among the promiscuous white inhabitants of this region there are many rough and vicious characters, in dealing with whom one recognizes the need of promoting peace and harmony just as in an Indian camp. Every man is armed; every man protects his own house and his property. He requites every insult with knife or shotgun. One who loves his life guards against giving offense. It is not their idea of honor to challenge the offender and give him still another chance to commit an outrage by killing an innocent person. Fighting duels is no means of obtaining divine judgment. Among white people here, one hears fewer violent disputes and witnesses fisticuff fights less frequently than in the civilized States, for the reason that people here guard against giving cause for strife, knowing the deadly consequences.

Knife brought ill news from our winter trading post on the Upper Bourbeuse. Ten Assiniboin died at their settlement in that region of a strange disease that they caught from the Cree on Red River. They say blood flows from the nose, ears, and eyes. As chance would have it, the disease appeared simultaneously with the arrival of horse thieves and impressed the Assiniboin anew with thoughts of bad medicine.

Knife, authorized as one of our soldiers, flogged a "buck" in Bruyère's house because the young boor insisted on trying to pick a quarrel with Pellot. By the English word "buck" is meant a young rowdy whose chief business is the conquest of the fair sex, as he is yet too young for exploits of war. At a loss to know what to do with himself, he kept on opening and shutting the door to Bruyère's house, as they frequently do at the fort with the dining-room door. The ill-mannered fellow was diverted by the singular lock, by the noise he was making, and still more by the sheer malicious satisfaction of admitting a draught of cold air into a warm room.

Pellot bade him leave the door alone. The buck laughed in his face. Finally Pellot gave him a piece of his mind, whereupon the buck said that if Pellot would come outside, he would thrash him. As it happened, Knife was also there. As a soldier bound to keep the peace, he sprang up, quickly seized a stick of wood from the fire, lay hold of the buck, and ordered him to come in and strike the Schajeh. Tomorrow, you say. Aha, you will in the morning! And with that, Knife dealt him such a blow behind the ears that the fellow lay on the floor as if he were dead. Knife was just on the point of dealing several blows more and in his anger would have killed the churl, had he not been restrained by his friends. That buck may well be on his guard hereafter against Knife, the brother of Ours Fou.

Have restored Mr. Culbertson's portrait as well as I could.

As the metifs get meat here now, I have learned the word for fresh meat in the Chippewa (Sauteurs) speech. The word is *"wiass."* Difficulties in learning a language increase daily.

November 23—A ring, a ring! A wedding ring! *Quien sabe?* ("Who knows?") Marguerite La Bombarde came to see me this afternoon and put a brass ring on my finger, saying, *"Tu la porteras pour moi."* ("Thou wilt wear it for me.") Does she want to marry me?

November 24—I painted a large eagle for Bear's Head; he has to pay twenty robes for the flag. Today I came upon Natoh's picture in a garret that serves as a storage room for drugs, paints, and crackers! Is it due to delicate sensibilities or superstition that they keep his image in hiding? Since Natoh's death, Mr. Denig has indulged in a new fancy: three splendid wolfhounds, in new harness with bells, hitched to a cariole! I am now to give a coat of paint to this one-seated sled. The last supply of oil at the fort is to be lavished on it.

Indian dogs differ very slightly from wolves in appearance, howl like them, do not bark, and not infrequently mate with them. Dogs of another type are brought here from the Rocky Mountains—small, lop-eared canines, covered from head to toes and tail with long, shaggy hair.

November 25—Last night Cadotte's Assiniboin wife came to my door and called out.

I opened the door; she had disappeared. He no longer has credit, so, no coffee, no wife? *Point d'argent, point de Suisse!* ("No song, no supper," a French idiom; also "No tip, no porter.") And for this wife of his, Cadotte was rash enough to put his life at stake! It happened last year, when Cadotte had to go along as usual with the Mackinaw boat that carried goods for the Blackfeet tribe and, in his capacity as huntsman, to provide fresh meat for the crew who towed the boat laboriously up the river by means of a rope.

Harvey was then bourgeois at Fort William. He was attracted to the beautiful Assiniboin woman and, during Cadotte's absence, enticed her to his fort. As Cadotte was returning, he heard his wife carousing in the Tiger's lair. Equipped as for the hunt, he set out at once in trace of her, entered Harvey's room, and in the latter's presence, inside the latter's own fort, he took his woman by the arm and bade her come with him. How the Tiger must have glared at the Lion going off with his prize! Harvey is not a whit less daring than Cadotte, who defies the devil, but he was restrained by the feeling that he was in the wrong!

Unfaithful women are now become a commonplace—nobody thinks much about such occurrences. Only old ugly women or those burdened with children remain with their husbands. They are exposed to no temptation, no seduction.

Much depends upon a girl's parents, whether they come of good family and enjoin upon their daughters the duty of being loyal to their husbands. Indian women who marry engagés are not valued at the purchase price of a horse, so they do not regard themselves duty-bound to remain. As a rule, such Indian women are riffraff. As a matter of course, children born of such unions inherit bad rather than good qualities of their parents. On the other hand, half-breed children of clerks and traders are a credit to the white race.

Rottentail and Grayhead are on a visit here once more. The first-mentioned chief regrets much that he did not find Mr. Culbertson's courier, so that he might have gone to the Platte. Then he would have been chief of the Absaroka and not Big Robert. The latter will gain considerable influence though the distribution of gifts provided by the United States. Many of Rottentail's adherents will move over to Big Robert's settlement. Rottentail has not more than 80 tents.

November 26—Received another wipe-down from Mr. Denig today because I gave out lard in too-large quantities. Perhaps so. Nobody has taken the trouble to give me instructions. As Bruyère was leaving, he delivered a bunch of 10 keys to me without showing me the lock to which a single one of them belonged, or giving me information concerning any of the duties I was to assume.

The two men in charge were always more or less befuddled; were unwilling for my nose to come within smelling distance of their gin, for my eyes to behold their tragicomic play; hence, were satisfied to let me find out everything for myself. I knew neither what the rations were nor the persons entitled to receive them. Consequently, some of the Indian women took advantage of me. Now I have found out about these matters myself.

I first had to learn the difference between tallow fat or suet, and market fat or lard; between tender meat and hard meat, packed in the bladders in which the Indians bring it to us; and whether the dried strips of flesh were cut from a cow or an ox. I had to watch over 12 men all at the same time and keep them at work, to deliver their tools and implements, the names of which I frequently did not even know, much less the place where they were kept. Ten thousand soldiers would not have given me as much trouble as those few laborers and women. Nor does the great number of different languages in which I am addressed make my way of life in this place any less confusing. Women eat at no stated intervals but if possible throughout the entire day. Each comes for meat when it suits her, and I am to make no change in that respect. It is quite a while before one knows all the various terms for fresh meat, cured meat, lard, corn, water, "open the door," etc., in seven different languages.

Tools and implements are scattered everywhere: in the saddle room, in the meat house, in the storehouse, in outhouses, in the bastions, on the floor; axes are even thrust under the beds. Before I had brought order out of this chaos by my own efforts alone, I was forced many times to scratch my bewildered head. Of course I make many mistakes. For instance, I forgot once to feed the pigeons, to count the pigs, to drive away a woman because she came twice in the same day to ask for meat, in order to give some food to visitors. I committed yet another error when I gave out lard instead of tallow fat to another woman. Only at that moment was Mr. Denig inclined to vent his spleen upon me. Indeed, at other times he has been kind.

He is in a bad humor now, because he has found out that when the Crows came here to trade, not only Joe Picotte but he himself doesn't have sufficient sugar, meal, etc., on hand. We are already forced to eat bread made from maize instead of wheat and to drink coffee without milk. Soon we shall have no sugar and shall have to put up with meat and water. He brags about how he puts up with any fare, but I was destined to catch him eating butter and bread with cheese and sausage on the sly. He stood before me an idle braggart. He supplies all the corn needed for chickens and pigeons that are laying no eggs, and besides, will most likely be frozen to death before winter is over, but none to preserve the strength of horses, cows, and draught oxen in daily service.

My prime fault, which caused dissatisfaction to my chief, was committed on the evening of the ball, when I neglected to praise the new ball gown as much as did Jim Hawthorn, whose only duty is to dance attendance on the bourgeois, to flatter him and submissively cut his tobacco for him. Jim came here with the expectation of getting a position right away. He finds no employment; no doubt I am in his way. Look alive!

Ours Fou, chief of the Assiniboin, sits beside me on the floor before the fire. What a melancholy picture! A chieftain "in sackcloth and ashes," greatness in humility! He sits here now in sorrow, with the same imposing dignity that characterized him as a prince in power. He is uncovered. On his head, breast, and legs are incisions in his skin to allow blood to flow as atonement for his deceased wife, his murdered sons, and his beloved grandchildren. The good old man has still other troubles to afflict him: His newly acquired title is not recognized; neither Absaroka nor Assiniboin accept him. For the first time in 30 years—since the war with the Crows and subsequent peace with that tribe—Ours Fou has pitched his camp in the Assiniboin hunting grounds.

Absaroka interfere with him when on the chase; his tribesmen find no food. He talks with Rottentail, who is discontented on his part because he was not chosen chief of the Absaroka. The latter is wary, a good businessman who makes light of the white man's chief in the territory of the Platte. "White Americans lie," he says. "Where are their gifts? Where are their warriors?" Absaroka sneer at a chief who is poor. Ours Fou is in sorrow. He dispensed all his gifts long ago; he is poor.

He cudgels his brain to find some way out of his dilemma. He juggles with this plan and that, trying to regain his prestige. He finds rivals among his own adherents who are envious of him. One of them, Le Premiere que Vole [First to Fly], Mr. Denig's brother-in-law, is an adventurous brave. He was in the Platte territory; but for his impetuous temper, he might have been chief. In accordance with Indian custom, he counted more coups, assembled more tents, brought together more followers, more braves, under his command than any other.

Severe snowstorm, biting cold, and howling north wind. How queer that yesterday this north wind was so mild that the snow began to melt. Can it be that the current of air had swept over a warm section of the country, bearing forward the warmth of the South? I can defy this frightfully cold weather when I am put in such a jolly good mood by this bright fire in my fireplace. How the wood sputters and crackles when it burns! It is a joy to behold. Or has my blonde disposed me to be gay? Ach, Marguerite, you would be beautiful enough to suit me, and sufficiently industrious, too, if you were only not quite so silly.

Made further progress today in "fort-unionization," Mr. Denig's expression. I had to take 81 buffalo tongues out of salt and hang them up in my room to dry. Then I was told to cut more than 170 fresh tongues out of buffalo heads and pack them thick in a cask filled with warm salt water. It's as though I were living in a pork house, which overhead suggests a heaven filled with joys I dare not taste. Mr. Denig refuses to sell these choice morsels even at a dollar apiece.

November 27—I have painted the bourgeois' sled (cariole) red and black. I am ordered to paint another eagle tomorrow. These flags with painted eagles are much sought-after as significant gifts. By means of such presents that cost him practically nothing, Mr. Denig is said to have attracted great numbers of customers.

November 28—Absaroka and Assiniboin are encamped across the river only a few miles from here. Now that the stream is frozen over, they are continually visiting this fort.

They transact no business but do a great deal of eating and tobacco smoking. I have become acquainted with Four Rivers, another Crow chief. He is a very powerful man, both in regards to physique and in relationships. Le Fourbillon, an Assiniboin, is said to count more coups than all the known warriors of any nation in this part of the world. He has slain 24 enemies with his own hand. Le Gras, Le Garonille, the knapper (one who has been scalped though not killed) are only parasites, beggars.

November 29—Engagés are giving a dance at their own expense in the dining room, which is near me. Meanwhile, I peel twigs of the upland willow and weave fancies over an occasional pipe of this Indian blend. Glad I am not obliged to join the dance, but the cotillion affords more graceful figures, I admit, than the silly waltzes.

November 30—Farewell November! If December brings me as many interesting prospects, I shall be well satisfied. How soft, how harmoniously blended are the colors on the wide prairie, under a light covering of snow. Yellows and browns, blacks and rose, among the grasses and weeds with their gray seed pods, blended with the snow, give every variety of hue and shade. On that radiant plain, a buffalo with his velvety winter coat of hair must stand in splendid relief.

SEVEN *December 1851*

December 1—This evening an Assiniboin from the lower camp came to me because he could find no place to sit in the crowded room, or anything to eat. He was tired and so hungry, he said, that his stomach was continually crying out *"rygrug."* As I have no authority to feed and lodge Indians on my own responsibility, nor had I received instructions to that effect, I could not show too much compassion for his empty stomach. I indicated to him that Minnehasga must give him food. In the meantime, he sat down by the fire and I filled my pipe for him. We smoked together. I do not understand how it occurred to him, a stranger, to get at my weak side. He began to specify certain words in the Assiniboin tongue and to give their meanings by signs, explaining that I was to write them down. I was so delighted with this unexpected civility on the part of a savage that my strict sense of duty began more and more to relent as my list of words increased. I hurried out to the storehouse to fetch a piece of sun-dried meat, though the cold was terrible and keys and lock stuck so fast to my fingers that I thought I should pull the skin off in getting them loose. *"Osmiedo,"* he said, when puffing and blowing I reentered the room. Yes, it was really freezing cold. I permitted him to sleep there. His hunger appeased, he rolled himself up in his buffalo robe and fell asleep on the hard floor.

When the Indians are at the fort in such large numbers, an especial need is felt for a room of good size with a large fireplace, where the redskins can be quartered en masse. As things are now, they have to be crowded into at least five rooms already occupied, an arrangement that is uncomfortable for both occupants and visitors. At this time of year, all of them like to squat about the fire, and they interfere with the cooking. In midsummer, they would find the heat and steam all the more unbearable. Mr. Denig is speaking of having an Indian lodge built. By so doing, he would not only satisfy a need but also win a great many friends for himself. We have already devoted our combined efforts to drawing a plan for the construction.

December 2—The same old story of an Indian woman I am to marry—if only it were not so difficult to keep her after I get her! They remain just long enough to procure all that a white man is able to give them. The first time he says, "It is impossible," then it is *"Adieu, je t'ai ou"* with them. They know that women are in great demand.

To return to my story, as I was coming back to my room after having closed the gates, I found an old woman and a young Indian girl sitting on my doorsill. They have been living for several weeks in the camp outside. I thought they were only waiting to ask me to open the gate again, but I was mistaken. They intended to come into the room with me.

The young girl was quite well-grown and had fine, noble features, soft, languishing eyes, and—for an Indian woman—a very high forehead. Her face was washed clean, a delicate crimson came and went in her cheeks, but oh, Lord, the rest of her was in such contrast! Her swarthy neck, shoulders, and bust; her doeskin dress, sleek and shining with grease and dirt; her shabby buffalo robe. The old woman talked a great deal, but the young one, though friendly in manner, only sighed gently, then more deeply, then aloud. I understood her quite well, but the family did not appeal to me at all.

When they saw that I could not talk to them, or would not, the girl went to fetch the mulatto, Auguste, that he might act as interpreter. I refused to let that fellow have anything to do with my affairs and sent him for Morgan. To be sure, Morgan does not know any great deal himself about the Assiniboin language, but I wished to have him come just for the fun of the thing. For a long while, they discussed the matter, but to no purpose. With the women, marriage was the word and gifts in return for the bride. On the other hand, a poverty-stricken Indian family with an endless family connection to be supported by the groom: fireside joys too dearly bought!

Morgan left. So did the women. I had hardly closed the door behind the latter and was starting over to see Morgan when I heard a knock at the door. There stood the two women again with the blind head of their family. They came into the room. The blind man said by means of signs: "I give you my daughter to live here with you." Fortunately, Packinaud had got wind of the matter and came limping over to take part in the trade. He must have the girl, he asserted, without paying a horse. When that plan failed utterly, he became angry and sent them all off.

From now on, I am allowed to sell buffalo robes among other commodities under my charge. The price has been advanced from $4 to $5 apiece, just at this time when they are most in demand. Mr. Denig claims he makes so little profit on them here that he would do better to send them to St. Louis. Yes, probably.

December 3—From my night lodger, I learned additional words in the Dakota speech. When he had taught me numerals up to 10, I laid down another chip, hoping he would tell me the word for eleven. In spite of all the signs I was able to make, he refused to understand further; he seemed to think I would lead him on to 30, 40, etc. His sense of color was not at all pronounced: Blue and green were the same to him; so were brown and black. Having done me such an immense service, he assumed that he was privileged to beg unceasingly for everything that came within his view. I gave him a present of some tobacco and let him go.

As a means of passing the time during these long winter evenings, I have begun teaching Packinaud English. If he learns enough to be able to write and calculate in that language, he can occupy a higher post. In return, he teaches me words in the Herantsa and Dakota dialects.

December 6—I got a real live fox to paint from Smith. He brought the fellow in just as he was caught by his nose with the trap, a very rare occurrence. Animals are usually caught by their feet. According to my observation of Master Reynard in this region, he has not half the cunning of a wolf, for five of his sort are entrapped to one of the latter. As I sat wholly absorbed in painting the frightened animal, which in quiet behavior as well as in form and color afforded me an excellent model, in came Mr. Denig, who bought the fox from Smith at once. He had a cage prepared in which Reynard is to live, directed me to take care of him and feed him, in return for which service I am to study him and paint pictures of him to my heart's content. In the meantime, I had taken advantage of the opportunity to make a sketch of him, together with the trap. I shall make another study, now that he is behind bars, happy to have his nose released.

Instruction in English and Herantsa.

December 9—My imagination is likely to be overburdened in preserving all the new pictures I am storing there. It is now a matter of conservation, rather than productivity. My demon of composition will not break loose until I shall have left this place for some years, and long for these scenes again.

December 10—Belhumeur's arrival here last night from the winter post below us caused a break in our quiet life. (I am already quite used to seeing great numbers of Indians.) Mackenzie sent him up here to notify us that Joe Picotte, regardless of his pledged word, had sent his traders to the more distant settlements of the Assiniboin and Cree to anticipate us in the purchase of robes on hand. At that news, everything here took fire. Morgan had to mount John and race to the horse guard with an order to bring in all the horses tonight. A decision was made at once to counteract by all possible means the treachery, deceit, and dishonesty of Joe Picotte, whatever the cost.

The fact is, Joe had only sent his traders out into the lower fur-producing districts. However, he is no longer to be trusted; consequently, Mr. Denig is going to contest his right to every inch of ground and to every hide. He sent away three expeditions with goods today: Cadotte to Knife River; Morgan to the Lower Bourbeuse to relieve Mackenzie, so that Mackenzie may be able to avert imminent peril to himself. Furthermore, he sent a courier to Bruyère, instructing him to dispatch clerks in every direction and to strain every nerve in his efforts to bring about Joe's defeat.

Only Packinaud the lame and Istaboba remain with Mr. Denig to protect the fort. At this time, the bourgeois is in a state of great irritation, of course.

After all our feasting, largesse, and advances to Ours Fou, he has brought us only 57 robes from his camp of 60 tents. It looks as though Indians so near the range of buffalo herds would never be in need of anything. They have any number of raw hides in their possession but are disinclined to tan them because their stomachs are full.

December 14—After a few quiet days, we have another stir in fort and camp. The sugar is out. No more sugar for coffee, no more sugar given away, no sugar either for sale or for buffalo hides. Frightful state of things! What is life worth without sugar? It will be almost half a year before a fresh cargo can be had. The sweet-toothed engagés have well supplied themselves. As soon as they learned from Packinaud that sugar and meal might give out, they went to him in the storehouse and had him put 50 pounds to their account in secret. In that way several barrels have been emptied without Mr. Denig's knowledge until yesterday, when Packinaud, unable to make the entries because he cannot write, had to specify the persons whom he had allowed credit.

What dismay in the land of Canaan! Famine was about to set in. What damage to trade! Ten barrels more of meal and 20 barrels more of sugar would have been no appreciable increase in the steamer's cargo. For want of a sufficient quantity of these commodities, several hundred buffalo robes are lost to the company, for the reasons that Indians put themselves to little trouble for other goods on sale. In winter, they prefer their robes to woolen blankets, and their own sort of clothes made of skin to those made of cloth. Leather is a better protection against wind and cold than wool, except in water.

I had much trouble with my watercolor sketch. Though I held the water over the fire in a tin cup, it froze when I applied it to the ice-cold paper, and it soon formed ice crystals on my porcelain palette.

Bad news has reached us from the other side. Yesterday, two of our metifs who are out of employment went to the Yellowstone with a dogsled and two pack horses to hunt on their own account, in order to provision their families with meat and to obtain some hides, if possible. They were attacked—so the report goes—by Blackfeet. David is severely wounded and Antoine is missing. Without delay, I harnessed three dogs to the cariole; Mr. Denig got in and had Joe conduct him to the Crow settlement, where David is said to be.

Mr. Denig brought our wounded man home. His nose was pierced through in the direction of his left eye and both his feet are frozen. What a wretched outlook, to be lame and half-blind in this wild region. As yet, no trace has been found of Antoine la Pierre. As soon as we had put David to bed, made an examination of his wounds and dressed them, he gave an account of his adventure.

They were fortunate enough to come upon a drove of 200 elks and shot 4 of the cows. Owing to the sudden alternation from cold to hot, their rifles became dripping wet and of no further use. They had hardly lighted their evening campfire, put their meat on spits, and stretched their hides as a protection against the rough wind when some Indians plunged out of a nearby thicket and fired upon them.

Antoine fled from the place at once, or at least disappeared in the darkness. Momentarily staggered by being shot in the face, David could not see how to defend himself. He was only conscious of clamorous voices, as of many Indians running toward him to take his scalp, and of the first arrival's crying out in Blackfeet, "A white man," and then sounds of a quick flight. In all probability, the Indians took the pack horses with them, and perhaps Antoine also.

Severely wounded as he was, David attempted to reach the Assiniboin camp. His feet froze on the journey; his moccasins must have been wet. David's wife and children will have a hard time this winter. David is out of employment, and though he owned nothing of much use, he has now lost all his belongings, together with the rifle and saddle Mr. Denig had lent him. Nor do David and his wife stand well with the Bombarde family. It is said that on the whole, metifs are not inclined to render mutual assistance to one another.

Mr. Denig was invited to dinner at Fort William by Joe Picotte. His family and I were included in the invitation. Family did not go, so I had to accompany the bourgeois. He drove over with his dogs and sled, conducted by Joe, while I galloped along on Cendre as outrider to the equipage. How splendid, how jolly to ride a fiery racer over the frozen snow! Sparkling sunshine but cold air! Joe expressed a desire to return to virtue and avert punishment.

As I was indulging my whim to ride slowly to the gates on our return home, I was suddenly aroused by seeing the sled with Mr. Denig seated therein almost under Cendre's paunch. The dogs had foolishly ignored their conductor and run between Cendre's legs. If I had not kept the horse well in hand, we should have been thrown topsy-turvy into a confused heap.

December 15—Antoine has at last appeared with his skin whole. Here is his story. After they had kindled a fire and stuck the meat on spits to roast, they took off their wet moccasins to dry them and warm their feet. Antoine put on another pair right away and told David to do likewise. The latter, suspecting no danger, replied, "*À tantot* [soon]." Antoine placed his gun, which was quite wet—not only from having been fired in such cold air, but also from having brushed against snow-covered boughs and shrubs as they traveled along—beside the fire to dry and began to cut up the elk cows they had killed and to hang up the meat.

As he was thus employed, he heard a crunching of footsteps on snow and a rustling of boughs. He called his companion's attention to this. David thought the noise was made by their pack horses; the dogs were not stirring at all. They had stretched a lodge skin, made of several [buffalo] cow hides sewed together one above the other in a row, to form a tent. These tent skins had become almost transparent, being much the worse for wear from age and long use in the packing of goods. So, as the men sat beside the fire or were busy at work, their shadows could be seen by the enemy but not clearly enough to indicate the race to which they belonged.

Suddenly there were shots and then a voice, shouting in Blackfeet dialect: "Advance, my men, and take their scalps!" Knowing well that sitting in the firelight, they were at the mercy of an enemy concealed by darkness, they ran instinctively into the night, each trying to save his own skin. They were thus separated from each other. David does not know himself how long he was running about through the snow in his bare feet, for he was almost insensible from pain and wearying wanderings in the dark when he arrived at the Assiniboin camp. Antoine fled to the Crow settlement, which was not so great a distance as the Assiniboin camp.

Yesterday morning, Antoine went with a band of Crows to their abandoned camping place. Along the banks of the Yellowstone, they discovered 15 different footprints. Antoine met some Assiniboin to whom he related his adventure and inquired after his comrade. He let the Crows follow the tracks on farther, while he returned with the Assiniboin to the abandoned campfire. He found other members of the Crow tribe in possession of his pack horses. The meat had been devoured, and the elk skins had disappeared. The sled, the dogs, everything had found great favor with someone. The Crow Indians maintained that it was all legitimate booty because metifs have no right to hunt in that part of the domain. They consented to give back only the pack horse belonging to our company, and they did that purely on repeated admonition of the Assiniboin, the real owners of the land.

The Blackfeet took no booty, merely shot one of the dogs that happened to be with the horses. The other two dogs were lying by the fire, and the only thing that can be said for them is that they certainly were very poor guards.

December 16—At breakfast, Mr. Denig told me I was to get ready to go soon with La Bombarde to the camp of Le Premier qui Vole, [Mr. Denig's] brother-in-law, to trade for buffalo robes, although, so far as that is concerned, he is certain of the robes anyway. How delighted I should be to spend several weeks in an Indian's camp just as one of the "savages!" What a chance to study camp scenes! However, La Bombarde has not yet come back from Blackfeet territory, where he was sent to bring back a pair of horses. Tonight, Ours Fou, his widowed daughter-in-law, and her two pretty daughters are sleeping in my room.

In the Absaroka language, "Bear's Head" is written "Machetetsi Antu'" "Rottentail" is "Tsite Yore"; "Sapsucker" is "Ubschita Thash." In Herantsa, "Quatre Ours" is written "Machbitse Topa"; "Queue Rouge" is "Sita Ische"; "Langue de Boeuf" is "Kirayi Lesche."

December 20—This morning I was forced into a fight with Badger. Morgan sent him here yesterday with other dogs harnessed to a sled, which was loaded with tongues and driven by Belhumeur. Today he was to return home. Out of pure sympathy for the beast, I gave him a good breakfast, whereupon he crept under my bed and refused to come out until I poked him with a sharp-pointed rod in such a way that he became furious and sprang at me.

I had to strike him sharply on the nose to make him mind me. Mr. Denig was outside stamping impatiently, while he complained of the delay. When he was told the reason for it, he said that dogs used for the purpose of drawing sleds must be fed only in the evening, after the day's work is done. Otherwise, as I had just seen, if they were fed beforehand, they became drowsy and lazy. I shall let this serve as a warning to me. While Badger was asleep in my room the whole night, his comrade Bull refused to be brought in but remained, in spite of the severe cold, before the door on guard.

December 25—Christmas. We were very busy the entire day. Our only variation from the usual routine was an extra course of cake at dinner, and stewed dried apples served with cream. Last Monday, when Rottentail came in with his band, they brought 130 buffalo robes. The Absaroka are famous for their robes. In no other nation are the dressed skins so soft and pliable. As I have no robes for my bed except the handsome one given me by Mr. Denig, I was biding my time to choose the most beautiful I could find in a pack of excellent ones, as a model of the best manufacture. As bad luck would have it, I did not find among these great piles a single buffalo robe that satisfied me. On most of them I found the hair imperfect. Furthermore, they were cut in two and sewed together in a seam down the middle.

Some of the Crow chiefs, and several girls as well, wore robes of extraordinary beauty. The skins were entire, including both the head and the tail. They were not cut at all, the hair was long and silky, the skin as soft and pliable as a woolen blanket. Such robes cost at least as much as a Mackinaw blanket. Since the Absaroka have found out that fur traders pay no more for a good buffalo robe than for one tanned just ordinarily well, they take little pains with those intended for trade. And they are right; fur traders pay more attention to quantity than quality.

The bourgeois sell thousands of buffalo robes in packs of ten robes each. Both at this trading post and in St. Louis at Chouteau Jr. & Co., salesmen first examine the packs and sort the robes, including in every assortment at least one robe of the best quality for every pack of 10. Sometimes, for the sake of the fine, curly hair, small hides of one-year-old calves are sold for robes made of cowhides. Raw calf's skins and robes made from scabby skins are not offered for sale. An old robe that has been in use is more sought than a new one, when the hair is in good condition, because after it has been worn, it shows always whether it was properly tanned, whether it is soft, and whether it can be cleaned.

We purchased some immense elk horns from a band of Cree. They are sold as wall decoration or for the manufacture of knives, tobacco pipes, etc. I am itching for a pair, but I am still contemplating the purchase. They are far too difficult to pack and too heavy to carry. Besides, they are dispensable, because sketches can be made from several different views.

We have old Sapsucker, Bear's Head, and their adherents with us today. The two chiefs are quartered in my room, so that they may not be obliged to lie down with common folk. Honor to whom honor is due! Crows are distinguished from other tribes by individual features of face and form, cut of their hair, vanity, penchant for personal adornment, and marked parental affection. The men, who value wealth above valor, sagacity, or honor, make a great show of their apparel and decorations. They hang hollow tubes of white and violet-colored porcelain (wampum) in their hair, and they wear long ropes of the same ornaments about their necks. They decorate their leather pouches with beads, and also those broad bands by means of which they swing their bows, quivers, and rifles across their shoulders.

That singular style of trimming women's doeskin garments with rows and rows of elk's teeth placed horizontally across front and back originated among the Crow Indians. For that purpose, they use the six lower incisors of the elk, which, since they are so few, are very expensive. One hundred of them cost $20, as much as a pack horse. Among the Crow tribe, the women cut their hair short above the eyes and on the neck. Only the men are allowed to make themselves conspicuous for long hair; to that end—just as do their relatives the Herantsas—they stick on false hair as a means of making their own seem longer than it really is.

Indians of no other nation so frequently call themselves by name as the Crows. With much self-esteem, they place their right hand on their breast and say, "Absaroka!" Then extending their arms from the side, they imitate the motion of wings when a bird is in flight. Women and children are not subjected to the rigid discipline that is customary among other nations. On the contrary, they are allowed to be present at the tribal meetings for counsel and even to interrupt the speakers with remarks of their own. Such liberty is unheard-of among other tribes. Rottentail's 12-year-old is always hanging around where his daddy is and constantly begging for something or taking part in the old man's conversation. These practices cause the Crow to be ridiculed by friend and foe alike.

David is blind in his right eye. His toes, black from having been frozen, are beginning to drop off. Twice a day I have to rid both feet of the putrefied flesh and dress the wounds with copaiba balsam salve. In return, David's family beg alms of me incessantly: "*Un petit brin de sucre; seulement une poigné de café.*" ("A little bit of sugar; just a handful of coffee.") How can I gratify their wants without stealing? These people really seem to believe that if a man has the keys to a storehouse, he may without scruple pocket a handful here and there, that the company can afford to lose it!

The metifs here are the most haughty beggars I have ever seen, an instance where the admixture of Indian blood, which is supposed to improve the white race, in reality has made matters worse. They have the opinion that their business is to serve as scouts, huntsmen, or interpreters. It is beneath their dignity to drive oxen or to cut wood.

Apparently David thinks that I am here solely for his benefit, that I am to provide food, fuel, medicine, and other things besides for him and his family. Yet he is not even employed here, and his wife and daughters refuse to sew a stitch by way of payment. Even Madame la Bombarde and her two daughters, who are employed regularly at the fort to make clothes for pay (credit on account), refused Mr. Denig the loan of her dogs to send goods to the Upper Bourbeuse. Mr. Denig retaliated by giving her no more work to do. Now she has to use her own supply of meat for food.

December 26—I had a quarrel with Jim Hawthorn about Bear's Head. While Jim was eating breakfast in the kitchen, he asserted that I had neither assigned the chief a place to sleep nor provided him with a buffalo robe. That was not true. I had done both, but after I went to bed, Bear's Head went out to talk with acquaintances in another room, where he remained quite late. When he came back, he may have found that his place and his robe had been appropriated by someone else. I could not help that. He said not a word to me but complained to Jim Hawthorn, who is always glad to pick a quarrel with a person whose employment here deprives him of a position at the fort.

The latter reported the matter, much exaggerated, to the boss with the hope of precipitating a reprimand upon me; this he succeeded in doing. However, I was able to exonerate myself. At supper, I inquired of Jim in a joking way whether he did not know some other complaint he might bring forward against me. He made the occasion for seeking me out after the meal to say he was ready to fight me with any weapon from "rifle down to needle," if I wished a row with him. I only asked him, "Who began the carping?" I am not in the least afraid of him. For some time I have been aware of his malicious ill will.

December 28—My prospects for remaining any considerable time in a locality as clerk seem more uncertain daily. Joe Picotte is now convinced that he is unable to compete with the big company. He has insufficient means. Besides, he lost several horses on his secret scouting trip. He has already recalled the traders he sent out. Joe comprehends now that Mr. Denig was right when he told him to be satisfied with what jealousy among soldiers and their advantageous position with the two companies can bring in. Owing to the competition between companies, for instance, Indians get European goods at more reasonable prices. Furthermore, a larger number of braves find employment at a fort as soldiers, or protectors, a position greatly desired by Indians and much envied, because it brings with it not only authority but many fights and other advantages besides.

December 29—Last evening, Antoine la Pierre brought the skin of a six-year-old moose buck and the head with horns intact. As I had a few moments to spare, I made a thorough study of the head in my room and painted two views of it. Now I shall not find it necessary to buy a pair of elk horns—that much saved. Collecting has ever been my weak point.

December 31—The last day of the year that had brought me much nearer the accomplishment of my life purpose. Six months more ahead of me for my studies of animals, and hardly any paper and pencils left. There is not one whole lead pencil in the fort and only ruled writing paper. Moreover, it is hardly possible for me to get a new supply of drawing materials before summer.

As soon as Mr. Denig learned that Joe Picotte and Ramsay had withdrawn from their ill-intentioned enterprise and had really recalled the traders whom they had sent out earlier to skirmish for buffalo robes, he had me go to Fort William and ask Joe to sign a written agreement for future dealing.

Upon my arrival there I heard bad news: The Blackfeet have again stolen a large drove of horses from the Assiniboin—155 head at one throw! Among them were two belonging to the Dobies and three of Carafel's. La Main qui Tremble [Trembling Hand], one of our soldiers, lost all of his, including several preeminent runners. The Assiniboin brought their remaining horses together in great haste (neither did they spare those belonging to the fur traders) and hurried out in pursuit of the daring thieves. They soon found that the main trail along which the robbers were traveling separated into three, each leading in a different direction so as to confuse pursuers.

The Assiniboin, following the way that showed the greatest number of hoofprints, found that it separated also, just as the other did. They came at last upon the worst conditioned of their horses but saw no Blackfeet. They gave up further pursuit.

Farewell, Old Year. At your beginning, you exposed me to severe trials, but all is well as you draw to a close. Once more my hopes are high, my courage unabated! If the New Year brings me to the completion of my studies, puts me in a position where I may have the required leisure to execute paintings to my own satisfaction, I shall be quite content.

EIGHT

January 1852

January 1—To begin the New Year aright, I brought the most perfect pelt of a grizzly bear that I could find from the press room where our furs are kept, so that I might complete studies I am making of wild animals now extant in this territory. It took me the entire day to reproduce with exactness the great variety of hues and shades, as well as the differences apparent in curly, wiry, smooth, and long hairs. It must be taken into consideration that I had to attend to my usual duties besides. The water I was using for my watercolor sketch often froze on the paper, in spite of my precautions to heat it. I was constantly disturbed by the half-breed girl with her kisses and New Year's greetings, and frequently summoned by Mr. Denig to write something down, because his sore thumb is giving him a great deal of pain. A great protuberance of proud flesh formed below the nail and later fell off, after having caused intense pain. For a long while, Mr. Denig feared he might lose his arm. He is in the habit of thrusting the thumb into his waistcoat, just as I represented him in the portrait I painted.

Joe Picotte was here to acknowledge with his signature an agreement that I was required to draw up in writing. The first clause had to do with his sending out traders to anticipate us in acquiring the stock of buffalo robes in those districts that supply our winter trading posts. The second obligated him to pay $1,000 in damages. The third, not to employ any deserters in any part of the territory over which he has control. This last-named clause is of great importance, because under conditions therein named, an employee's running away is made so difficult that he would need the utmost courage to attempt it. Heretofore, people who had played a trick on the opposition were all the more gladly taken into service. Their new bourgeois knew how to use their hostility toward the opposing company to his own benefit in the way of intensifying zeal to thwart a competitor. In fact, so long as a man was able to find another employer, he was not looked upon as a deserter. He might even take a hostile attitude toward an earlier master and then dare to go back to him later on.

Not even while we were drawing up and signing this trade agreement would old dame la Pierre leave us in peace. She kissed, in turn, every man in the office. I came near to having an attack of nausea!

January 2—Today old Sapsucker came marching across the frozen Missouri to our fort, at the head of a stout band of Absaroka. To do him honor, I was commissioned to fire a salute of three guns. That is, I fired three times with our four-pounder that stands on the gallery above the river gate. As there were neither cartridges nor match cord at the fort, I had to wrap a load of powder in paper and thrust it into the barrel, then ram it in with shreds and rags of leather, clear out the vent with an iron pin, put powder on the pan, and touch it off with a burning brand—and all by myself. It was in loading the gun after this clumsy fashion that old Gareau (Pierre's father) lost an arm. After having fired, he thought it unnecessary to stop the vent while reloading. But what does Mr. Denig care?

Sapsucker and his entire family are again my guests. This name "Sapsucker" is the usual designation in the United States for the downy woodpecker.

January 3—This old chief's medicine is dried buffalo dung! When I lighted my Indian pipe and offered it to him, he rubbed some dry powder over the smoking tobacco from a bullet-shaped substance in his hand.

Thinking he did this to obtain some sort of aroma, yet sensible of no resulting fragrance, I asked him what it was. He laid a piece of dried buffalo dung in my hand, indicating that I must never neglect to put some of it on the tobacco when I desired to smoke with him. Two of his children wear bits of this miraculous medicine in their hair, just above the brow, as a talisman.

Today Mr. Denig bartered with one of the Absaroka for a charming pipe bowl of red sandstone. As he had no use for it, he offered it to me at cost price for my collection. "If my credit is so far good," I replied. "Certainly," he said. So I bought the beautiful pipe bowl for $7 and had it charged to my account. Among the Crows, I should have had to pay the price of a pack horse for such a treasure. The red sandstone comes from a cliff near the St. Peters River in Sioux territory. These bowls are drilled out, shaped, and polished by the Sioux but are offered as articles of trade among all the rest of the natives as well.

Le Petit Mandan [Little Mandan] came today from the Herantsa village. He says great numbers of buffaloes are seen in the near neighborhood. I am glad, indeed, to have been driven to this place, even through the influence of Indian superstition. I only regret not having been able to make a finished drawing of the village with all its medicine poles, while the Herantsa were camped within.

January 4—With the hope of being able to complete sketches of several antlered stags' heads that we have on hand, I hurried through my day's tasks, such as the distributing of meat, feeding the chickens and pigeons, etc. Even though it was Sunday, Mr. Denig did not fail to continually find something else for me to do. He is kept in a sort of feverish unrest by pain in his thumb; proud flesh is causing the loss of his thumbnail. On account of this he cannot write, so I have to serve as his secretary.

He never fails to find fault with something. He is vexed if I cannot account for every rope, every nail, tool, implement, stock, ring, saddle, nay, even every mouse at the fort. I am to keep a sharp lookout in all directions, so as to know what is in stock, what is wanting, what is out of place. From actual observation, I am to know everything—even to the smallest object—that is stored in the attic under the roof, in boxes and chests, in barrels and casks, in the cellar, in places to which I am not admitted, in outhouses, even among dung heaps in a stall: Shovels and hose or something else may be left lying there neglected or forgotten. If I cannot give an account of a thing forthwith—who has it, or where it lies, stands, or hangs, as the case may be—then he says, "It is too infernal bad."

When I was given the keys, there was no inventory from which I could inform myself. There was no way for me to know offhand whether certain things were here or not, or the names of many tools and implements I had not even heard of, at least in the patois—half-Yankee, half-Canadian, half-Indian—that is spoken here. The fault with me is not that I am lacking in diligence or punctuality but that I am undiscerning, or rather that I am not sharp-sighted. I lack curiosity (or a propensity to stick my nose into everything), and what is more, my thoughts are always intent on my studies in art.

My day's work should engross my attention. Unfortunately, that is not true; art always occupies my best thoughts. Wherever I am, wherever I go, my eyes instinctively seek beauty of form and color. To be sure, I might force myself to live entirely absorbed in the duties of clerk and foreman, if it had to be done for any great length of time. I have no intense desire to tarry here several years, but only so long as I need to stay to finish my studies. In spite of the romantic adventure of my situation, I should become bored in the course of time. Besides, I cannot execute my paintings here, or finish my collection. I notice there are people enough in the land to do the work of clerks. Hawthorn has been hereabouts for a good long time and yet has no employment. My departure is his dearest wish.

January 6—Mr. Denig bartered with an Absaroka for a long necklace of 30 bear's claws. When an Indian offers such ornaments for sale, one always gets them for much less than when one asks the redskin to set his price.

As a matter of course, they never offer an article like that for sale unless at the moment they need something else much more; therefore, the purchaser has the advantage. If one proposes to buy some object from an Indian that he highly values and is not obliged to part with, he demands in return as much as he likes or else something that he would much rather have. Mr. Denig barters for such trinkets and trappings as an accommodation to the Indians only when he sees that he can dispose of the object in question at a profit, or at least without loss. He offered me the necklace at the cost price ($10). I took it at once.

Ours Fou is again with me. To his great annoyance, he found a young Crow already installed in my room, because, according to the custom of the Crow tribe, this young fellow dares not live in the same room with his mother-in-law. He dares not talk with her directly or allow her to see his face until his young wife bears him a child. The same custom is observed among the Dakotas, but only at the first marriage.

Ours Fou wishes me to send the buck away. He sought the solitude of my room for the express purpose of being undisturbed. Furthermore, he thought it beneath his dignity to sit beside this young fop and smoke with him. The latter is most richly appareled: coat, leggings, and hood fashioned from a new Mackinaw blanket. He trails another Mackinaw blanket negligently after him in such a manner as to display its wealth of ornamentation.

The buck went doubly armed, as when he arrived. He swung his rifle in a sheath over his shoulder, bow and quiver in two broad bandoliers, the straps of both entirely covered with coral beads in various designs. The sheath was decorated with fringe and scarlet cloth. He carried three pouches with him, all richly ornamented, absolutely covered with beads arranged in different patterns. The largest pouch opened at the side; the shot bag, with cover, was attached to his belt in front. A third pouch, closed with a long, tapering cover, was fastened at his belt in the back. His knife sheath was just as elaborately embroidered. It was also trimmed with fringe and, like his knee bands, with falcon bells from Leipzig. The tinkling of those bells behind and before gave him an especial pleasure. In face and form he was quite attractive and manifestly the darling of many sisters, or else of other girls who hoped to be his future wives.

He was constantly trying to be companionable with me. He asked me how many horses I owned, with the evident purpose of considering whether, if he offered me a present of one of his, I would make it up later on by giving him another in return. I did not encourage him, though Mr. Denig had advised me to say, if the young Absaroka made me a present of a horse, that next year (when there will be none left) I would give him a good one in return. My oilcloth painter's wallet appealed to him very much as a novelty. Because I had a good practical pouch made here, I gave him one I had formerly used. I had experienced how little suited to its purpose it was when one traveled on horseback.

His stirrups and saddle were also elaborately ornamented with beads and tassels. The Crows' saddles are made without wood and without pommel. They consist of two leather cushions bound together with a broad, solid leather girth. They are most comfortable for the rider; being soft and pliable, they inflict no discomfort or hardship on the horse. Besides, the Crows never fail to use a piece of buffalo hide with hair or some other skin as a saddle blanket (apischimo).

January 9—Yesterday Grayhead and Bear's Head arrived for the purpose of trade, together with the tribesmen belonging to their respective bands. The two chiefs and their families were shown to my room, which became so crowded that one could hardly stir. I found no chance to celebrate my thirty-fourth birthday with reflections on this transitory life.

Among 130 robes, more or less, I fail to find one of the first quality. On most of them the hair, here and there, is like black silk velvet, but they are either tanned in a superficial way or cut in two and sewed with a seam down the middle. Some of good, soft skin lack the best hair.

As Crows care little for other commodities just now, but demand horses in exchange, we are longing for the return of La Bombarde from the Black-feet territory, whither he went with Mr. Culbertson to trade for a drove and bring them to this fort.

As the chief of a band is favored in the presentation of gifts according to the number of robes he brings, these leaders naturally bestir themselves to make their people hurry with the preparation of skins. In their eagerness to get together the number of robes required, they pay no attention to the quality of work done. Among 400 that were prepared by Assiniboin and sent in from Mackenzie's post, I was unable to find one to my taste. Though I must admit they were all tanned in a painstaking manner on the whole, all were sewed together in the middle. To save themselves trouble, the women cut out that part of the hide which, even on a cow's back, is very thick, and then sew the two parts together with thread made from dried sinews or tendons. Canadians call this Indian thread "*du nerf.*" There are several qualities of it. Tendons of the long muscle that extends the length of the backbone are used preferably for that purpose. The finest thread is made from the dorsal muscles of Virginia deer and antelopes. Now and then it happens that the women sew together parts of hides that were taken from different animals, which produces a singular effect.

When Madame David came to get "*le dur*" from me so that she might improve some robes Mr. Denig thought too imperfectly prepared for market, for a long while, I could not understand what "*le dur*" meant. I was conducted by her to the meat house, where she pointed out the liver. This organ, and also the brain of a deer, or in case of emergency, fat of any sort, tallow, etc., are all used to soften hides. One woman dresses a buffalo hide in 3 or 4 days just as well, making the skin as soft and durable as our leather dressers do in 6 months. First of all, they stretch the raw hide on the ground and fasten it down with pegs or wooden pins. With some sharp instrument, a piece of bone perhaps, they scrape off every particle of flesh, which is eagerly devoured by the hungry dogs. If the skin is not to be dressed until later, they leave it spread in the air to dry until it becomes quite hard.

On the other hand, if they intend to prepare the robe at once, for one entire day they rub the hide with liver, fat, or the brains of a deer to soften the skin. They leave it 2 or 3 days (according to the season or extreme tem-perature) until the grease soaks in; then they dry it in a slow fire, constantly beating it or rubbing it with a stone until it becomes uniformly soft and pliable. This rubbing is of the greatest importance in the dressing of skins, Indian-fashion.

As soon as the hide has been prepared in this manner and is quite dry, they begin the fatiguing process of rubbing it around a taut horsehair rope or braided leather to make it smooth. Oftentimes, it receives a final polish with pumice stone. Such work is most burdensome from start to finish. Even the scraping of the hides has to be done in a stooped position that is very fatiguing. As the brain of a deer is fine and more rare than liver or tallow, it is used primarily in the preparation of deerskins (except skins of elks). In the final stage of preparation, deer hides are placed over a slow fire covered with green sprays of sumac and are thus smoked. Owing to this process, they suffer less injury from water. They become golden brown in color and retain the smell of smoke for quite a while, which repels mosquitoes and moths.

Grayhead was given his name on account of his gray hair, which, however, is a perfect yellow in spots. As he is not gray headed from age, the singularity of his appearance has acquired this nickname for him. He always wears a fur cap with a red feather. He insists on much ceremony when he joins in the tobacco smoking. First of all, he makes the statement that he smokes only after meals. La Queue Rouge, who has returned from his visit, lights the pipe. With his right hand, he extends it to Grayhead according to custom, the mouthpiece forward, whereupon Grayhead explains to him that he is supposed to hold the pipe out in front of him, not offer it directly to a chief.

When that position is assumed, Grayhead seizes the pipe with his right fist in a backhanded manner (thumb down) as one grasps a cudgel, passes it gently into his left hand, and pulls a whiff. Instead of exhaling the smoke through his nose in the usual manner, he holds the pipe aloft in front of him, the stem in a vertical position, and blows the smoke upward through his mouth. Again a whiff; holding the pipe so that the stem points straight before him, he puffs out the smoke in the same direction. Grasping the stem with his left hand, he takes a fresh draw, holds the mouthpiece aslant toward his right side, and blows the smoke to the right. He then inclines the mouthpiece toward his left side, blows the smoke to the left, pulls another whiff, touches the ground with the pipe bowl, emits a cloud of smoke as before, turns toward the fire, and blows a puff in that direction. He then begins to smoke in customary Indian fashion, exhaling the smoke through his nose.

When Grayhead saw that I carried the key to the meat house, he begged continually for meat for his daughters. In expectation that as daughters of a chief they would be supplied with food, they put aside the liberal portions of mush served them at the feast for their children. I had instructions from Mr. Denig never to let an Indian have meat without his special permission, so I referred Grayhead to my boss.

The latter informed the chief that we did not buy cured meat from him for the sake of providing him afterwards with other meat that was fresh. Grayhead continued to beg from Packinaud and others, who replied by way of excuse that they were not in possession of the key to the meat house.

When he comes on a visit to white people, an Indian regards it as a discourtesy not to be duly entertained at feasts and spreads. What concerns us in these matters is not merely our duty from the standpoint of hospitality but the vital question of sustaining life at a fort. If we were required to entertain everyone who comes with the hospitality due to a guest, we should soon have nothing but visitors—no trade, no compensation. Consequently, we should soon go to ruin, literally eaten out of business.

January 11—In Zimmermann's workroom I saw four Assiniboin women playing a new game. They sat in a row before the fire. They had four disks six inches long, attached to the ends of wands sharpened to a point. On two of the wands, there were disks having the figure of a man on the upper surface. On the other two, the upper surface of the disks bore the figure of a hand. The under surfaces of the disks were not marked at all. One after another, the women would seize the four wands at the upper ends and throw them on the floor with points turned adroitly downward, so as to make them tumble over with all the decorated surfaces of the disks turned upward.

Whoever succeeded in doing that won double the stakes of all the others. If all unmarked surfaces turned upward, that counted simply as a score. If both marked with the figure of a man or both marked with a hand were turned, that counted half as much. The winning woman continues to throw until she fails to turn the disks uniformly, then another player throws them in turn. According to agreement, the stakes consisted of grains of corn, a certain number designating stipulated objects, such as ornaments, clothing, etc. Women play this game just as eagerly as men, perhaps more passionately, when they have no other pastime. They play day and night, and lose articles of apparel. It has happened here that they even put up their children for stakes.

January 12—Again, a significant instance of the Indian's sense of obligation in matters of trade. An Assiniboin has been living in his tent at the Dobie fort ever since his arrival in these parts on the steamboat *Robert Campbell*. During this entire time, he has been provided with food, with his smoking tobacco, and with many gifts at the expense of the fort. When he had finished five buffalo robes, he demanded a high price that Joe Picotte refused to pay, whereupon the Assiniboin brought his hides here and exchanged them at the current market price. Despite his indebtedness to Joe, he left him empty-handed.

L'Ours Fou is back again with the members of his encampment. He did not venture beyond the other settlements of Assiniboin and Absaroka, hence had slain no buffaloes. This great but do-nothing chief sees, ever-hovering before his eyes, quantities of cured meat packed in our storeroom, together with supplies of cornmeal mush. Since he has been appointed supreme chief of the Assiniboin by the white man's doing, let the white man attend to the duty of having him properly clothed and fed. He confuses all of us white men in this region with Americans, with Uncle Sam.

Ours Fou appears to be a stupid rather than a crazy bear. First, he came and asked that all his followers be provided with food. When he saw that plan would not work, he said, "Give me food at least, and let the others go." Then La Jambe Blessé [Wounded Leg] and La Poudière [Powder] followed; only they were to be supplied in addition. It was no use; we could not risk the consequences, so we were obliged to have them depart with long faces and empty stomachs. If we had satisfied their demands, we should never be rid of these beggars. They would rely on us for supplies and no longer hunt at all. As a consequence, we should suffer a twofold loss: constant reduction of our stores of provisions without any return, and no replenishing of our stock of buffalo hides.

As soon as they see that no foodstuffs will be delivered to them except as payment, they are forced to go in search of buffalo herds. These Assiniboin grow more lazy each day. As excuse for their inactivity, they use the unfortunate circumstance of their owning so few horses fit to run buffaloes. In that case, owners of swift horses have a distinct advantage, which they should put to good use by hunting on behalf of their less-fortunate comrades in the camp. At an earlier time, every man stood on his own feet. Everybody had an equal chance upon the encircling of a herd on a buffalo hunt. Footmen remained in the rear of horsemen, and those riding ponies took a position behind the huntsmen mounted on American racing horses. One of our customers here has related how on foot, during an earlier season, he slew 140 buffaloes in one winter and sold their tongues and hides at this fort. An entire settlement (40 to 60 tents) takes not so much booty in a whole winter nowadays.

Le Gras [Greasy] brought bad news from the Yellowstone. The river is out of its bounds and has overflowed and inundated Rottentail's camp. Everything was carried off by the high waters: his largest tent, made of 25 skins sewed together, all his commodities but recently purchased, his stock of raw buffalo hides together with those already tanned, his clothing, and decorations. They say he sits on a hill and wails. Sapsucker lost 2 of his 37 horses.

A Crow was taken unaware so suddenly by the swiftly rising water that he no longer had time to slip out through his low tent door but had to clamber up poles on the inside to the smoke hole in the roof and shout for help. He was later rescued by a friend mounted on a large, heavy horse. Wallace, whom Mr. Denig had dispatched with letters to a trading post in Crow territory, lost his steed in the flood (but at that time he had no business at all anywhere near the river).

January 15—Le Gras brought only two leather cabrets to exchange. As soon as he received as much as they were worth, he came to me and asked for a rope with which to tether his saddle horse. Then came the Platte Man (Garçon du Fraissée) and wished something to eat. Mr. Denig answered, "Yes, when you bring hides for my trade."

"But will you at least let me have some smoking mixture?"

"The upland willow grows quite near your tent."

"Then give me a flint and steel."

"I haven't one. Neither have I any coal, that I might have such a thing made."

"Well, can I get a file? I need something of the sort."

"Good! Then bring in some robes."

Mr. Denig fled to my room, hoping to escape such insistent begging, but Le Gras soon hunted him out.

"Say at once what it is you want," Mr. Denig interposed before the former could speak. "First?"

"A calico case for my pipe stem," Le Gras began. "Long enough to hang over both ends."

"Second?" Mr. Denig went on, counting off on his fingers.

"Eye water."

"Third?"

"Tobacco."

"Fourth?"

Le Gras could not help laughing and thereupon gave up any further petitioning.

Smith, Cadotte, and Antoine returned this evening from a four days' hunt with only two elks. This shows how difficult it is to start game in a region inhabited by large numbers of Indians.

January 16—Painted my first study of the elk. I am very anxious to make my studies of animals from life, as well as my sketches of natural scenes, so thorough that they cannot fail to satisfy the naturalists.

If we should have a heavier snowfall, say, several feet deep, Indians would wander about here less, and wild game in our vicinity would be left in peace. In other winters, so I am told, wild animals have approached the fort within shooting distance. One could stand just outside the gate and kill buffaloes and antelopes.

January 17—Despite this frightfully cold weather, Rottentail and a number of his adherents came here to arrange for an advance payment so that he can revive his business. At the same time, he gave us an account of the disaster that befell him.

The Absaroka were taken unawares by the Yellowstone flood while they slept. It is true that they had heard the thunderous roar of the waters breaking through the ice, but they had attributed the sound to a violent gale that was sweeping through the forest. Occupants of the village lost more or less, according to whether their tents were pitched on high ground or low. Some were hard put to save even their children. Others brought away some of their bedclothes also.

As luck would have it, Rottentail, his horses, and six fine mules were on the high shore. The berdache lost everything except the buffalo robe in which she was sleeping. Everything was swept away by the swift stream: two horses, her supply of raw hides, finished buffalo robes, commodities, provisions, and knives. She had to struggle against the rushing, ice-cold water to save herself. It came up to her chest and so chilled her limbs that they became swollen.

At great risk of their lives, some of the more daring youths tried to snatch their most valuable belongings from the stream. Repeatedly they sprang back into the flood to rescue something. They could not fish out Rottentail's tent because it was too heavy and the ground on which they stood was too insecure. Though it was carried off, they found it again six days later, entangled in some bushes.

What a picturesque scene: fathers and mothers struggling to save their children, young men to rescue their sweethearts, oldish bachelors and widows to hold onto their goods and chattels. Stripped of everything, some few were happy to escape with skin whole, while brave men mounted on strong horses contended against the current to assist those whose strength was failing, to encourage them anew and succor them.

January 18—Rottentail presented Mr. Denig with a military headdress containing 36 eagle feathers—three full eagle tails valued by Indians at the price paid for three good pack horses. For such a present as that, Rottentail naturally expected to receive some gift in return. Indians are never generous toward a white person. They always expect a gift in return, sooner or later. Even among his own people, an Indian is liberal with gifts (meat excepted) only to win friends or partisans, to secure for himself a large number of adherents.

Inasmuch as I am not able to pay $36 for this interesting head attire, I am going to paint a picture of it.

Rottentail brought nine robes to sell. As soon as he received the worth of them, the berdache claimed one as her property. Rottentail laid the blame on his wife. She admitted that the robe belonged to the berdache but claimed to have delivered nine robes besides that one to Jim Hawthorn.

For the first time, Mr. Denig now sees that Jim Hawthorn does not understand the Crow dialect at all. Rottentail is a Yankee; he is smart. Mr. Denig has to pay twice the usual amount for the robe—the flatterer's shares in this joint business are declining in value.

Rottentail bade us farewell until spring. He will not come back until he has become rich once more. Now that is sensible of you. Do but go; the fewer Indians we have in this vicinity, the more animals there are to be seen. For my studies, beasts of the chase are more welcome now than Indians.

January 19—All of a sudden there is profound quiet at this fort, truly a calm after the storm. Mr. Denig most kindly invited me to make a copy of the Indian war headgear in his warm and comfortable office. He had Packinaud come in and put it on properly, so as to serve me as model. His countenance as seen beneath the features caused much pleasant merriment—flattered his vanity not a little.

My studies progress slowly, yet they steadily increase. Indeed, they are becoming so abundant that my first plan for a collection begins to seem impracticable, that is, too limited. Which pictures shall I paint? Which omit? Besides, there is the life of the fur traders, the Mountaineers, and the half-breeds; their hunting expeditions, their adventures, their pleasures and their sufferings, their amours, their good fortune and bad, their travels, their work, dangers they face on water and land, in heat and in frost, in a region of redskins and wild beasts—are not all those matters of exceeding interest?

When the last buffalo passes, the last wild beast of the chase will have disappeared. Furthermore, the last trapper will have disappeared, and the last fur traders.

January 20—Smith wants my fire steel for his benefit early in the morning, for he is going on a hunt. Throughout the entire fort, not a fire steel is to be had for its weight in gold. Not a fire steel—a utensil of such importance—and no coal, in so extended an enterprise as this fur-trading business. Hunters find their flint and steel indispensable. Matches are too easily affected by dampness to be practical; furthermore, we have no supply in stock. Smith is at a loss unless he can get mine. All the other hunters need their own themselves or else—in consequence of the high value placed upon fire steels at the moment—are unwilling to expose so necessary an object to the risk of coming within the reach of an Indian's long fingers.

Smith can be of great service to me if he brings back the heads of the large animals slain, and the entire bodies of the smaller ones, thus providing me models for my studies. Without hesitation, I made him a present of my flint and steel. In doing this, I was perfectly aware of the fact that in this place, a man never knows where he will sleep the next night, or whether he may not be sent unexpectedly into the open, where a fire steel is just as necessary as knife and gun.

Smith says that at this season, buck elks live apart from the female elks and range in groups of 4 or 5 to 8. The females range in droves of from 10 to 20, together with the brockets (2-year-old stags). He also gave me an account of a large cave in the red earth at the source of the Missouri. Only Blackfeet go into this cave in any great numbers. That they may not lose their way in the numerous adjoining caverns, they make fast a long rope at the entrance as they enter the cave, and take the other end along with them. Quite frequently, Indians find the skeletons of men and animals in there, which discoveries lead them to believe that those unfortunates got bewildered in the labyrinth, could not find the way out, and starved to death.

For the sake of conserving his stock of dried meat, Mr. Denig plans to send some of his men and horses "into the country," where both man and beast can find food for themselves. Although he still has nearly 15,000 pounds on hand, he is forced to use at least 60 pounds a day, on account of the multitude of people who eat here. At that rate, the supply will be rapidly exhausted. Moreover, he can get a good price for this meat just now at Fort Pierre, where buffaloes are rarely seen. As soon as our men come back from the winter posts, many of us will find very little to do here. Consequently, some of us should support ourselves.

How happy I would be if I might do that. Then I should get all the chance I want to study beasts of the chase, their ways of doing, their mode of living, how they are traced out, pursued, and slain.

January 21—Spent my whole day painting a sketch of a pair of elk horns. Smith has come back with nothing to show for his pains; the entire region is inundated. He could find no way out of the marshy depths.

January 25—Yesterday evening, Bruyère arrived from his winter trading post for a visit. La Bombarde returned at last from the Blackfeet domain, bringing 17 horses with him. As I have mentioned already, he accompanied Mr. Culbertson thither for the purpose of bringing back horses. After 24 days, Mr. Culbertson got back to Fort Benton in safety and dispatched a messenger (express) direct to St. Louis. At every post under the direction of this company, the expressman will be supplied anew with provisions and if need be, with fresh horses.

After I had taken care of the different saddles and camp fixings and made a memorandum of everything, I found, to my utter astonishment on entering my room, that Master Reynard had escaped from his box and was cutting all sorts of capers in the middle of the floor. He had gnawed through one of the narrow slats nailed across the side of the box and wriggled out. I slammed the door and seized my buffalo robe with which to catch the renegade. I saw at once that was going to be no easy matter, for he made tremendous leaps over the table, over the chairs, over the pile of firewood, always bearing his superb tail with fine effect.

To my utmost perplexity, he finally took refuge under the bed, where he crouched in a corner and gave forth sharp, guttural sounds. I had a hard time getting him out. After we had chased each other for a long while up and down the room, I succeeded in throwing my robe over him, whereupon I seized the crafty fox by his neck and put him in confinement again. It was lucky he did not jump through the window into the open. I should have been severely censured.

January 26—Painted a study in still life of a female elk. Observed in detail her shape, color, quality of hair, and proportions, then her movements, in order to get a correct idea, from actual observation, of the beast and its habits.

January 29—Last Tuesday evening, Morgan returned from his winter post on the Lower Bourbeuse. We found the first and second tables so overcrowded with bourgeois, clerks, interpreters, hunters, workmen, and horse guards that Mr. Denig saw the time had come to send out a "starvation band," together with their half-frozen saddle horses, as he had so often spoken of doing. The nearby region where our garnered hay had been flooded by the inopportune overflow of the Yellowstone was selected as good pasture, and within easy reach of a hunting ground well stocked with deer. The hayricks are surrounded by a great shallow sheet of water covered with a thin layer of ice. As Cadotte, Smith, La Bombarde, and La Pierre are our four best deer stalkers, there will be a gay, jolly rivalry. Those hunters would soon devastate any region, so far as deer are concerned. I would have liked to go with them, and yet I am glad to make myself useful at the fort. Otherwise, my services would be dispensed with entirely too soon.

Today, the expressman went on his way to St. Louis, with one fellow traveler and a pack horse. A difficult undertaking at this time of year: 2,500 miles on foot all the way to St. Joseph, from which point he may travel by steamer.

Hawthorn also left with one companion for Blackfeet territory, where his family lives.

I asked Packinaud to tell me something of the Herantsa themselves. Twenty years ago, they are said to have been a most powerful tribe, more feared than either the Sioux or the Assiniboin. At that time, they took up their habitations in five different settlements: village where the Mandan live now, 250 tents; village one mile farther up the Missouri, 80 tents; village on Knife River, 130 tents; village one-and-a-half miles above Knife River, 60 tents; village six miles from the one last named, 30 tents.

This made 550 tents in all, and the tribe reckoned 1,650 warriors. This number was reduced to 80 warriors by epidemics of smallpox and measles. Subsequently, it was increased to 150, 20 of whom were carried off last year by cholera. The Teton Sioux are said to have been forced up into this region from St. Louis, the Arikara from Council Bluffs.

The Arikara now inhabit the same village that heretofore the Mandan owned, that is, they chose the same location on which to establish their dwelling place. Under the best conditions, clay huts last not longer than 7 years. Mandan and Herantsa have always lived most amicably together.

January 31—The other day, Morgan came to barter a choice pelt of the gold fox, ermine fur, and a black pipe in addition for my beautiful pipe bowl.

NINE

February 1852

February 4—Weather usually fine and warm. I was enabled to sketch the interior of the fort from the southwest bastion. Should such agreeable atmospheric conditions continue for any length of time, we may expect a slow, cold, or wet springtime, for as yet, very little snow has fallen. Smith brought in venison. The hunters in the hayfield have already shot twenty-four deer and two elks. They are feeling quite at ease, camping in two tents with their women and eating all the choice portions of the game they kill. They are glad to be where they have not the bourgeois continually directing them.

February 5—Morgan had to take oxcarts and pack horses to fetch Mackenzie and his remaining stock of goods from his winter quarters on the Lower Bourbeuse. This warm weather has melted the snow, and in consequence, the river overflowed to such an extent that the occupants of this winter trading post were beginning to think they might have to be rescued from the roof. There is hardly anybody at the fort today. The days begin to lengthen. Weather continues warm.

February 8—Mackenzie is here with what remains of his stock of goods and what furs and pelts he has accumulated in his barter trade. His progress across the prairie, accompanied by armed foot passengers, oxcarts, pack horses, Indian women, ox drivers, and dogs, was original, to say the least.

He brought me a stag's head, which I shall sketch. There are already four tents, occupied by Assiniboin hangers-on, pitched near the camping place of our hunters in the hayfield. The smell of meat attracted them. They make themselves quite comfortable and look on while our white men hunt and our worn-out horses drag in meat for them. Smith has received instructions to keep no supplies there with which to provide food for good-for-nothing Indians, but to send what they do not need to the fort at once.

Fig. 5. Fort Union interior courtyard as seen from the southwest bastion. Without Kurz's detailed sketches and drawings of Fort Union's buildings—which were dismantled in 1867—the partial reconstruction of Fort Union by the National Park Service in 1986–1991 would have been nearly impossible. (Drawing from the collection of Gilcrease Museum, Tulsa, Oklahoma)

February 9—Four separate expeditions equipped and dispatched, Mackenzie had but arrived at the fort when he was sent off with three oxcarts laden with commodities for Bruyère. Morgan with his workmen set out for the timber yard to get lumber ready to build the new Indian lodge at the fort. Boneau and Valette were sent with the two dogsleds loaded with maize, also to Bruyère. The fourth traveled to the hayfield to bring up fresh supplies of meat. After all these had been dispatched, then commodities and robes brought back by Mackenzie had to be itemized, entered on the books, and put in their proper places.

February 10—This afternoon, Le Gras brought news that we were to expect the early arrival of Ours Fou and members of his band, the Gens des Filles, an Assiniboin band, for whom we were directed to make ready a feast of fresh meat, mush, and sweet coffee. As the dark-skinned Indians came forward in the glittering sunlight across the smooth surface of the frozen river—some on horseback, others on foot, accompanied by women and numbers of children, pack horses, and laden dogs—they formed a most picturesque cavalcade. As they failed to bring robes for exchange, nothing came of their bidding us to prepare a feast.

All appurtenances to flat painting have been put in order and all remaining paints that were left on the floor in the store have been put away, indicating that my duties of official painter are at an end.

February 11—Crazy Bear's band occupy only 11 tents. Bear would like to sit for his portrait but fears to take such risk. Natoh is dead, and though Mr. Denig's thumb has healed, it is a strange coincidence that such an affliction should have come upon him just at that time.

Furthermore, the coincidence was promptly misinterpreted by womankind at the fort. To be sure, Crazy Bear declares that he is not so foolish as to think my paintings exert a perilous influence, but at the same time, he has to confess that his people believe they do. Instead of painting his likeness, I drew the picture of a turtle on a piece of wood for him. Mackenzie carved it out and filled it with lead. Now the chief wears this leaden turtle around his neck for a charm, his "medicine." He dreamed of a turtle. His earlier "medicine" had failed to ward off the death of so many relatives, so he wore it no longer. If this charm proves more efficacious, he can then say whether it brings good luck.

February 12—In the Indian encampment just outside the fort, there was a fight today between two wives of one husband as to which of them was the owner of a horse. When the man saw his wives seizing each other by the hair, he took bow and arrow and shot the unoffending nag through the heart, then gave the woman who was in the wrong a good, sound thrashing. He would have been much more sensible if he had inflicted the beating without sacrificing the horse, all the more as it was the only one he possessed.

L'Ours Fou is much cast down because the Assiniboin band north of us refuses to conclude a peace with the Blackfeet tribe. Now that he is supreme chief, appointed by the United States, he thinks the Assiniboin should obey him. Those wild bands are not inclined as yet to change their condition, having no conception of the power and extent of the United States. Moreover, his appointment to the rank of supreme chief is contrary to their wishes, in violation of their right of free choice, an infringement of their liberties, and in contravention of their ancient customs. As Ours Fou can unite only the smallest of the Assiniboin bands under his leadership, his appointment as supreme chief meets with all the more opposition.

L'Ours Fou's plan, first of all, is to influence his people to establish a village as the Herantsa have done and to plant acres of corn. But Assiniboin are an idle people and easily distinguished by their indifference to appearances from the proud, gorgeously bedecked Absaroka and Sioux. So far as clothes are concerned, the Assiniboin would just as soon have his old, worn robe as a woolen blanket. He cares only for the possession of horses. He is too poverty-stricken to purchase the beasts, so he has to find those that he can steal; in other words, he must have an enemy. In the event that the Assiniboin should consent to stop their wars against the Blackfeet, the Crows would necessarily conclude a like peace, for the latter are by no means powerful enough alone to hold at bay the great Blackfeet tribe.

Without war, an Indian is no longer an Indian. War is his means of educating himself. His supreme aim in life is success in war. By nature imperious and full of energy, he finds in martial exploits his only chance to win distinction. In renouncing war, he gives up his chief life purpose; he is forced to rearrange the plan of his whole existence.

February 13—Weather so warm today that we could dispense with our open fires and revel in the genial sunshine. If this continues, my hope of hunting buffaloes, antelopes, and stags on snowshoes will not be realized. As those animals bound over the snow with their thin legs and sharp hoofs, they sink so deep into the drifts that they can easily be overtaken on snowshoes, and with no trouble at all by swift hounds.

February 22—There has been nothing new to record for a week. Weather continues fine. Time passes quickly. My studies increase in number, because I make a sketch of every little thing that I shall use later on in paintings representative of life in this region. For instance, today I made a drawing of that stuffed head of a bighorn, or Rocky Mountain sheep.

Packinaud would rather play poker with common laborers than learn English. I have given up on him. That American card game called poker enables only the rich to win, i.e., those who can always put up a higher stake, irrespective of the hand they hold. Though the poorer man may have the higher cards, even three aces, three kings, etc., and stakes everything that he possesses on the game, his opponent wins if he puts up a still higher stake than the man of lesser means. As no money is in circulation here, the gamesters stake their credit at the store; they gamble their wages or salaries. They use grains of corn to keep score.

Two Cree Indians brought more than 100 robes, for which they received a better price than is usually paid. In reality, this was due to the fact that they were previously customers of the opposition.

The Sioux have the intention of keeping the Treaty of Horseshoe Creek [1851 Fort Laramie Treaty]. At least, they are willing to try to keep it for one year, so as to find out whether they derive any benefits from it or whether it is nothing more than empty promises: white men's lies.

They have about 80 tents pitched on this side of Fort Clarke. They were visited by Assiniboin who presented 12 horses, laid stress on their ancient relationship, and insisted upon the combined tribes using the same speech. Occupying 20 tents, Assiniboin are on a visit to the Herantsa, probably to beg corn.

L'Ours Fou has already selected a site for his future village, in the vicinity of this fort as a matter of course, and not too far but that he can get the smell of sweet coffee and warm bread. He understands perfectly well that sooner or later he can no longer depend on hunting for a living, but he assumes that as chief, he is entitled to an annual supply of coffee, sugar, and meal at the expense of Uncle Sam, especially since it is beneath his dignity to work. Of course, molasses will be provided him: He dreams every night of molasses. I am of the opinion that the treacle he likes so much and dreams about is going to displace in his esteem the turtle he wears about his neck.

L'Ours Fou is friendly with me. Every time he comes to the fort, he sleeps in my room. He talks about his plan to voyage down the river with Mr. Culbertson in the spring and return on the company's steamboat, bringing back with him all the wealth of possessions promised by Uncle Sam, to distribute among his people. Woe be unto the white population if that promise is not kept. If representatives of the United States government are again guilty of false statement, their double-dealing will have become proverbial among nations in this region also.

Not long ago, L'Ours Fou was sleeping in my room as usual. He waked up every now and then during the night, tended the fire, teased the fox, smoked his pipe, and jabbed me in the ribs with the pipestem to wake me, so that I might chat with him. To entertain me, he would teach me words in his native tongue. For example, *"nuspeh"* means "ax"; *"kukusch"* (French *"cochon"*) means "swine." He had great fun teaching me the last-named word. To make me understand what animal was meant, he grunted in such perfect imitation of a hog that I laughed until tears rolled down my cheeks.

February 26—The Sioux visited me while I was sketching this afternoon. He brought two interesting drawings. He was not satisfied with my work; he could do better. Forthwith, I supplied him with drawing paper. First he made a drawing of his coup. Then, with ink, he drew a buffalo very well indeed, for a savage. In their drawings, Indians attempt to make some outstanding distinguishing feature especially prominent. For instance, in drawing the figure of a man, they stress not his form, but something distinctive in his dress that indicates his rank. Hence, they represent the human form with far less accuracy than they draw animals. Among the Indians, their manner of representing the form of man has remained so much the same for thousands of years that they look upon their accepted form as historically sacrosanct.

We must take into consideration that the human form is not represented in the same manner by all nations. To prove this, one has only to examine the different drawings of a man on horseback. In one, the man has no legs at all. In another, both legs are on that side of the horse which is in view. In still another, both legs are on the other side of the horse. Therefore, my manner of representing a rider was not at all satisfactory to the Sioux.

"But you see," he said, "a man has two legs." That the other limb was concealed by the horse's body was not the question.

In the end, I annoyed him not a little by my remark that among our people, only women ride horseback as he represented riders in his drawings.

February 29—After several chilly, lonely days, I once more have a change of conditions in my room. L'Ours Fou, his daughter, and two of his grandchildren are going to share my quarters with me until the chief departs for St. Louis with Mr. Culbertson. For the time being, I welcome their company. Since there is nothing to sketch, nothing to interest me, the hours pass so slowly just now. During these last few days, we have had a recurrence of such extremely cold weather that there is no possibility of my being able to paint, however ardent my zeal.

The storing of ice in the icehouse is our only occupation at the moment. Some of the men cut out thick blocks of ice from the river and bring them up the riverbank; others load them; a third drives the cart. I have to count the number of loads delivered at the icehouse and supervise packing the blocks. In summer, ice is indispensable for preserving fresh meat and for cooling the tepid drinking water brought from the river.

Today Bear's half-starved Assiniboin returned at last to the Lower Bourbeuse. They would have liked to be supplied with food; in that case, they would have felt quite at ease. Not a man in the camp had the least idea of going out hunting. They kept hoping that meat would be offered to them from our stores of provisions, which we purchased from them last summer.

Bear himself is much more concerned about filling his own stomach than he is about inspiring his tribesmen by his own good example to be up and doing. With backs sharply arched and tails between their legs, their emaciated dogs watched every door, every movement made, hoping for a chance to steal something to eat. Nothing was safe. Even pieces of leather that they could snatch were acceptable to them. Since I have the duty to distribute meat to the various employees, I was forced into a constant scuffle with those beasts. I was immediately surrounded if I went toward the door of the meat house. I dared not leave the door open for an instant.

Old Indian women were no better. They themselves would have suffered a beating for a piece of meat. We felt obliged to pen up all the pigs and calves, otherwise much fine skill might have been put to the test for the sake of a goodly portion of fresh veal or pork. The Assiniboin complained of our hardness of heart, especially mine. They should consider that the meat does not belong to me; furthermore, their need is a result of their own laziness. They were not employed here. They have to be made to work; sluggards deserve neither sympathy nor assistance. On the other hand, those who wish employment should never be at a loss for something to do, should never be in need of food.

For the sake of providing more space in my room for my guests, I packed my collections. Now I am ready to start on a journey at a moment's notice. I hope the three girls will bring in enough wood, so that we may keep ourselves comfortably warm.

I am glad to have some variation from everyday employment. Life at this fort has become more and more a dull routine, as less that is new or novel has presented itself for my study. There remain yet four months to live through before the steamer arrives. Am I certain of going to St. Louis? Is it not probable that Mr. Kipp still may find employment for me one more year? I am at his service; there are all sorts of things I should like to study at the Herantsa village. Even though I might not dare to make sketches except in secret, I could devote all the more time to collecting facts concerning Indian legend and tradition, religious belief, social organization, etc.

It would be most unpleasant to serve under Pierre Gareau, an unreasonable, self-conceited half-breed. The truth is, I am totally unaccustomed to taking directions from anybody. Still, I can accommodate myself to circumstances to accomplish my purposes, as I have already submitted to greater humiliations. At all events, I must get a chance to attend the hunt and take part in everything just as the others do, either here or at Fort Berthold. I must hunt the stag, the elk, perhaps the bear, wherever it may be, whatever it may cost.

TEN

March 1852

March 1—The Blackfeet call themselves Siksigisqu, i.e., Siksika.

March 2—The Queen of Sheba, as Morgan and I designate Bear's daughter, is gradually overcoming her shyness in my presence, or rather, her high-bred reserve.

She received a calico dress from Mr. Denig. Accordingly, she took off her soiled black mourning costume of dressed doeskin, exchanged her buffalo robe for a blanket indigo blue in color, and no longer always remains crouched behind her bed curtains. Mad Bear asked Mr. Denig beforehand whether his daughter was in danger of being annoyed by me. Mr. Denig assured him of the contrary, saying that I was absorbed in other matters. Besides, his daughter is old enough to know how to conduct herself properly, and if need be, to defend herself.

The old chief would be really pleased to have his beautiful daughter married to a white man who is in a position to keep him well stocked with coffee, meal, and molasses, but that would be a joy dearly bought. His daughter would have to be more richly endowed in mind and heart, as well as in beauty of form and feature, to induce a man to burden himself with a pauper family of high rank.

During the first few days, the dark-skinned princess sat behind the curtains, as if she were possessed of beauty too rare to be exposed to profane gaze. Since she sees that I pay no especial attention to her, and that I have no designs upon her, she is moved to descend from her throne of buffalo hides and take charge of household affairs at our warm fireside. She had once been married to a young brave who was killed in an Indian fray. In truth, the young widow is not distinguished for personal loveliness. She has, it is true, a finely developed figure, beautiful, pensive eyes, splendid teeth, and small hands. There are tattoo marks between her eyebrows, forming a half-moon.

It is well that my thoughts are absorbed in my studies at the moment; otherwise this association with an attractive, unguarded young widow might result quite differently. As all our traders are now provided with wives, and Morgan and I intend to leave in the spring, this young widow has little prospect of being married to any man here. Both Mr. Denig and Mackenzie made proposals earlier that were rejected by her father, because at that time, he expected a far greater number of gifts than those men offered. Times have changed.

No doubt Matoh Mito and Schitschaka [the widow] will soon find this place dull enough. There is nothing to amuse them, and our fare is neither rich nor abundant. We drink coffee without sugar and eat bread made without lard.

March 4—Le Gras brought the news from Fort Berthold that a courier had arrived there from Fort Pierre. As that is so unusual an occurrence at this time of year, Mr. Denig has high hopes that the opposition is crushed.

What a victory! What a triumph! But can it be true? This company has already put down many competitors, or else bought them out. It is still steadily extending its trade and increasing in wealth. The opposition, whom we designate as "Dobies," were employees of this company at an earlier period. Owing to some disagreement, they withdrew and combined to form a new firm. It seems that their earlier friendship—relationship in fact: the two Picottes—serves to make these two companies all the more bitter and jaundiced in their attitude toward each other. Indians know full well that when there is no competition, they are obliged to pay much more dearly for what they buy. They have good and just reasons for doing what they can to keep competition alive. As to this report, it seems to me that if Primeau, Harvey & Co. have suspended payments, they have in mind only a change of firm. Campbell of St. Louis, their principal creditor who advances their goods, would not allow the business to go to ruin.

March 6—I have just had the pleasant but most unexpected news that I may go with Morgan to the horse camp tomorrow. What glad tidings! I can sketch and hunt there to my heart's content. The only duty imposed is that I am to take charge of the camp when Morgan is absent. He supersedes Smith, because the latter fed too many Indians. Owing to Smith's forbearance, several tents were occupied with redskins all the time.

When we first get there, I can be all the more free to roam about or follow the chase, because my friend is not fit just now for much hunting and will stay in camp. What unexpected good fortune! How my heart thrills! What I most ardently desired, what I am most urgently in need of to accomplish my aims is now awaiting me. Adieu, Fort Union!

March 8—Horse camp, 12 miles from Fort Union. Morgan and I left the fort yesterday, with our bedding loaded on an ox sled driven by Tetreaux. The sky was clear; there was little snow. A sharp, cold wind was blowing, but our blood was warm. We had to adapt our gait to that of the oxen, as we were supposed to be a kind of escort accompanying the sled. Five dogs leaped about us joyously.

Smith had moved his camp to the forest when the hayfield was flooded by the Yellowstone's overflow. In order to take along enough hay for the oxen overnight, we had to go a little out of our way at that point. We were proceeding across the marsh when Morgan caught sight of a wolf in the distance and instantly gave his dogs the signal. Away went the hounds in full cry, raising a whirlwind of flying snow in their wake. We followed full-tilt to see the fun. The young greyhound was in the lead, eager to win his spurs. Then came Badger, Castor, and Bull. As soon as Kadosch got scent of the wolf's track, he lagged behind. The greyhound soon overtook his quarry and was instantly bitten on the nose, whereupon Badger seized the wolf by the leg. Bull and Castor caught him by the throat and killed him.

It was only a prairie wolf. In spite of the terrible cold, Morgan tarried long enough to flay the beast. While he was engaged with that, the dogs found another wolf and set out at once in pursuit. We called them back, however, because we dared not stray too far from our course.

When we came to the hayfield, where Tetreaux was already working, we found the flooded bottomland frozen over. The water was about a foot deep and covered with a crust of ice not thick enough to bear our weight. Consequently, we broke through at every step. We had to go forward for the distance of a mile, sinking through the ice crust into the water at every stride, a most fatiguing progress. We changed our course and blazed another trail.

We found Smith's camp four miles farther on. It was situated on this side of the *bois peinture* ("painted tree"), at the foot of the steep slope—probably the river shore in prehistoric times—at the edge of a forest below the high prairie. Though well protected from the wind, our situation afforded no view at all of the plateau where the horses were to graze. Morgan decided at once to transfer the camp to another spot. We did not pitch the tent we brought but laid it on the ground along with our bedding, brought dry wood, put together a good pile of it, and kindled a crackling fire. We found quantities of meat on a scaffold. Smith had concerned himself little about sending it to the fort.

Nearby on the height above, we found traces of several tents just recently removed. The occupants, too indolent to hunt on their own account, had lived entirely on food brought in by our huntsmen. We ate our supper with the old Spanish horse guard, then sat down beside our dogs before the blazing, crackling fire, the sparks from which swam high up among the trees. How tall the dark tree trunks seemed in the gloom of the forest! How glorious to smoke my pipe in that romantic place! What flowing fancies filled my brain, of hunts I was to follow, of studies I was to make, of pictures I was to paint! How could I ever have been able to sleep!

The others disturbed us very little with talk. The fact that we had come to relieve Smith of his post, to put a restraint on Cadotte's and Pierre's women, to buy sugar from the opposition in exchange for deerskins, to prevent Indians from consuming meat brought in by our hunters, to spur the Platte Man on to a better use of the powder and lead he borrowed, gave occasion to each of us for more or less displeasing reflections. Morgan was to put things in order. Inasmuch as he knew no French and the hunters and metifs knew no English, I was to serve as his interpreter as well as assistant.

Yesterday (Sunday) we transferred our camp to the bank of the icebound Missouri. We pitched our tents in a beautiful spot that affords an outlook over the hills, the prairie where our drove of 36 horses and mules is to graze, and a far-reaching view of the river.

We found quantities of dry wood there and brought pure river water from a hole in the ice. When we reached our chosen location, each selected the place where he wished to pitch his tent, and cleared away the snow and underbrush. While the women busied themselves dragging in their household effects, some of the men cut down dead trees and others got the tent poles ready.

As soon as the ground was cleared for a tent, pieces of bark were laid all around the place where the fire was to be built, so that the *apischimos* (raw buffalo hides), or whatever was used for bedding, would not lie directly upon the wet earth. The size of the tent was determined by the number of occupants. Accordingly, each required a larger or smaller amount of bark.

To construct a tent, three or four poles were bound together at the ends, then set up to form the first framework. Their lower ends were extended as far apart as the diameter of the tent was intended to be. In the spaces between them, other poles were added until a circular framework was formed. Then the tent cloth—made of several dressed skins sewed together, [buffalo] cow hides from which the hair had been removed—was bound fast by its upper edges to another tent pole, which was erected inside the framework and fitted in at the top where the other poles join. This awning was then pulled over the poles and fastened together with wooden pins or cords, an opening having been left at the top for the egress of smoke, and at the bottom for entrance to the tent.

Incisions were made along its lower edge through which wooden pins were driven into the ground to hold the tent cloth down. The two flaps at the top were sewed together like a pocket and weighted down by means of long, slender rods, to prevent their being blown about by the wind in such a way as to drive the smoke back into the tent. This pocket and the ends of tent poles left uncovered were frequently used by Indians to display their decorations and ornaments. An animal skin stretched between two staves was hung before the lower opening that served for a door, a most uncomfortable arrangement. One had to bend almost double to crawl through under the pelt.

The wind was blowing violently and the ground was too solidly frozen to permit our putting much faith in the wooden pins we had driven down. In order to hold it fast to the ground, we secured the awning further by weighting it with heavy boughs, even sections of tree stems. As a further precaution, we heaped up snow all around, so as to ward off the wind as much as we could. Our tents were then ready, so far as the exterior was concerned.

On the inside, we spread our beds over against the fireplace. We put up two posts nearby that were to serve for a cupboard. Higher up, about five or six feet from the ground, we extended a thick beam straight across the fireplace, made each end secure to a tent pole, and suspended another smaller one from this with a hole in the middle, over which we set our kettle. We deposited our stores of meat opposite the entrance.

From now on, the hunters are to deliver all the game they kill to us. In turn, we distribute the rations due. As a matter of course, every hunter is entitled to certain amounts that belong to him by right, according to their accepted law of the chase: for instance, the head of the animal killed, the heart, stomach, stone, unborn calves, etc.

Morgan and I occupy our tent, together with five dogs. Joe Dolores, the Spaniard, his Mandan woman, and Belhumeur live in the one next to ours. Cadotte and his Assiniboin woman live with two Assiniboin families in the third. Antoine La Pierre, the half-breed, and his family live in the fourth. Our company is made up of people differing widely as to race and lineage.

Today, Joe had a mind to impress me at once with his courage. Though he is only a horse guard, he wished me to believe that he is just as experienced in hunting and setting traps as any other man. He succeeded no better in convincing me this time, however, than when he rushed into the fort just after my arrival there with Bellangé and shouted "Blackfeet!"

I am sorry to say that today's bear hunt was all false alarms. It is true that we found a great hole made by the uprooting of a tree, in the depths of the forest on the other side of the Missouri. The mouth of this den was half covered with snow. I fired one load into it from my double-barreled gun but unearthed no bear, either vigilant or sleeping, black or grizzly. At least we saw no evidence of anything astir. But suppose an old son of a gun had rushed out to attack us? Is it likely that we should have given him a mortal wound forthwith? We stood there, ready to brave the worst.

To compensate ourselves for not having fallen victim to bruin's paws (as our foolhardy act deserved), we followed very fresh deer tracks that we discovered on our way home. After having followed the deer for a long time as noiselessly as we could along a course full of twists and turns, we were startled by two white-tailed hinds springing out of their retreat just in front of us and darting off with mad leaps over shrubs and fallen trees. We fired instantly, but without result. Joe ran after them, but I crossed the river and came back to our tent, opening a way for myself through brambles and grapevine stems with great difficulty.

Naturally, Smith is not particularly pleased about his removal from command at this camp. Now he is not permitted to go hunting whenever he likes. He must take off only the hides of the beasts he kills and keep only those portions of meat to which the hunter is entitled, leaving the rest for

Indians or wolves. Besides, he must now go hunting on foot, to spare the horses. Moreover, he has to hunt every day, unless weather conditions are altogether unfavorable. I cannot help but be grateful for his negligence, since that is the reason I am here.

March 9 (?)—This morning I went to the slope where the painted tree (bois peinture) is located to examine a trap that Joe set. I found only a magpie there. Made a sketch of the tree. It is a large cottonwood. On the trunk near the foot of it, an Indian had cut away the bark and sketched different figures in vermilion and chrome yellow on the bare wood. Because the tree stands near the trail, people passing that way have added various other figures in charcoal, verifying the proverb, "A wall is a fool's writing paper." It seems to me that the original drawing of a sun, a hand, an enclosure, and the forms of different animals were meant to record adventures on a hunt that the redskin who made the sketch experienced during one sun (day) in this forest.

March 14, Sunday—Clear weather; sunshine quite warm wherever the abominably cold northwest wind does not penetrate. Things go on as usual at our camp. Because he is unfit for active duty, Morgan has to take charge of the camp. I have better opportunity to wander about with the hunters than to sketch or write. Besides, I have covered nearly all the pages of my sketchbook on both sides, so I have to guard against making superfluous drawings, especially when so much of great importance may occur.

We have killed 16 elks and 10 deer and dispatched the meat to the fort. Though hunters have turned this region to good account already, they enable us to deliver more meat to the fort now than was sent there earlier. They are no longer allowed to slay the beasts for the sake of their hides only (hides belong to the hunter) but are required to bring the meat here on pack horses.

Hunters are not paid salaries and provided with guns and ammunition merely to go hunting for the love of the sport. They are employed to hunt in order that business at the fort may derive a profit. Morgan has appointed certain days on which the hunters always go out to shoot the game, and others on which they bring in the spoils. I am invariably on hand on such occasions and on the lookout for picturesque landscapes, views, etc. To secure the slaughtered animals from wolves, hunters hang the carcasses as high as they can on limbs of a tree, or else cover the meat with the hide of the animal in such a way as to prevent the smell of it from reaching wolves within 24 hours.

To verify their right of possession, in the event that other Indians find the game, hunters hang some article of their clothing or equipment on a pole or stake set up nearby. To drive away wolves or ravens that may approach his booty, a hunter will sometimes inflate bladders taken from the slain animals and attach them to the stake or pole. Their movements in the wind will frighten the vultures or prowling beasts. To the same end, he is said to strew gunpowder about the place where the meat is left.

If we fail to find sufficient game here to supply the fort with meat, we shall remove our camp to a region on the other side of the Yellowstone, where little hunting has been done, on account of frequent forays into that neighborhood by hostile Blackfeet. We should have the disadvantage there of being obliged to take the pack horses across two rivers, not expedient except at this time of the year, when the ice is firm.

This horse camp is likely to be maintained for some time yet, inasmuch as we can be more easily dispensed with when Bruyère and his men return to the fort. Morgan wishes to go to St. Louis with Mr. Culbertson next month, so that he may make a visit to his Scottish homeland during the summer, when he is free from duties here.

Last Thursday, Schitschaka came to see the Platte Man (Le Garçon du Fraissée). She stayed twice as long in our tent. With the desire to do something in acknowledgment of the honor, we served coffee with sugar. Later the Platte Man came to inquire whether one of us would not like to marry her. Oh, is that it? That is why she came to see us?

March 18—A cold, penetrating north wind has prevailed for several days. It makes me all the more uncomfortable, because despite every precaution, it blows directly on my bed. Besides, we are out of coffee; our only drink is ice water. The river ice is so thick now that we can no longer get drinking water from the hole we scooped out. We either have to melt ice in a kettle over the fire or let it waste away in our mouths. To make matters worse, we suffer unending thirst as a result of an enforced diet of lean, sun-dried elk meat. As a consequence, we are continually wanting to drink.

If this chill to which our bodies are subjected both internally and externally does not penetrate even the marrow of our bones, I know nothing of the human constitution. It is out of the question to get bread at this camp.

We have nothing but meat, which at this time of year is stale and tasteless enough. I have never been so tormented with thirst. Even in seasons of excessive heat, I have not suffered such intense desire for drinking water as now, in the climate of severe dry cold. Even the corn that is now and then graciously sent us from the fort serves only to inflame the stomach. We shall soon have coffee. We set as much store by the coffeepot as old wives do. If the meat had more nutriment, a broth would satisfy our appetites. The worst effect on me of this severe weather is that I see so much, so very much, that I wish to record with my brush, but it is out of the question to attempt painting in this temperature.

Yesterday, Boneau and Valette arrived here to stay for a while; Bruyère no longer has anything for them to do. Smith has to go to that winter post and hunt; all the Indians are temporarily absent from that vicinity. Finding things dull at the fort, L'Ours Fou sent for the Platte Man, whom he wishes to take with him to fetch the Gens des Filles, a society of the Assiniboin, the Girls' Band. In this wise, changes have come about in the personnel of our camp.

All my ideas revolve about one central thought: How much sketching I might be able to do if the weather were warmer. Since this excessive cold spell set in, my chief occupation has been cutting wood. We attend to everything ourselves in our tent, so that we can be alone and undisturbed.

March 21—Have been here two weeks already. All of a sudden, the weather turned warm today, real thawing weather. If the ice in the river should break up, we would be obliged to get away from this place and seek a new hunting ground. Even now, the hunters are forced to go a distance of 20 miles to find deer. That is too far, when the meat must be delivered to the fort. In the event that my studies are pretty nearly completed by the end of next month, I have decided that I shall make an effort to go with Mr. Culbertson on his trip down the river. It makes me uncomfortable in the highest degree to feel that I am a superfluous guest. Furthermore, there is no prospect of my being able to earn my livelihood in this country. Finally, the noiseless motion of a keelboat will afford me better opportunity to see wild beasts than if I were to travel on a puffing steamer.

Joe Dolores and his wife have left for the fort. The former will go to the Yellowstone to trap beaver on his own account, and the latter will remain at the fort. L'Ours Fou dropped in to see us yesterday, in passing, and smoked with me for the last time. Heartfelt leave-taking.

March 24—Owing to the sudden rise in temperature, we were obliged to change the location of our camp. We had to be constantly on the watch that the Yellowstone, flowing up from more southerly latitudes, might break its bounds at any moment where it empties into the Missouri, and overflow all the surrounding lowlands. Though our camp stood 8 feet above the ice-bound Missouri, we did not regard our situation as being safe any longer. Morgan decided on the old camping ground near the hayricks. We folded our tents, loaded our goods and chattels on pack mules, mounted horses, and rode along with the rest of the drove to that spot. We had to make a detour of 4 miles around a wide bend of the Missouri. Snow was melting everywhere; because the water had no outlet and could not be absorbed by earth still frozen, we were compelled to trudge all the way through slush.

We had the luck to find tent poles that Smith had made use of when he pitched his camp here earlier in the season. This advantage, together with that of having hay nearby, influenced Morgan to select this place. There are quantities of good firewood, but we are surrounded by water. I do not approve of this site at all.

We spent a horrible night. I lay down early under my buffalo robe and fell asleep listening to an Indian air sung by three metifs in the tent next to ours. I had been fast asleep for some time when Morgan waked me with the shout, "Water! Water!" He had been trying to make up the fire, because he wanted to fry another piece of meat. Though the wood was dry, he could not get the fire to burn. At first, he thought this was due to the dampness of the ground where the fire was built, and he removed the wood to a more elevated place in the tent, with no better result. Finally the light went out. Morgan started out of the tent and found that he was standing in water.

It was high time to save ourselves. The river had overflowed its banks and the flood had crept gradually and stealthily upon us without the least warning. He shouted at once to the singing metifs and told them to bestir themselves. We hurried to higher ground, taking with us our bedclothes, books, supplies of gunpowder, and rifles. We waded through water above our hips in one place. We left the heavy tent behind, and also our stores of meat.

The rising flood came slowly forward until it was restrained by undergrowth and thickets. We were at least an English mile from the river. In the midst of this dismal scene, lighted faintly by a crescent moon, we hurried to and fro like robbers escaping with their booty, plunging through the water with our dark forms enveloped in buffalo robes. Meanwhile, the metifs kept on singing their long-winded Chippewa song, taking no heed of our warning. They were perfectly sober. Did they continue their song in defiance of the elements?

Having reached dry ground, I bound together all my possessions of value, my sketchbook, journal, drawing materials, and put them in my much-prized calfskin pouch, which serves me regularly for a pillow.

We spread our apischimos on the ground out on the open prairie and covered ourselves with riding cloaks and buffalo robes, having first removed our wet clothes. For the first time since I left St. Joseph, I slept without my trousers, now—of all times—when the weather is cold. We lay as close together as we could, to keep each other warm. We called our dogs to lie on top of us, as usual, for the purpose of keeping guard and for warmth. Every instant scenting wolves nearby, those canines bounded off with a great outcry to fight the beasts or drive them away. They lay down on top of us again, scratching themselves and contesting one another's places. Under such restless, disquieting conditions, we were unable to sleep at all, especially in our disquieted state. Morgan and I consoled ourselves with the thought that journeys affording no adventure are worth nothing to a fellow. One must have something or other to relate afterwards, else one would not have a really comfortable feeling.

It was late in the day before we went to see about our abandoned tent. Several times we had peeped out faintheartedly from under our bed coverings, but we dared not expose ourselves to a cold, piercing wind on the prairie while we put on clothes stiff with frost. Once dressed, I strode swiftly through the water to our tent, where I found nothing to eat or drink, no meat, not anything. Then I went to the metifs' tent to dry my clothes by their fire and to get warm. It was evident that they had moved their tent to higher ground.

Morgan came on after me. During the hours in which our place was unguarded, dogs had devoured all our meat. Never in my life did black coffee have so delicious a taste, even without sugar. Never did a fire seem so glorious. In this instance, even the intense cold stood us in good stead. Ice is always preferable to mud and slush—anything but mud and mire, mud and marsh.

We were hardly through eating when we heard swans passing overhead, the first we had heard. Morgan ran out to see whether they were likely to come down anywhere near, then returned quickly for his gun and hastened away. Meanwhile, I sent Boneau and Valette to bring our roving horses together and see whether all of them were to be found. I assisted Belhumeur to pitch our new tent, where I am now writing. We have placed this one on somewhat higher ground than the other, but we are still much too near the water. Morgan distrusts wind on the open prairie, where tents are blown down frequently. After great pains and trouble, we have a good fire burning between our two beds. At last I am drying my shoes and hose while I get myself warm.

Just now, the evening sunshine feels unusually warm. We are encouraged to expect the early arrival of ducks, geese, and swans. In summer, the neighboring moor must be alive with those migratory birds, and mosquitoes and frogs, no doubt. The water now flooding that low ground is purely the result of melting snows.

March 26—Night before last, the Yellowstone overflowed its banks and poured into the Missouri with such volume that the ice layer was crushed. We were forced to remove our own tent and two others to the spot where Morgan and I had such a miserable lodging last Monday night.

This bottomland is now underwater throughout its entire length. Carrying blocks of ice, boughs, tree stems, scum and foam, the flood sweeps over it like a wild mountain stream. I hope we may be able to stay for a while in one place; this constant breaking camp and pitching tents again has become a bore. In my opinion, our present location is not well chosen. We are exposed to the full fury of prairie winds. While we have plenty of firewood conveniently near, we find it hardly feasible to snatch our fuel from this roaring flood. It is of little use and too dangerous to force our way through a stream blocked with ice and tree trunks to bring only wet, sodden wood from the forest. We have to go two miles to the nearest coulee to get wood that will really keep our fires burning. Where are we to find our game? We can easily be discovered for miles around, on the wide-open prairie. We have water in superabundance.

Morgan thinks only of shooting ducks. Loaded gun in hand, he stands gazing always southward. Only a few ducks were seen; they sneak under the willow bushes today to escape this cold southwest wind. In truth, our prospects for hunting seem rather discouraging at the moment. We have no shot either here or at the fort. I don't see how Morgan is likely to hit fowls on the wing with bullets, especially when the birds are flying singly.

The metifs are employed for a limited term, which ends on the 15th of next month; they draw their pay in horses. They now own 26 animals in this drove under our care, while only three horses and six mules remain to the company. When the metifs depart with their drove, I wonder what is going to be done with our horse camp? During the recent fearfully cold spell, an old gray horse belonging to us was nearly frozen to death. In consequence, he was unable to defend himself against wolves that gnawed away the shank of one of his hind legs. And yet the pitiable old creature still lives.

March 27—After a long hunt yesterday, Morgan came back late in the evening with only one duck. He said his failure was due to our lack of shot. Because I am on good terms with Joe Picotte, he wished I would go and try to buy some shot from him. Morgan has expressed that wish several times before, but I am unresponsive for several reasons. I despise Joe Picotte's double-dealing. Also, I am no hunter and have no need of shot for myself but wanted the supply for his competitors. Finally, [if I did go to Joe,] Mr. Denig would say at once that I went after bread and sugar, or that I was currying favor with the opposition during my absence from the fort.

Still, since Morgan has shown me so much friendliness, I ordered a horse saddled today and rode over to the adobe fort. There I found the Missouri 30 feet above its usual level and rushing by with a thunderous roar. I was told that the upper Missouri rose 20 feet yesterday in 2 hours and overflowed all the lowlands, bearing huge blocks of ice with it. Blocks of ice are piled as high as a wall in thickets and coppices on the outskirts of the forest. "The oldest inhabitants have never known the river to be so high or to rise so rapidly." The adobe fort stands 100 feet from the steep riverbank, but today the stream was sweeping by within 20 feet of the southward gate.

I was received in a most friendly manner. Joe presented me with 3 pounds of sugar, but I could not get any shot. Even though night was falling, I rode back immediately, because I had concealed something interesting on the prairie and dared take it to our camp only after dark. On my way over, I found a medicine doll lying on the trail. Such images are said to have the power to invoke spirits and also to exert curative effects on sick children. It is a stuffed doll made of the dressed skin of an animal. It is about 2 feet high and adorned with the usual ornaments children wear: bracelets and necklaces of "dove's eggs," made of blue and white porcelain. An Indian woman doctor who attends sick children lost this conjuring doll, so I dared not let the women in our camp know that it is in my possession.

It was as dark as Erebus on the prairie; I should have found my way with difficulty, except for my horse. He neighed to his comrades as they came thundering along to meet him. In the blackness of night their bodies could not be distinguished; they seemed really ghostlike. Only their resounding hoofbeats and eager neighing gave evidence of what was approaching. They might just as easily have been taken for stags, which often graze with our horses.

After a time, I detected a gleam of light in the distance, a fire burning inside a tent. At last I could guide my unwilling courser in a definite direction, he being more inclined to go roaming with his own kind. He was soon at liberty to do so, for we were again at our camp. The dogs had already scented us and came bounding forward with loud outcry. They changed their wrathful baying to joyous yelps when I called them by name.

March 28—As Morgan and I were out together on a hunt, we met the semisavage Kipland, who brought us a note from Mr. Denig. He gave us directions to remain in camp, in spite of the outbreak of the rivers, until the metifs left, or better still, until Mr. Culbertson arrived from Blackfeet territory and took us two along with him. If Mr. Denig only know how little we yearn for his society, he would not have been in such a hurry to send that message. I suppose he assumes that we are just as sensible of the want of bread as he would be in our place.

Because of a raw, cold wind, the river is again covered with ice sufficiently thick to restrain the upper current and to cake ice blocks and masses of wood together, but not firm enough to bear our weight yet. We had quite a picturesque adventure crossing the wild coulee by holding on to overhanging boughs as we clambered over huge blocks of ice. We heard La Pierre firing his gun frequently in a corner of this frozen lake that covers the upper pasture.

We hurried across the thin ice crust that spread over the prairie, breaking through at every step and causing a great deal of noise by the constant cracking of ice. Unfortunately, this attracted our dogs, who broke loose from the tent where we had confined them and came running along, too. As they were not in the right direction, their presence would only destroy our prospects for a hunt. We drove them back, but they only retreated to a certain distance and remained there, howling most dolefully.

Pretty soon we discovered two hinds, standing bewildered at the brink of the frozen river and looking anxiously toward us. On one side of them, La Pierre was firing upon a herd that had sunk through the ice crust into the water. In the rear was the treacherous ice, and Morgan and I were in front of them, with the dogs howling on the other side. Morgan took my gun, concealed himself behind a clump of bushes, and told me to go around to the other side and drive the two hinds toward him. I ran forward quickly, facing the sharp wind. The dazed animals did not scent me but remained perfectly still until I was within 20 feet of them. I put them to flight by shouting and hurling chunks of ice. I could easily have shot them, if only I had had my gun in hand. Morgan missed and the little creatures escaped. For my part, I did not grudge them their life. Then Morgan went in pursuit of his everlasting ducks, a sport that is not worth so much freezing oneself and getting one's clothing soaking wet.

I made my way through the thin ice layer to Marguerite La Pierre, who shouted across to ask that I come and lead the pack horse she had brought through the water to her father, so he might load the meat and hides. La Pierre stood far out in the river up to his knees in water, where he had slain a herd that was unable to get out of the depths. With every plunge to extricate themselves from the surrounding ice crust, the animals sank again into the streambed. I had great difficulty crossing the thin layer; I sank through repeatedly into the icy water. Still, I could not expect that girl to do such work.

When I reached La Pierre, he was already taking off the hides. Standing leg-deep in ice water, I assisted him. As soon as the horse was laden with hides, legs, shoulders, and portions of ribs, I made my way as fast as I could to the tent, for I was miserably cold and even more uncomfortable from the irritation to my skin caused by frozen trousers. I found the tent cheerless and cold; the fire had gone out. I had to return to the frozen river, snatch some tree limbs embedded there, split the wood, and build a fire again. In a short time I had a blaze that would have done credit to Hades. Such terrible cold as I was enduring was no joke. I trembled in every limb, my teeth chattered, and yet I was obliged to dry my clothes on my body. I was so numb that I thought I would like to put my arms around that fire and hug the blaze.

ELEVEN

April 1852

April 1—Since last Saturday, winter has returned with rigor: heavy snowfall, frightful cold, violent north wind. Everything seems to be working together to make our life here quite romantically miserable. In such atrocious weather as this, one would refuse to turn a dog out, to say nothing of human hunters. Accordingly, Morgan feeds the dogs better than usual and diminishes our rations from day to day. Most probably, he means to give the former less inclination to steal.

To procure wood for our fire, we have to run the risk of slipping down, perhaps falling through the treacherous ice crust at any minute, with our burden on our shoulders. Or we could wade through deep snow to the distant coulee, cut down an ash or a linden, and lug the wood to camp.

I can tell you that I was in no jocose humor yesterday morning. Upon awaking, we saw what inspired great alarm: The interior of our tent was entirely covered with snow. Everything was under snow: the vessel containing our meat broth, the fire, bedclothes, man and beast. To get out of our beds, shake off the snow, clean up the tent before we could light the fire again, thaw our meat broth and make it palatable—what a dreary outlook! Our prospects become constantly more dreary, more comfortless.

April 2—Bad news has reached us from Joe Dolores. When he arrived with his laden dogs at his destination on the Yellowstone, he found the region under water and had to turn back. Until he feels he may risk crossing on the ice, he has been lingering for several days in an Assiniboin's tent on the other side of the Missouri opposite Fort Union. That Assiniboin's tent is the only one left of five that were pitched there. The report goes that Blackfeet have killed 25 people.

The waters of the Missouri receded to their normal bounds last night. After much splitting and cracking, the ice crust finally gave way. The thick fogs have been dispersed by the sun, which now shines with more splendor and more warmth than we have recently experienced. The snow is melting fast under the sun's genial rays. Blades of grass are already protruding from the soil.

Quantities of driftwood lie in piles throughout these recently flooded lowlands. Great blocks of ice rest among the boughs of trees, where they were lodged when carried thither by the high waters. There they remain, along with other heaps of such ice blocks and snow mounds found everywhere among the undergrowth and coppices. Is the winter really at an end? Hardly. The month of April is the most unsettled of the entire year.

Dried venison and suet is our only fare. We should do pretty well, even so, if we did not suffer so dreadfully from thirst. Drinking ice-cold water chilled us to the bone. Black coffee is a rare delicacy that we drink with all the pleasure of old maids. As a rule, we have to make out with hot broth made from dried meat.

April 3—Joe Dolores is with us once more. He told us about his misadventures on the beaver hunt. In the first place, he set out on his trapping expedition one day too late and reached the Yellowstone just as the waters burst through the ice and overflowed the surrounding land. He attempted to cross in a skin canoe but found the stream so full of floating ice that he had to turn back. Even then, he was forced to abandon his boat in order to save his dogs and the travois—together with three traps—from the raging flood.

He then had to wade a long distance through breast-deep water until he reached higher ground on the prairie. Under a great elm, sheltered by a gigantic ice block lying near, he kindled a fire to dry his clothes and get himself warm. Next morning, he walked around to get a view of his situation and decide what to do. He came upon an abandoned campfire. Upon such discoveries, this question arises in one's mind: friend or foe? Dolores was unaware of Assiniboin lodges in that neighborhood, so he assumed at once that Blackfeet had recently passed that way.

Adding a handful of buckshot along with his bullet ball, he loaded his gun and went cautiously forward. Soon he caught sight of an Indian. At the instant he raised his gun and took aim, he heard the whimpering of a dog.

"Blackfeet have no dogs," he said to himself. "That man must be one of the Dakota."

With that, he stood up and greeted the Indian with the well-known words, *"Dagodeh kuna?"* (Whither, friend?) The Assiniboin was severely wounded in his left arm, which was so swollen it was all a strut. He gave Joe an account of the Blackfeet attack. The men of seven Assiniboin tents under the command of La Main Poque were hunting in the vicinity of a small lake this side of Butte des Mammelles, where they were detected by a troop of Blackfeet, who were lying in wait for the Crow Indians. At sunrise the next morning, the Blackfeet made a surprise attack on the seven tents, cut three of them asunder at once, and sent a bullet into the brain of one Assiniboin but were unable to get his scalp.

On the whole, though they had the advantage of a surprise attack from higher ground, and superior numbers, the Blackfeet seem not to have fought valiantly. They were reported to have numbered 50 men, but I do not for one moment believe that, because the casualties were so few. They killed only one warrior, one woman, and inflicted severe wounds upon 15 others. They themselves lost three men and one scalp. It is reported that after the first onslaught, they made no further combined attacks but merely kept themselves concealed within rifle range behind trees and underbrush. The Assiniboin were protected only by heaps of snow. Perhaps the Blackfeet lost courage when they found out they were attacking Assiniboin instead of Crow.

I must say that La Main Poque chose a most unfavorable situation when he camped in the bottom of that deep circular valley, shut in by hills covered with groves and thickets, while the ground surrounding his encampment was perfectly level. The women lay down flat on their stomachs and covered themselves and their papooses with buffalo robes. That is why so many of them were grazed with bullets on their heels, hinder parts, and shoulders. Bluefoot was the one and only man who did not fight, but covered himself on the ground, just as the women did.

Joe says that he saw the Blackfeet's fortified camp, which was entrenched with tree trunks. From the quantities of bones there, he concluded that the enemy had tarried a long time in ambush. If we had crossed the Yellowstone according to our plan some time ago, that band would have cost us our pack horses, if not our lives.

As far as I am concerned, witnessing such an encounter would not have been an unwelcome experience. At the same time, the thought of being crippled or made blind is far more disagreeable in prospect than the possibility of being killed suddenly. It would be a hundred times more bitter than death to be a burden to others throughout a long life. Besides, I have no desire to appear as an enemy to the Indians. Up to the present time, I have had no cause to take such an attitude.

April 7—Mild weather and substantial food has again awakened my dormant imagination. Last Sunday was indeed a dismal, lonely day. We had only tough venison to eat and precious little of that. Morgan decided to ride to the fort under the pretext of wanting shot, to give Mr. Denig the ducks he prizes so highly for his table, and to provide for our wants. I remained dejected and lonely the entire day, lying wrapped in my buffalo robe beside our fire. The weather was too cold to make the out-of-doors agreeable, and I needed to guard our belongings from La Pierre's long-fingered wife and daughter. Those two had already committed several bold thefts. One night they stole a duck that Morgan has been saving quite a while for Mr. Denig. Another time, they took the last of our parched coffee which we had powdered with a stone and hidden under my pillow.

On that occasion, I was aroused from sleep when the skin pouch containing the coffee was pulled out from under my head. I recognized Marguerite from the dress she wore. I fell asleep again immediately and was under the impression later that I had dreamed the whole thing. When the pouch was nowhere to be found, the light dawned on me. At first, both women denied that they stole the coffee. Soon afterwards, my attention was attracted by something moving outside our tent. Then I saw a "beautiful hand" thrust the purloined pouch under the awning. The older women confessed at once that she took the duck, because she claimed we did not know how to prepare it. On the dreary day of which I speak, anyone can easily understand that I found much time for reflection. I drank warm water sweetened with sugar to enliven my spirits.

On Monday, Morgan brought some select portions of dried meat taken from the *deponille* or fat layers over the ribs, some coffee in return for my money, and corn that had been soaked in lye to remove the outer covering. I could hardly get enough of the dried deponille, which was such a luxury in comparison with our daily fare of dried venison, which is all the more unpalatable at this time of year.

Today I fabricated a novel kind of shot for Morgan. At least it is something new to me, though this was probably the sort that was first used. I flattened one-pound lead bars into thin plates, cut the latter into narrow bars, from which I then struck off little cubes. I threw them into our frying pan, together with ashes and sand, and rubbed them over and over with a flat stone until those small angular pieces became round. Cadotte must also fabricate his own shot, or rather, buckshot. He takes such cubes of lead, whatever size he needs, and rounds them off in his mouth with his teeth.

Today I saw a large herd of elk grazing on the hills. With the aid of my telescope, I studied their different postures and movements for a long while.

Only a few moments ago, La Pierre brought news that he saw two Indians running on the southern side of the river; they concealed themselves the instant they saw him. Now our entire settlement is in a state of alarm. Blackfeet!

Once near Fort Union, Blackfeet Indians drove off a number of horses right under their owners' noses. Remembering that occurrence, the men here feel that our drove is no longer safe. We have loaded our guns afresh and secured the best horses and mules to stakes near the tents, and we make the dogs sleep outside. Our camp's unfavorable situation is perfectly apparent, now that it is a question of defense.

We have pitched our tents on the prairie on the slopes of what was, in early times, a high river shore. The plain below us is covered with forests and undergrowth, so dense that an enemy could actually conceal himself almost within arm's length of us. By night, our illuminated tents expose us just as certainly to their attacks. When fully armed, white men have no fear of Indians in the habit of coming near to steal.

April 9—Snow again, but snow is preferable to rain. Continual rainy weather would be the most abominable state of things that could be revisited on us: no hunting, nothing to eat, no firewood, no fire in the tent. If the downpour continued long enough, water would flow down even under the beds where we slept.

At the moment, things are not going well with our hunters. Cadotte ran a splinter into his foot, and he is lame. La Pierre is dejected because he must give up all hope of being employed at the fort. Enthusiastic and untiring on the hunt for ducks, Morgan is ruining his health standing in ice-cold water in some hiding place, and always without success. One day he shot a beautiful otter. As the animal was being carried down the swollen stream near the "bois peinture," Morgan plunged into water up to his shoulders to recover it. He lost his valuable prize, because he could not swim. Another time, wearing his horned fur cap, he enticed two dainty hinds within rifle range, but his gun misfired and the animals ran off.

When he shoots a duck, goose, or swan, they fall at some place where he cannot lay hands on them; he has no trained dog to help him. Because of such mischance, he is not in a better humor when he comes back to camp. In reality, he is a good shot but not a cool, well-trained huntsman. When he returns disappointed, he always finds fault with me, his fellow tent-dweller; either the fire is smoking, or the blaze is too strong, or the meat is underdone or cooked too long. Since he has often much to endure from my lack of skill in selecting firewood and cutting it up, I pass over such outbursts with patience.

Besides, I have everything to gain in the success of Morgan's plan to put his chief in a fine mood by sending him ducks, and win him over to granting our early release. I have now observed the manner of hunting all species of game in this part of the world, and my supply of art paper is exhausted. Why should I remain longer?

I cannot help feeling sorry for Morgan. In defiance of frigid weather, hail, ice and snow, high waters, morass, and wind, he hunts zealously the live-long day without bringing back any game at all to enliven our fireside with a roast, while Cadotte shoots enough wildfowl from his own tent to feed himself, his wife, and visitors besides. Cadotte never ruins his clothes, never tires himself out, never gets soaking wet, or numb from cold for the sake of roast duck. He laughs all the more about Morgan's ill luck.

When stalking deer, Cadotte's swift gait and endurance under such strain is truly remarkable. He can pursue the ambling elks untiringly for 20 miles and turn the curiosity of the animals, their habit of standing still and looking about, to his own advantage. However, Cadotte is now lame and must remain in camp.

April 10—Morgan and Cadotte rode together to the Lower Bourbeuse to shoot wildfowl. According to report, the birds nest there in great numbers at this season of the year. In the meantime, La Bombarde arrived from the fort to make an arrangement with Belhumeur, to convince him to go to the Red River with his family. In other words, La Bombarde is employed by Mr. Denig for another year, but his family is not included in the contract and must go. The metifs leave with their horses tomorrow. Morgan, Cadotte, the Spaniard, and I are to remain here until Mr. Culbertson arrives. We have to provide food and protection for ourselves. What La Pierre is going to "land," he himself does not know yet.

April 11—Fifth Sunday in camp; without bread. Belhumeur, Valette, and Boneau have gone, taking all the horses that belong to the metifs. Only three tents remain. Morgan and Cadotte have returned from the Bourbeuse, where they both passed a dismal night. That region is also flooded. There is waterfowl in multitudes, but after the first discharge of the guns, they flew to the other side of the stream. Without water spaniels, it was no use to kill birds. This time Morgan came home happy, because he outstripped Cadotte.

April 13—I spent another utterly miserable day yesterday. We had roast goose, so my discomfort was not due to scanty fare. We were thrown into disquiet and confusion by a frightful windstorm that howled unceasingly and swept across the prairie with a roar like distant thunder, carrying snow before it. Once more, the sunny sky became dark, and the air thick with rain, or snow, or hail. Not one of us found it possible to stand upright in the storm; it was necessary to secure the tent further by weighting down the tent cover with tree stems.

There was such a fiendish uproar that we could not understand what the other said. Incessant howling of the wind, flapping of the awning, fluttering of the cover flaps, and cracking of the tent poles made it impossible for us to be comfortable inside the tent. We were frightfully cold. We had every reason to expect that the awning would be snatched from over our heads at any moment. That actually happened to La Pierre's family in the afternoon. It was impossible to erect their lodge again in such a gale, so they came to us seeking shelter. We detest having them around because of their pilfering. We were not inclined to share goose or coffee—which came so dear—with those common womenfolk, so we sent them to Cadotte.

Antoine [La Pierre] was absent. Out of pure spite, the old woman pushed away a tree stem that we had laid on the awning to weight it down. We noticed at once what had been done and were able to prevent disaster, for the time being. In the evening, they had better success with their bad joke. Just as Morgan and I were sitting comfortably together, eating roast goose and drinking strong meat broth, a violent gust of wind lifted our tent and suddenly snatched it from over our heads. At the same instant, it drove the fire into our laps and caught up everything together in one chaotic whirl—fire, gunpowder, cloaks, clothes, and buffalo robes.

What were we to do now? It was good-by to roast goose and hot meat broth! We had to look out for our goods and chattels flying about our heads, and to exert our utmost efforts to collect them. We had to regain our fallen awning and pile tent poles upon it, put out the fire, beat sparks out of the buffalo robes, and put the gunpowder in some safe place.

There was now no alternative for us: We had to seek protection in Cadotte's tent, the only one left standing. We were so crowded together in that small space that we were obliged to sit up the whole night through and to feel heartily glad that the gale had not torn away our last refuge.

The wind fell this morning. The sky is gloriously blue, and the sunshine delightful. We pitched our tent again in a very short time, with the help of Garouille's wife and daughter. We have had a lot of practice. We only made a provisional arrangement of things, hoping to be delivered soon from this place. Life in a wigwam begins to bore me, now that I have no further incentive to make new studies and no further chance to employ myself except to keep the fire burning. Since I possess no family to enliven my fireside, I gaze into its glowing depths, solitary. My enthusiasm wanes all the more certainly under such conditions of inaction and insufferable weather, since I have nothing more to gain by remaining here. It would be much more gratifying to me now if I had taken more interest in things: for instance, in studying the different species of ducks, etc.

Morgan and I spent the entire morning drying our clothes, putting things in order, and helping each other find our belongings. I discovered my gray felt hat hanging on a far-distant bush. In the evening, we had Smith and Joe Dolores in our tent. The former brought with him a fat beaver that he had shot on the way. I could afford to pass over this opportunity to make a sketch, because he had earlier furnished me with a beaver for a model. I enjoyed the tender beaver meat, which made a fine dish. Smith gave me the tail for preservation.

The sunshine seems genial today, after such dreadful weather. Its effect is not only to send one's blood coursing through one's veins, but also to present the future as brighter, more inviting.

They say everything comes to those who wait; perhaps that is not universally true. How often I have thought that I would have to give up any hope of attaining my aims because I lacked necessary funds. How often I have been forced to suspend my studies in order to earn my bread. Now that I am in possession of the studies, I need to look forward to the fulfillment of this dream which I have treasured for 20 years.

I have completed the scientific part of my work; the aesthetic execution remains to be done yet. Up to this time, I devoted myself more to study; as yet, I have executed but few paintings. My studies in America include such a great number as well as such a various assortment that it will be no easy matter to choose what I shall paint. Where shall I begin? My head is crammed full of it all.

April 14—Very warm weather this morning, golden sunshine, clear bright blue sky. Took my sketchbook under my arm, called Schungtogetsche, our tamed wolf, and wandered over to the coulee to make a sketch. On the way I heard two cannon shots, a salvo at the fort, but in whose honor? Culbertson or Harvey? Will Mr. Culbertson come and go without taking me along with him? The time must be near at hand. I shall soon know what fate has in store.

April 15—Oh! Here I sit in a chair at the table beside the fire in my old room at the fort. Yesterday, no sooner had I replaced my journal in my skin pouch than an aging Assiniboin—his entire face blackened, with the exception of the tip of his nose—arrived at our tent and, in Morgan's absence, delivered a communication to me from Mr. Denig containing the welcome order to break camp and return, bag and baggage, man, horse, and dog, to Fort Union today. We gave the odd-looking courier something to eat and fired our guns to summon Morgan, who was lying in wait for ducks beyond the hayricks. We had to pack up, break camp, and depart this morning in most unpleasant weather. For that very reason, I left our hunting ground all the more willingly, and with no regret.

I might have withdrawn from the scene of our struggles with some reluctance had the sun shone warm, had the ground been dry, affording the prospect of one more hunt, or other interesting sketches. We faced a sharp west wind that drove forward—now rain, now snow—constantly recurring storms that made our advance slow and difficult. Smith was bitten by one of his dogs at the coulee. The riders hurried forward with the pack mules. Presently I found myself in the rear, combating the elements in company with old dame Garouille and her daughter.

Prairie and sky became blurred and indistinct under the heavy downpour of rain. Sometimes we were unable to see 20 feet ahead. Propelled by violent wind, heavy raindrops struck sharply against our faces. As ill luck would have it, my riding cloak was packed with the buffalo robes carried by a pack mule in the vanguard far ahead of us. Under such conditions, facing wind and rain, I had to walk five long miles through water that on the level and still half-frozen ground could neither flow off nor sink in, but steadily increased in depth and extent until it spread over the prairie like a vast inland lake. The nearer we came to the fort, all the more violent became the wind, all the more heavy the downpour, and all the more rapid the rise of water on the prairie.

Though we found it impossible to look far ahead through the impenetrable rain and mist, we were fortunately able to follow a path that had been made by marauders; otherwise, I could not have kept my bearings at all. Except for such weather, I was in no haste to reach the fort. I did not care to be received by Mr. Denig with the cheerful greeting: "Bread makes you stir your stumps."

On the east side of the fort, where they are protected from the raging west wind, I found a group of Assiniboin lodges occupied by La Main Poque and his wounded braves. Several Indians walked proudly about the place, parading their blackened faces, with the exception of their nose tips, as evidence of having survived a hand-to-hand combat with the Blackfeet enemy.

When I entered the mess room, I found that my fellow travelers had pretty well emptied the dishes of rice and beans. From my reflection in the mirror, I saw how thin I had grown. When I undressed, I noticed that my legs were quite stiff from prolonged exposure to cold and dampness and that my feet were badly swollen.

April 16—The old north wind still rumbles and roars as of old, but not to my dismay. It is not likely to snatch this shelter from over my head, as he blew away my tent. He cannot penetrate these thick walls and disturb my slumbers. Mr. Denig agreed to my proposal that I be released without further remuneration, if Mr. Culbertson is willing to take me along with him.

Mr. Denig presented me with a pair of snowshoes. I am in no hurry to travel down the river in such weather as this.

April 17—I made a visit to the press room to jot down the names of different wild animals in this section, for the pelts stored there provide a rather complete list of those four-footed beasts which are native here. Those found in greatest numbers are buffalo, elk, Virginia deer, antelope, gray wolf, prairie wolf, gray fox, red fox, mice; then grizzly bear, beaver, bighorn (Rocky Mountain sheep), black-tailed deer, ermine, hedgehog, muskrat, white hare, otter, marten, skunk, and cross fox.

I also came upon a wolverine's skin. Its hair is long and entirely black, except where it merges to dark brown on the underparts along the sides of the paunch; the tail is long and bushy, the head like that of a pug dog. A living animal of this species has never come under my observation. Among those whose pelts I failed to find are rabbits, squirrels, badgers, rats, black bears, and black and red wolves. Other wild creatures native here in great numbers are tortoises, raccoons, cougars, lynxes, prairie dogs, buzzards, parakeets, turkeys, doves, fireflies, and bees.

April 18—Fare thee well, Fort Union! Mr. Culbertson arrived by boat yesterday. He will take Morgan and me with him, provided we are willing to pull an oar. We shall be off tomorrow morning. Adieu, Fort Union! Farewell, ye red men! Farewell, ye wild beasts of primeval woods!

April 19—Left Fort Union at 11 this morning to begin my return journey home. My studies in this country are now completed. From this time forward, my thoughts will concentrate on painting pictures—one half of my work accomplished at middle life, and at the expense of my health.

Our keelboat provides a wooden cabin which will protect us from wind and frost. The door is in the wall toward the prow; two apertures on one side serve for portholes; a cooking stove stands near the wall at the back. Forward, at the left, is a bed for Mr. Culbertson and supplies of meat and cornmeal. The cabin has a flat roof; the pilot steers the lengthened rudder from on top of the cabin's roof. There are three benches for oarsmen in the bow; our firewood is stored under those seats.

Upon setting out, we found more people aboard than the boat could accommodate comfortably. Several Indian women took passage as far as Fort

Berthold. With the exception of Mr. Culbertson, we men had to content ourselves with the roof for our lodging place at night, during that part of the journey.

April 20—I found it hard work to steadily keep stroke with the oars. My hands were soon blistered, badly swollen, and stiff. Rowing is no joke, even for practiced Canadians, if they are required invariably to keep stroke. First I was too slow, then I was too fast. Now I plunged the oar too deeply, now I dipped the oar too lightly. Again, my oar either struck the back of the rower in front of me or else became entangled with another man's oar. Battiste Champagne was at the helm. Morgan and I, together with Hawthorn, Cadotte, Joe Dolores, and three Canadians, took turns at the oars, assisted now and then by a young Blackfeet (brother-in-law of Mr. Culbertson). Our cook was a Negro. Mr. Culbertson was in command. Sometimes he was at the wheel, sometimes pulling an oar, trying to keep himself warm by exercise. At the command, the oarsmen were relieved every twenty minutes. At night we lay to, collected quantities of wood on shore for our fire, then lay down to sleep. Very good meals, under the circumstances.

April 21—Strong contrary winds; boats moored to shore. Rested. Took a walk. My swollen feet were much in need of exercise.

April 22—We were often interrupted in our navigation today, according as the wind was stormy or calm.

April 23—Rather pleasant sailing. Cadotte killed a bighorn that had left the herd and was clambering down a steep bluff.

April 24—Cadotte and Battiste had a jolly hunt and killed a buffalo. We had to bring the meat aboard from quite a distance. We are still making our way around the Big Bend. We are often forced to stop, owing to counterwinds. I saw numbers of elks.

April 25—Beautiful weather. Rowed vigorously. Reached Fort Berthold at sunset. I found my large trunk in good order. The Indian apparel I had engaged from Bellangé, together with three handsome buffalo robes and other things besides, were all in readiness for me. I confess I was a little surprised at this. One of the robes delighted me especially: a complete buffalo skin without cut or seam and ornamented with drawings in color. I was glad to get it, even though I had received a beautiful robe made from a forest bison's hide that very day from Mr. Culbertson. I now have seven robes and two calfskins.

In exchange for his services, Bellangé received my gun and its accessories, and also other things that I no longer need. I gave him my much-valued telescope for a keepsake. Joe and the three women went ashore at Fort Berthold. Their departure enabled us to be much more comfortable, though the Canadians maintained that the more heavily laden the boat, the faster the speed. In the vicinity of the fort, I saw a great many tents occupied by Assiniboin and Absaroka.

April 26—Left Fort Berthold at sunrise. This has been the first bright, warm day we have had on our voyage. We came rapidly down the river. Stopped at Fort Clarke. While the bourgeois went to talk with Dorson, I watched a ball game played by Arikara girls. We rowed about 25 miles farther downstream, passing by great numbers of prairie fires. At this season of the year, Indians set the prairie on fire in order to remove the old, dried grass and provide room for the young, tender growth. That constitutes the Indians' total cultivation of the land they are accustomed to wander. We spent the night at the Cannon Ball River.

April 27—Again strong counterwinds. We had to moor the boat fast to shore. Morgan shot a lynx. At first we took it to be a young cougar, but the short tail and pointed ears were sufficient to identify the species. Either disquieted or bewildered by the high wind, multitudes of gulls swarmed over the surface of the river. When one sees them flying together over the water and hears the confused din of their cries, one may safely reckon on a violent gale. The wind was strong on the river but hardly noticeable on shore.

April 29—Wind—consequently rest for us. Cadotte, Battiste, and company went into a little glen sheltered from the wind, lighted a big blazing fire, lay down beside it, and went to sleep. While they slept, the dried grass about them caught fire but burned slowly, surrounding them with a circle of flame. It spread, fanned by a gust of wind, driving onward in winding curves. I followed a long way at an even gait, walking over the charred ground, springing across the flames several times, simply to find out whether prairie fires are really as dangerous as writers declare them to be. I think such conflagrations can endanger peoples' lives only when the grass is very high and there is additional brushwood or dried undergrowth. As everybody knows, green, lush grass is just as little likely to catch fire as water is. All animals, both domestic and wild, flee in terror from a prairie fire's smoke and flame.

Although the wind was rather high, the fire in the dead grass did not spread any more rapidly forward than I could easily follow without walking very fast. In facing the fire, one finds the smoke more disagreeable than the flame. At no point was the fire more than 3 feet in depth. It spread in every direction, more swiftly where the wind blew hard, for instance, up the hills and slopes, then descended more gradually on the opposite sides of those heights. It lingers longer in vales and dells, where it finds more replenishing substances but less that is dry and dead, as there is less agitation of the atmosphere.

TWELVE

May 1852

May 1—Little Cheyenne River. We find great blocks of ice here caught in the boughs of trees along the shore, where they were deposited on the outbreak of the high waters. They melt slowly, on account of their great size. On the other hand, the grass is coming out in well-sheltered nooks.

May 2—Great Cheyenne River.

May 3—We reached Fort Pierre this evening, after much exertion and strain. Throughout the day, I have seen groups of antelopes along the river's shore.

May 4—Have been held fast here at the fort the livelong day by a violent storm. Our wooden cabin was broken to pieces, so we had to put up a tent in its place. We expect warmer weather as we sail southward. We hardly see a sprig of green grass here; no foliage at all; only catkins on the willows. The gale blew with unabated fury even until the evening. After sunset there was a sudden calm, quite warm weather, and mosquitoes. Just at this time, Mr. Picotte is sick.

May 5—Left early. About 10 o'clock, we passed Campbell & Primeau's new winter trading post. Many Sioux in the section are suffering from hunger; they are now resorting to horse meat. We found the abandoned Forts Lookout and Nedeune in ruins already.

May 6—We set out again by moonlight before the break of day. Having lost so much time—owing to contrary winds—everybody is now eager to reach the United States. Mr. Culbertson would like to overtake Harvey, who is ahead of us, hastening along the same route in his skiff. I would be in no hurry at all, if I did not have to be in such a strain rowing, and if my feet were not swelling for want of exercise. We will make no more stops during the day but will keep steadily on our course until we are forced to shore by darkness. Foliage! No more blocks of ice among the boughs along the steep river shore. The first whippoorwill and turkeys.

May 7—We overtook Decoteaux, P. Sarpy's clerk from L'Eau qui Court, in his long skin boat, and got some fish from him. Once more I beheld that lovely scene at the mouth of the Basil River. I was sorry the trees were not in full leaf, as I saw them last summer. Even though destitute of foliage, this is the most beautiful part of the Missouri.

May 8—Stopped awhile opposite the Isle de Bonhomme, Schlegel's new post. Picturesque landing place, with oaks thrown over a wild brook, behind which rise precipitous bluffs.

May 9—In the forenoon, we passed Vermilion; the quarters of Bruyère the elder; Sergeant's Bluff at 12 o'clock; wood bluffs with their burning coalfields about 4 in the afternoon; Blackbird's grave at 7 o'clock. Foliage is advancing in the forests.

May 10—Big Sioux. We came upon one place in the Missouri so blocked with snags, both vertical and horizontal, that we could hardly steer our way through. I saw millions of little swallows on the bluffs. First blockhouse. Old Council Bluffs. Toward evening, we arrived at the first settlement (Mormons). The Mormons' ferry above was crowded on both sides of the river with tents, covered wagons, throngs of people, and herds of cattle, all bound for New Zion. For five dollars, I purchased a very beautiful pelt of a grizzly she-bear from one of our oarsmen; from another, I bought a Snake Indian's scalp. Slept in this keelboat for the last time.

May 11—This morning we saw the funnel of a steamboat in the distance at the landing where passengers go ashore for the inland settlement of Kanesville. Owing to the position of the boat, we saw only one smokestack. Consequently, we took it to be the *Utha*, Corby's steam ferry, which we were expecting from St. Louis. Instantly there was a unanimous hurrah; none of us had dared hope for release from rowing as early as this. However, we found that it was the *Eloira*, a vessel with two smokestacks, that had brought a great number of Mormons and their vehicles, cattle, household luggage, etc.

We thought the captain's charge for the journey to St. Louis was too high, so we waited for the *St. Paul*, which we had already sighted on its way up the river. We could get a more reasonable rate on the *St. Paul*. The captain promised to take us aboard at Belle Vue that evening. At Council Bluffs, we found a considerable part of the shore torn away. My former boardinghouse, which had stood at least a hundred feet from the river when I lived there, was now hanging over the riverbank. Had dinner in Belle Vue with my friends Decatur, Wacoma, Joseph and Mary La Fleche, and Witthae. Witthae expected that I would speak to her, but I am not the man to offer my hand once more to one who had deserted me as she had done.

At 4 o'clock we went aboard the *St. Paul*, leaving our Mackinaw boat behind. Exchanged souvenirs with Decatur, "the first man to settle in the future Nebraska territory." I gave him one of my necklaces made of bear's claws, and he gave me a pair of moccasins. I gave the first scalp I purchased to Morgan, which he accepted with great merriment, as an acknowledgment of his good comradeship.

Epilogue

From Council Bluffs to Switzerland, 1852–1871

ON MAY 11, AFTER SPENDING a last night on the keelboat, Kurz and his companions took the steamboat *St. Paul* downriver to St. Joseph, where he remained for nine days, packing his entire Indian collection, visiting old friends, and worrying about his health. During the voyage from Fort Union, his legs had begun to retain water, and he feared a return of dropsy. He wrote in his journal, "My future prospects are anything but favorable, if water continues to rise in my trusty legs."[1]

St. Louis was hot and muggy when he arrived by steamboat on May 25. He remained there most of the summer, taking long walks to improve his health. Gradually, the bloating left his legs, and he felt some relief, as evidenced in his journal: "It would be really very hard to depart this life just when I have come to the end of my period of study and have reached the point where I shall be able to begin creative work in my art."[2]

His money was running out, but he also seemed inclined to remain in America longer, if he could have found employment. Kurz lamented the situation of an artist in the unsophisticated American Middle West: "Earning my living painting houses, ships, and mural decorations, or undertaking once more the duties of a merchant's clerk, is an outlook I cannot contemplate. What is life to me without art?"[3]

Discouraged at his prospects and knowing that he would have to sell more of his hard-earned collection to afford passage to Europe, Kurz left St. Louis on August 11, 1852. Traveling variously by stagecoach, ferry, steamboat, and railroad, he arrived in New York less than two weeks later. With what must have been real dismay, he sold part of his Indian collection for $150. By August 24 he began the thirty-day voyage to Havre, France.

The crossing was difficult. From his journal description, Kurz may have been suffering from malaria, or at least a reoccurrence of the ailment. Alternating between chills, fever, sweats, and bouts of vomiting, he could sip nothing but tea, coffee, and a little broth made for him by two sympathetic Germans. In return for their kindness, he gave them most of his food. They had brought little on board, and he couldn't stomach it, anyway.

As he recorded in his journal, "I arrived at Havre half-starved, emaciated, and weak." Two days later he was home in Bern, to the surprise of his mother and sisters, who quickly assumed the task of restoring his health. Kurz's journal ended on a dismal note: "To earn my livelihood as an artist in Bern. Alas! What a prospect."[4]

In the next few years, using his sketches, watercolors, and objects remaining from his Indian collection, Kurz completed some one hundred paintings. His goal, as expressed earlier in his journal, was to create a gallery for his own vision of the West, as filtered through his classical background and his interest in primeval times. Unfortunately, an early exhibition was savaged by a critic. In an 1856 addition to his American journal, he wrote: "Audacious critics, ignorant of the subject, went so far as to contend that my pictures were not true to life—as if I would have devoted six years to a genre merely for the sake of indulging fancies in the end."[5] Always sensitive to criticism, Kurz was so distressed that he vowed never to exhibit his paintings and collection again.

His prospects for employment improved in 1855, when Kurz became art instructor at the Bern Canton School. In his monograph on Kurz, Scott Eckberg included this reminiscence by Franz Schenk, one of Kurz's pupils:

Mr. Kurz was our teacher at the Canton School, and while we practiced drawing he occasionally related his adventures in the wild west. Cooper's *Leatherstocking Tales* was our favorite book, and our thin, taciturn teacher so resembled the ideal western hunter, we swarmed to him. Once he invited us to his room on Market Street . . . in a corner was an iron bed covered with a buffalo robe, other robes were on the floor; sketches and Indian artifacts covered the walls. He let us sit on a robe and smoke Indian tobacco from an Indian pipe—we were speechless with pride. Only later did it make us sick.[6]

In one of those curious twists of life, Eckberg noted, Schenk must have taken Kurz's western vision lessons to heart. The young boy from Bern immigrated to America in 1870 and became an Indian agent for the Sioux at Fort Randall, South Dakota.

Kurz's steady employment as drawing-master gave him some measure of confidence and relieved him of his fears of unemployment: "Independent of a public composed of pedants, I determined to complete my collections of paintings from Indian life. . . . I look forward to the future with hope that, without neglecting the duties of my position, I shall be able to devote myself still further to my ideals, giving no thought to this public with its petty formalism."[7]

Along with his art instruction, Kurz painted landscapes and animals. It is these subjects, rather than his Indian depictions, that constitute his prominence in Switzerland today. As he mellowed through the years, he channeled his idealism and passion into the efforts of the Bern Artists Society, where he served on the board of directors. He proposed and encouraged the creation of an independent art school in Bern and was named its first director in 1871.

This acknowledgment of his abilities and local esteem may have given Kurz the courage to begin exploring his western themes again. However, the recognition that might have come through his more mature outlook and ability eluded him one last time. On October 16, 1871, Kurz died of an apparent heart attack while painting an oil of Indians and stampeding horses. He was only fifty-three.[8]

Today, most of Kurz's works and collections hang in museums in Bern, Switzerland. Additional art can be found at the Thomas Gilcrease Institute in Tulsa, Oklahoma; Boston's Museum of Fine Art; and smaller public and private venues worldwide.

The largest American monument to Rudolph Friederich Kurz is Fort Union Trading Post National Historic Site, located on the North Dakota–Montana border. The partial reconstruction of the trading post, which was torn down in 1867, owes much of its accuracy to information gleaned from Kurz's journal, sketches, and watercolors. No other artist or journalist who came to the Upper Missouri left more detailed proof of the events of the fur trade. What Kurz saw, lived, recorded, and sketched helped make possible Fort Union's reconstruction. Without Kurz's skillful drawings of the fort itself, there would probably be no tangible monument to the men and women of the fur trade—both Indian and white—who worked together in relative harmony for thirty-nine years. Proud, prickly, sensitive, observant Rudolph Kurz left an unparalleled visual and written record of the times, the structures, and the people. Our debt is profound.

Plates

THE ILLUSTRATIONS AND SKETCHES on the following pages come from Kurz's sketchbook, which he carried with him throughout his travels. Although some of them have a more "finished" appearance than others, Kurz's stated intention was to quickly capture scenes and faces that could later become part of paintings created in a proper studio. These sketches— done in pencil, pen and ink, and watercolor, were for future interpretation in oil, his preferred medium.

Kurz underestimated the ease of acquiring pencils and paper upriver. In several journal entries, he lamented that he had only one remaining pencil. He also fretted that the only additional paper to be found at Fort Union was lined paper, probably ledger paper. While at Fort Union, Kurz did produce some oil paintings at Edwin Denig's request. For these, he used what paint was available at the trading post, paint surely intended for less aesthetic projects.

In one of his concluding entries while at Fort Union, Kurz wrote that his writing paper was nearly gone, so he needed to use what was left sparingly and not sketch objects similar to others that he had already copied. Finally, he wrote in one poignant entry that he might as well leave the employment of the American Fur Company, because he was out of paper.

Kurz usually dated his sketches and labeled some with names and places. The plate captions in the original Bulletin 115 were probably provided by the editor, J. N. B. Hewitt. Where more information is known now than was available in 1937, I have supplemented Kurz's dates and labels and Hewitt's additions. Many of the sketches are merely figure studies of people and animals and require little additional explanation.Plates 1 through 93 are from the National Anthropological Archives, Smithsonian Institution Museum Support Center, Suitland, Maryland, accession numbers 2856-1 through 2856-95.

Pl. 1. Indian figure studies: *upper left,* July 23, 1851; *upper right,* Herantsa (Hidatsa, or Gros Ventres), July 17, 1851; *lower left,* Sioux, July 4, 1851; Herantsa (Hidatsa), July 13, 1851.

Pl. 2. Horses in motion and riders, August 17, 1851; *lower right,* round hide boat (also called a skin boat, or bullboat), August 19, 1851.

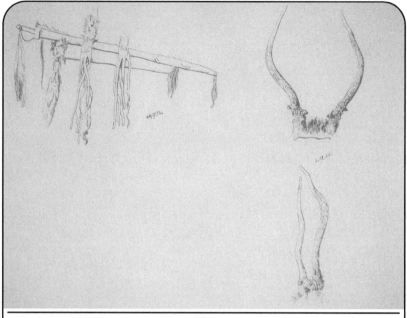

Pl. 3. *Upper left,* decorated bow and arrow cases, July 29, 1852. Because of the date, these items would have been sketched in St. Louis and were probably part of Kurz's Indian collection. *Upper right,* antlers, December 4, 1856. If the date is correct, this sketch would have been added four years after Kurz's return to Switzerland.

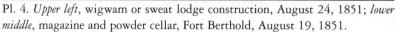

Pl. 4. *Upper left*, wigwam or sweat lodge construction, August 24, 1851; *lower middle*, magazine and powder cellar, Fort Berthold, August 19, 1851.

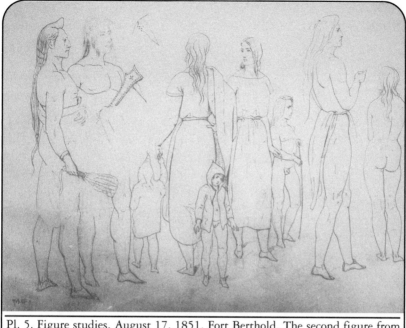

Pl. 5. Figure studies, August 17, 1851, Fort Berthold. The second figure from the left carries a war club called a *pockamogan*.

Pl. 6. Animal studies: *upper,* wolverine, February 26, 1852; *lower left,* elk, January 27, 1852; *lower right,* deer, February 9, 1852.

Pl. 7. "Swimming across Papillon Creek at the Omaha village," May 22, 1851; Kurz self-portrait.

Pl. 8. Prominent figure displays pictographs on his buffalo robe, August 2, 1851.

Pl. 9. Sketches of women and children; *lower right,* James Kipp, bourgeois at Fort Berthold, July 15, 1851.

Pl. 10. *Upper,* Omaha Indian studies, June 2, 1851; *lower,* "Overflow of the Musquaiter," May 31, 1851, Council Bluffs, Iowa. The Mosquito River flows into the Missouri River.

Pl. 11. "Returning from the Dobies' Ball," October 14, 1851. On the far left is Charles Morgan with his dogs, followed by Owen McKenzie mounted on Toku, with his wife seated behind him. Next is Rudolph Kurz, followed by Jeff Smith's wife and Denig's wife, on the same horse. This detail is found in reverse in figure 4.

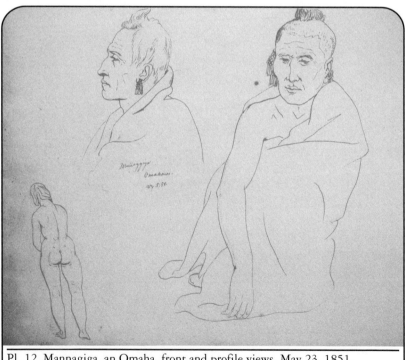

Pl. 12. Mannagiga, an Omaha, front and profile views, May 23, 1851.

Pl. 13. *Top left and top center*, Alexander Culbertson, bourgeois of Fort Benton, November 11, 1851; *top, left of center*, L'Ours Fou; *top right and below*, La Bombarde family, métis from the Red River Valley, November 9, 1851; *center*, Denig's cariole, November 27, 1851; *bottom*, sled, November 23, 1851.

Pl. 14. *Upper center*, Durham ox in harness, October 30, 1851; *upper right*, headdress; *lower*, women in European clothing.

Pl. 15. *Top,* "Mouth of the Big Platte," Nebraska. Niobrara. *Bottom,* Mus-lú-la and Wik-wi-la, Omaha Indians, May 23, 1851.

Pl. 16. Herantsa (Hidatsa or Gros Ventres) at Fort Berthold, August 1, 1851.

Pl. 17. *Top left,* chest tattoo; *top right,* Cree, December 17, 1851; *bottom,* horse herd and Indian handler.

Pl. 18. Horse with Crow saddle, October 5, 1851.

Pl. 19. *Top left,* Crows, November 29, 1851; *top right,* Crow women, with elk-tooth ornamentation on dress, January 7, 1852; *bottom,* pony with winter coat, January 23, 1852.

Pl. 20. Ring-and-spear game players, August 8, 1851, Fort Berthold.

Pl. 21. Californians, with Council Bluffs in the background, May 18, 1851.

Pl. 22. Self-portrait of the artist carrying his sketchbook, August 26, 1851.

Pl. 23. *Top left,* Herantsa (Hidatsa); *top center,* Badger, a dog belonging to Charles Morgan; *middle,* Cedar Island, Nebraska Territory, June 27, 1851; *bottom,* incidental studies.

Pl. 24. Two views of Fashion, Kurz's favorite horse (which he sold when he went up river), August 31, 1850. Man wearing decorated robe and woman.

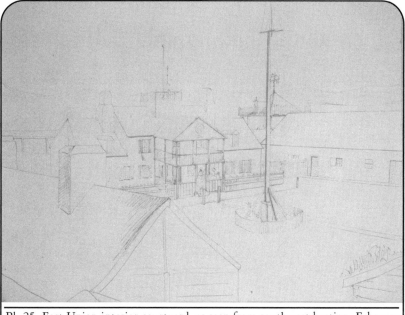

Pl. 25. Fort Union interior courtyard, as seen from southwest bastion, February 4, 1852. The long, single-story building on the right is the store range.

Pl. 26. *Left,* La Queue Rouge, August 20, 1851; *right,* horse and rider studies, August 21, 1851, Fort Berthold.

Pl. 27. *Top,* horse and rider studies, October 13, 1851; *center,* bullboats crossing the river with swimming horse; *bottom,* Herantsa (Hidatsa) with horses, August 23, 1851.

Pl. 28. Herding horses, August 23, 1851.

Pl. 29. Indian—possibly La Longue (or Grande) Chevelure—wearing *habits de Cheffre,* a European coat of military cut, August 1851.

Pl. 30. Probably Chief White Cloud, Iowa, December 19, 1850.

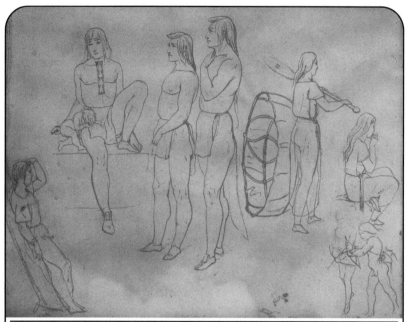

Pl. 31. *Left, center, and far right,* sketches of Herantsa (Hidatsa) at Fort Berthold, July 23, 1851; *right,* woman with bullboat and paddle; *lower right,* Indian boys shooting at frogs, August 1851.

Pl. 32. Medicine bags of La Queue Rouge (left) and Tête Jaune (right), August 29, 1851; *lower,* Mackinaw boat. Typically, these boats were built at the trading posts, loaded with packs of buffalo robes and other hides and pelts, and steered downriver to St. Louis.

Pl. 33. Fort Union, September 7, 1851.

Pl. 34. *Top,* Arikara at Fort Clarke (Clark); *bottom,* young girls' dance, July 13, 1851.

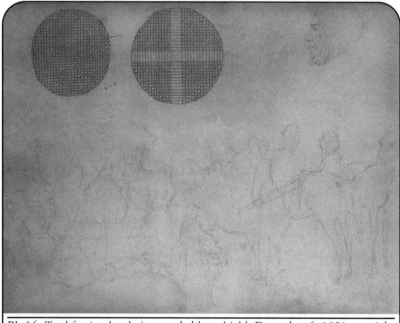

Pl. 35. *Left,* Omaha horseman; *right,* dog travois with faint sketch of Belhumeur, métis at a winter horse camp near Fort Union.

Pl. 36. *Top left,* circular design, probably a shield, December 6, 1851; *top right,* Edwin Denig; *bottom,* Cree with horses and travois.

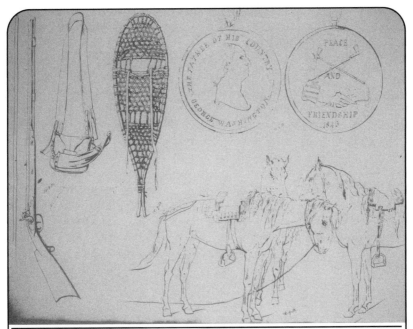

Pl. 37. *Top*, landscape below Fort Clarke (Clark), July 8, 1851; *bottom*, horse guard at Fort Berthold.

Pl. 38. *Top, left to right:* Edwin Denig's rifle, powderhorn and pouch, and snow-shoe, September 14 and 15, 1851; *top right*, peace medals, September 24, 1851; *bottom right*, saddled horses, September 26, 1851.

Pl. 39. "Trading Post for the Omahaws," labeled P. A. Sarpy, Belle Vue, May 16, 1851.

Pl. 40. *Top left,* "Mandan," July 12, 1851; *top right and bottom,* crossing the river on bullboats.

Pl. 41. Potawatomi on horseback, May 21, 1851.

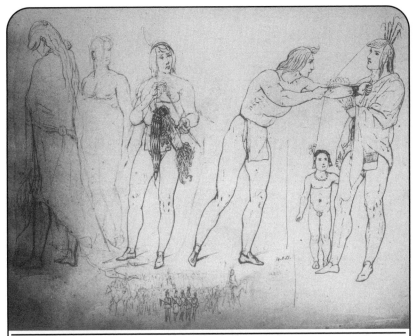

Pl. 42. *Top,* male figure studies, Aubust 4 and 14, 1851; *bottom,* Sauteurs (Chippewa or Ojibwa) coming to trade.

Pl. 43. *Left and far right,* female figure studies; *center,* Herantsa (Hidatsa) ring-and-spear game players, August 5, 1851.

Pl. 44. Animal sketches: *top right,* dog, March 12, 1852; *center,* saddled Blackfeet pony, February 15, 1852; *lower left,* fox; *bottom right,* dog.

Pl. 45. *Left, top and bottom,* figure studies; *top center,* La Bombarde, February 18, 1852; *right,* Herantsa (Hidatsa) cutting up a drowned bison; *bottom center,* Sauteurs (Chippewa) woman, July 27, 1851; *bottom right,* Herantsa (Hidatsa) woman.

Pl. 46. Omaha warrior and mixed-blood with horses.

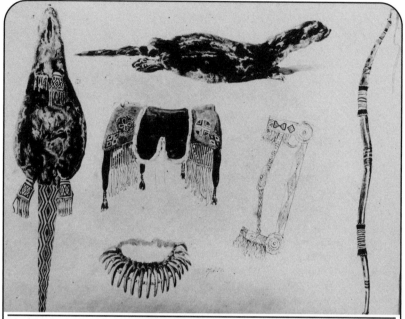

Pl. 47. This page of the sketchbook is dated June 27, 1852, after Kurz returned to St. Louis. Kurz recorded in his journal that he had to sell part of his Indian artifact collection to travel home. Before he did so, he must have painted or sketched these objects. *Top center,* live or stuffed river otter, probably the latter; *left to right,* otter-hide medicine pouch, saddle blanket, quiver, ceremonial bow; *bottom,* bear-claw necklace.

Pl. 48. Various Indian and animal studies, July 7 and 16, 1851.

Pl. 49. *Left,* horsemen, August 6, 1851; *right,* ring-and-spear game players, August 7, 1851; *bottom,* scenes from ring-and-spear game.

Pl. 50. Oto Indians with a boat, May 15, 1851.

Pl. 51. *Top, left to right:* figure wrapped in blanket, August 10, 1851; Pierre Gareau, clerk at Fort Berthold; Indian face in profile, August 13, 1851. *Bottom,* view of the Missouri River bottomlands from Fort Berthold, July 23, 1851.

Pl. 52. *Top,* Crow bags and medallion, December 27, 1851; *bottom,* Iowa woman and saddled horse.

Pl. 53. The packet boat *St. Ange,* July 2, 1851; top right, skin boat (bullboat).

Pl. 54. Mandan horsemen, July 14, 1851; *right,* James Kipp.

Pl. 55. *Top left,* woman with burden basket; *center and lower,* horse and rider studies, July 15, 1851; *top right,* Le Serpent Noir (Black Snake), July 16, 1851.

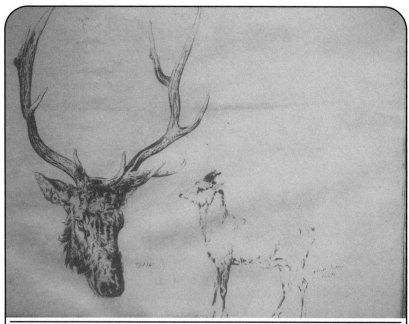

Pl. 56. *Left,* elk, January 27, 1852; *right,* female bighorn sheep, February 22, 1852.

Pl. 57. Herantsa (Hidatsa) riders and apparel, July 12, 1851.

Pl. 58. *Top row,* sketched faces of Herantsa (Hidatsa): *far left,* Corbeau (Raven), August 7, 1851; *center,* horseman driving herd, July 14, 1851.

Pl. 59. Cree, July 23, 1851.

Pl. 60. *Top,* horses at the river, with bullboat; *bottom left,* woman with burden basket; *bottom right,* removing a saddle, July 22, 1851.

Pl. 61. Herantsa (Hidatsa) figure studies and sketches, July 1851.

Pl. 62. *Left and left of center,* Herantsa (Hidatsa) figure studies, July 23 and 24, 1851; *right of center,* Cree woman; *far right,* Herantsa (Hidatsa) warriors, August 23, 1851.

Pl. 63. Engagés led by fur trader, August 28, 1851.

Pl. 64. *Top center,* L'Ours Fou, December 8, 1851; *right center,* Waaschamani, second chief of the Omaha, June 9, 1851; *bottom left,* Wakusche, an Omaha, June 8, 1851; *bottom right,* faces in profile, June 9, 1851.

Pl. 65. *Left,* Herantsa mourning, shown wearing stripes of white clay; *right,* river crossing, July 17, 1851.

Pl. 66. *Top left,* Assiniboine song, September 9, 1851; *center,* self-portrait of Kurz with horse, October 1850; *right,* figure of Indian man.

Pl. 67. *Top row,* sketches of faces; *left two,* Assiniboine, December 3, 1851; *center,* Pellott; *right center,* L'Ours Fou; *right,* Cadotte, a Fort Union hunter. *Center left,* a calumet; *bottom,* Cree figures, December 8, 1851.

Pl. 68. *Top right,* Assiniboine, November 16, 1851; *center,* Charles Martin, a Fort Union employee.

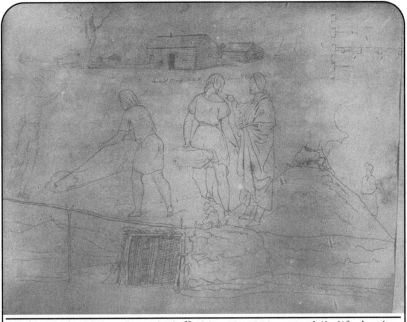

Pl. 69, *Top,* buildings, Council Bluffs, May 19, 1851; *center,* daily life sketches, May 26, 1851; *bottom,* earthen lodge.

Pl. 70. *Left,* Indian artist, May 9, 1851; *center and right,* women and children; *bottom,* dogs, May 10, 1851.

Pl. 71. *Top, left to right:* Sioux, May 25, 1851; engagé; trader, June 1851; Guyotte; Canadian engagé, May 26, 1851. *Bottom, left to right:* buildings at Council Bluffs; Lambert; Herantsa (Hidatsa) woman.

Pl. 72. *Center,* buildings at Council Bluffs, May 19, 1851; *bottom,* sketches of faces, labeled as Cree, July 28, 1851.

Pl. 73. *Upper left,* woman, November 13, 1851; river crossing at Fort Berthold, July 13, 1851.

Pl. 74. *Left,* Young Elk, chief of the Omaha; *right,* Omaha man, May 5, 1851.

Pl. 75. *Top left,* Tamegache, son of Washinga Saba, who is called Young Elk, June 11, 1851; *top right,* Dakota woman, June 24, 1851; *far right, at top and center,* W. (Honoré) Picotte and his Indian wife; *right of center,* seated Omaha women; *bottom left,* Captain La Barge of the *St. Agne,* July 7, 1851; *bottom center,* Père Pierre Jean De Smet.

Pl. 76. *Left,* warrior with hafted stone tomahawk, August 20, 1851; *right,* Indian studies.

Pl. 77. "Bellangé [and R. F. Kurz], from Fort Berthold to Fort Union," September 7, 1851.

Pl. 78. *Top,* figure sketches; *bottom,* Omaha village, May 20, 1851.

Pl. 79. *Top left,* Charles Morgan, September 13, 1851; *top, left of center,* Four Rivers, Absaroka, November 25, 1851; *bottom left,* oxen and covered wagon; *right,* nude study.

Pl. 80. *Top left,* horse and rider; *bottom left and top right,* faces, August 16, 1851; *right,* Long Hair (La Longue Chevelure, or La Grande Chevelure), carring a turkey-wing fan, August 15, 1851.

Pl. 81. Crossing at Council Bluffs, May 19, 1851.

Pl. 82. Fort Pierre, July 5, 1851.

Pl. 83. Rudolph F. Kurz and Iowas, March 20, 1851.

Pl. 84. *Top right,* Bull and Badger, Charles Morgan's dogs, October 10, 1851; *left,* outline of earthen lodge and crowd.

Pl. 85. Interior view of Omaha earthen lodge, May 16, 1851.

Pl. 86. Oto camp below mouth of the Big Platte, May 13, 1851.

Pl. 87. Two young braves returning with their first scalps, July 16, 1851, Fort Berthold. Their faces—with the exception of their noses, which are painted white—are blackened to indicate the counting of a coup.

Pl. 88. Faces: *center,* July 22, 1851; upper right, August 1, 1851; *lower left,* Gros Ventres, July 12, 1851. *Lower right,* "Below Fort Pierre at Garden Island," July 1, 1851.

Pl. 89. *Top,* figure studies; *bottom,* Omaha village, May 24, 1851.

Pl. 90. *Left,* mourning women at burial scaffold, July 28 and August 30, 1851; *right,* man and woman with horses.

Pl. 91. *Top left,* horse, February 16, 1851; *top right,* ox yoke, February 19, 1852; *right center,* Sauteur (Chippewa) snowshoe construction; *bottom,* métis with dog travois.

Pl. 92. Figure studies, August 3, 1851, Fort Berthold.

Pl. 93. Absaroka (Crow), probably Chief Rottentail, October 26, 1851.

Notes

PROLOGUE: FROM SWITZERLAND TO COUNCIL BLUFFS, 1851

1. Kurz, *Journal,* 1.
2. Ibid., 2.
3. Ibid., 2.
4. Ibid., 138.
5. Ibid., 4.
6. Eckberg, "Rudolf F. Kurz at Fort Union," 4.
7. Kurz, *Journal,* 64.

CHAPTER ONE: JUNE 1851

1. Kurz alone refers to Honoré Picotte as William. In other accounts Honoré Picotte is also called Henri. French Canadian by birth, Honoré Picotte came to the United States following the merger of the North West Company and Hudson's Bay Company. He was a partner in the Columbia Fur Company with Kenneth McKenzie, then partnered Pierre D. Papin in the French Fur Company. The American Fur Company bought out the French Fur Company in 1830 and hired Picotte. He served as the company's agent for the Lower Missouri Outfit, which included Fort Pierre, Fort Lookout, Fort Vermilion, Fort Clark, and Fort Berthold. See Hafen, *Mountain Men and the Fur Trade*, vols. I, 304–305; II, 218, 294; VIII, 62–63; IX, 105, 110, 292–93, 309, 310, 312, 316–17.

2. Alexander Culbertson, one of the most widely known and respected fur traders on the Upper Missouri, was born in Chambersburg, Pennsylvania, in 1809. He went upriver in 1833 as an employee of the Upper Missouri Outfit of the Western Department of the American Fur Company. Early on, he traveled beyond Fort Union to Fort McKenzie; he later built Fort Benton. His diplomacy with the Blackfeet earned their trading loyalty and brought that touchy nation into the American Fur Company fold. In addition, he served as bourgeois at Fort John (Laramie) and Fort Union. His prestige and value with the company earned him a share of the profits and a position as overall manager of trading posts on the Upper Missouri. Culbertson led the delegation of Upper Missouri tribes to the Fort Laramie treaty conference in 1851. Retiring from the fur trade in 1857, he engaged in several business schemes that left him nearly penniless. He died in 1879 in Orleans, Nebraska.

See Wischmann, *Frontier Diplomats;* Chittenden, *American Fur Trade of the Far West*, vol. I, 388; and Mattison, "Alexander Culbertson," in Hafen, *Mountain Men and the Fur Trade*, vol. I, 253–56.

3. Kurz wrote earlier in his journal that Decatur was a nephew and namesake of the famous Commodore Stephen Decatur.

4. Fauquicourt is a misspelling (by either Kurz or his translator) of L'Eau qui Court, an early name for the Niobrara River. Kurz also incorrectly listed the Pima as trading at the post on L'Eau qui Court; it was the Ponca who traded there.

5. The Robidoux family was well known in the fur trade, in part because there were so many of them. At least four Josephs are recorded, adding to the confusion. The Joseph in this story refers to the St. Louis patriarch and entrepreneur, whose younger brothers, sons, and nephews ranged across the West as independent traders, much to the irritation of the powerful St. Louis trading families. This Joseph—rival to Manuel Lisa—was born in St. Louis on August 10, 1783, and died in 1868 in St. Joseph, Missouri. Although Robidoux made some fur-trading trips, he principally served as the businessman who organized the expeditions of his numerous family. He settled in St. Joseph, perhaps as early as 1825. The town was officially incorporated in 1845 and named after his patron saint. "St. Joe" became known in the late 1840s and 1850s as the jumping-off place for travelers on the Oregon and Santa Fe trails. See Mattes, "Joseph Robidoux," in Hafen, *Mountain Men and the Fur Trade*, vol. VIII, 287–314.

6. Manuel Lisa (1772–1820) was a shrewd opportunist, a consummate entrepreneur, a successful government agent among the upriver Indians during the War of 1812, and an early fur trade visionary. Born in New Orleans of Spanish parents, Lisa saw the potential for fortunes to be made in fur. He spent his life enthusiastically engaged in the pursuit of wealth. Although he made many enemies, he also knew more than most of them about the Upper Missouri, the Rocky Mountains, and the Indians of the region. Lisa saw the value of keeping the Missouri River open, safe, and profitable for fur traders. He envisioned groups of white trappers contracted to established trading posts, finding fortunes in the mountains for their companies. See Oglesby, "Manuel Lisa," in Hafen, *Mountain Men and the Fur Trade*, vol. V, 179–201.

7. Kurz was probably referring to Christian Hoecken, a Jesuit missionary priest who baptized François Chardon's second Sioux wife, Marguerite Maria, at Fort Clark in 1840. See Chardon, *Chardon's Journal at Fort Clark, 1834–1839*, xliii.

8. The well-known peripatetic Jesuit priest Pierre Jean De Smet (1801–1873) was born in Belgium and spent five decades on the American frontier. No missionary was more respected or better received by native peoples than Père De Smet. No one knew the Indians of the Rockies and northern plains better than De Smet, and probably no one loved them more. See Carriker, *Father Peter John De Smet;* and Pfaller, *Father De Smet in Dakota*.

9. Two Fort Vermillions are known to have existed. The first, commonly known as Dickson's Post, was a Columbia Fur Company trading fort built in 1822 by William Dickson, a mixed-blood. It was located on the Missouri River halfway between the James and Vermillion rivers. The American Fur Company absorbed this post in 1835 and ran it until

1850. Fort Vermillion No. Two, also an AFC post, was built in 1833 and abandoned in 1851. It was located between present-day Elk Point and Vermillion, South Dakota. Number Two was probably the post where the Prussian trader Schlegel boarded the *St. Ange*. Schlegel was put ashore sixty miles farther upstream to build a post at Isle de Bonhomme. See Roberts, *Encyclopedia of Historic Forts*, 734–35.

10. There were four Fort Lookouts, located approximately ten to twelve miles above present-day Chamberlain, South Dakota. The first was a palisaded structure built in 1822 by the American Fur Company and abandoned in 1825. Fort Lookout No. Two was built in 1831. It was also known as French Post and, by 1851, when Kurz would have seen it, as La Barge's Post, after the steamboat captains, John and Joseph La Barge. Fort Lookout No. Three was built closer to the first one. Number Four was established in 1856 as a military post and abandoned less than a year later. See Roberts, *Encyclopedia of Historic Forts*, 730–31.

CHAPTER TWO: JULY 1851

1. John James Audubon, the nineteenth-century artist/naturalist, traveled upriver in 1843 with his entourage in preparation of his final work, *Viviparous Quadrupeds of North America*. He arrived at Fort Union in June 1843 and with his party spent the next two months hunting specimens and drawing them. He left Fort Union in August. Boehme, *John James Audubon in the West*, 35–65; see also McDermott, *Audubon in the West*, 3–19.

2. John Bachman, a longtime friend of Audubon's, was the pastor of St. John's Lutheran Church in Charleston, South Carolina, and a gifted amateur naturalist. He served as scientific advisor for *Viviparous Quadrupeds* but did not go upriver with Audubon. See Peck, "Audubon and Bachman: A Collaboration in Science," in Boehme, *John James Audubon in the West*, 71–115.

3. Fort Pierre was built in 1831 by the American Fur Company and named for Pierre Chouteau, Jr. It replaced Fort Tecumseh, an earlier trading post abandoned because of its proximity to the meandering Missouri River. See Schuler, *Fort Pierre Chouteau*.

4. Fort Clark was built by James Kipp in 1831 for the purpose of engaging in the Mandan/Hidatsa (and later Arikara) trade. It was located on the west side of the Missouri River, eight miles below the mouth of the Knife River. It was abandoned in 1851. See Mattison, "Kenneth McKenzie," in Hafen, *Mountain Men and the Fur Trade,* vol. II, 221, and vol. IV, 210–11; and Roberts, *Encyclopedia of Historic Forts*, 629.

5. The Mandan and Hidatsa, earth-lodge people living along the Missouri River, were devastated by the 1837 smallpox epidemic. See Dollar, "High Plains Smallpox Epidemic of 1837–1838," 15–38; and Ferch, "Fighting the Smallpox Epidemic of 1837–38," 2–7, 4–8 (two installments).

6. Prince Maximilian of Wied-Neuwied (1782–1867) was a German scholar-scientist. Interested in literally everything, Prince Maximilian traveled extensively in Europe and then in Brazil, documenting and sketching plants and animals and the cultural life of the natives. In 1832, accompanied by the equally remarkable Karl Bodmer, he went to America and spent twenty-eight months there. He journeyed as far west as northern Montana and spent significant time at American Fur Company trading posts, among them Fort Clark and Fort Union. His book, *Travels in the Interior of North America during the Years*

1832–1834, contained both his observations and Bodmer's stunning paintings. See Schierle, "The Fascination and Reality of Native American Cultures," in Maximilian Prince of Wied, *Travels in the Interior of North America*, 16–35.

7. Johann Karl Bodmer was born in Riesbach, Switzerland, in 1809. He studied art in Paris, and his landscape work came to the attention of Prince Maximilian, who invited the young artist to accompany him to North America in 1832. Bodmer's eighty-one paintings illustrated Maximilian's two-volume travel narrative. Kurz was an admirer of Bodmer, a fellow Swiss, and likely met him in Paris, where Bodmer lived and worked. See McCracken, *Great Painters and Illustrators of the Old West*, 72–76; and Maximilian, *Travels in the Interior of North America*, 263.

8. Fort Berthold was built in 1845 by François Chardon, primarily for the Hidatsa, and named for Bartholomew Berthold, of the influential St. Louis trading family. Berthold, Pratte, Chouteau, and Cabanné formed the nucleus of French-American families who controlled the Upper Missouri trade before the American Fur Company challenged their monopoly through Ramsay Crooks' marriage into the Pratte family. See Mattison, "François A. Chardon," in Hafen, *Mountain Men and the Fur Trade*, vol. I, 225–27.

9. Born near Montreal in 1788, James Kipp was in the Upper Missouri region by 1818. Kipp established a reputation as a builder of trading posts and became a well-known veteran of the fur trade. At one time or other, he managed most of the trading posts on the Upper Missouri. He was early on associated with the Columbia Fur Company, which came into the fold of the Western Department of the American Fur Company and was renamed the Upper Missouri Outfit. Kipp retired about 1865 and died on his Missouri farm in 1880. See Mattison, "James Kipp," in Hafen, *Mountain Men and the Fur Trade*, vol. II, 201–205.

10. I could find no information about Fort Medicine.

11. David Dawson Mitchell was an agent for the Upper Missouri Outfit of the American Fur Company, serving as bourgeois of various trading posts, including Fort Union. In 1841, Mitchell was appointed superintendent of Indian affairs. In this capacity, he participated in the Fort Laramie Treaty of 1851. See Mattison, "David Dawson Mitchell," in Hafen, *Mountain Men and the Fur Trade*, vol. II, 241–46.

12. Kurz is referring to Zephir Rencontre, a veteran employee of Fort Union. Barbour, *Fort Union and the Upper Missouri Fur Trade*, 144.

13. In 1812, Thomas Douglas, Fifth Earl of Selkirk, began the transplantation of nearly one thousand Scots settlers into a huge land grant awarded him by Hudson's Bay Company, comprising parts of what is now Manitoba, North Dakota, and Minnesota. Selkirk's hardy colonists suffered through years of crop failures and violence by métis and proponents of the rival North West Company. Selkirk's colony was largely successful; a direct result of the venture was absorption of the North West Company by Hudson's Bay Company. See Ross, *Red River Settlement*; and Newman, *Caesars of the Wilderness*.

CHAPTER THREE: AUGUST 1851

1. Fort William, an opposition fort at the mouth of the Yellowstone River, should not be confused with an earlier Fort William built by William Campbell and Robert Sublette.

Those men were bought out by the American Fur Company in 1834, and the fort was dismantled, with a portion of it moved close to the east side of Fort Union for use as corrals. The Fort William that Kurz knew in 1851, also an opposition fort, was operated by Harvey, Primeau and Company, with financial backing from Robert Campbell. It was built within the adobe remains of the Union Fur Company's old Fort Mortimer, another earlier opposition post. See Barbour, *Fort Union and the Upper Missouri Fur Trade*, 60. See also Sunder, *The Fur Trade on the Upper Missouri*, 1840–1865, 163–65.

2. In the late summer and early fall of 1851, Fort Laramie was the scene of the first major treaty between the U.S. government and northern plains tribes. The purpose of the treaty was to establish tribal boundaries, permit safe passage of Euro-Americans through Indian land, and curtail intertribal warfare. It is sometimes called the Horse Creek Treaty. See Hafen and Young, *Fort Laramie and the Pageant of the West, 1834–1890*, 177–96.

3. Tedding hay is to spread it out to dry.

4. Artist George Catlin recounted the myth of Prince Madoc of North Wales, who set sail in the fourteenth century with ten ships and crossed the Atlantic Ocean. According to legend, Madoc and his followers eventually settled up the Missouri River and became the founders of the Mandan Nation. See Catlin, *Letters and Notes*, 2:259.

5. Raymond DeMallie and Doug Parks of Indiana University suggest that "banneret" is a form of Panani/Panana, the Sioux-Assiniboine name for Arikara. The word appears in other Upper Missouri accounts and may have assumed generic status among whites to mean a young Indian not old enough to go on war parties. The word "banneret" is an obscure word describing a knight, which would fit the military metaphor.

CHAPTER FOUR: SEPTEMBER 1851

1. The rendering of these French lines into English has been supplied by the editor, J. N. B. Hewitt.

2. This may be a reference to Fort Floyd, where Kenneth McKenzie traded. Different accounts put Fort Floyd at different locations. In 1828, McKenzie constructed Fort Union on the Missouri River, where he became known as "King of the Upper Missouri." See Thompson, *Fort Union Trading Post*, 10–11.

3. An earlier name for the Little Missouri River.

4. Joseph Picotte was a nephew of Honoré Picotte. As bourgeois of Fort William, Joe Picotte was in partnership with Alexander Harvey and Charles Primeau. Harvey, Primeau, and Company remained in active opposition to Fort Union for eight years, the longest of any opposition post. Although in fierce competition with each other, the proprietors of Fort Union and Fort William carried on a wary social life that included dinners and dances. See Mattison, "Alexander Harvey," in Hafen, *Mountain Men and the Fur Trade*, vol. IV, 121–22.

5. Edwin Thompson Denig was born in Pennsylvania in 1812 and entered the fur trade in 1833, going upriver to Fort Union as a clerk. He became bourgeois in 1848. An advantageous marriage to Deer Little Woman, daughter of the Assiniboine chief Iron Arrow Point, gave Denig important status among the Assiniboine, Fort Union's chief trading partners. Denig was a careful student of the culture he lived among. His work, *Indian Tribes of the*

Upper Missouri, was the result of a request from Henry R. Schoolcraft, who was commissioned by the secretary of war to compile a report on Indian tribes in the United States. See Miller's new introduction to Denig, *The Assiniboine*, ix–xxi.

6. Owen McKenzie was the son of Kenneth McKenzie and an Assiniboine woman. He was born and raised at Fort Union and remained there when his father went downriver to St. Louis. Well known and popular among his Fort Union peers, McKenzie was a crack shot and an excellent buffalo hunter. He was killed in 1862 or 1863 near the Milk River by Malcolm Clarke during an argument. In his journal, Kurz spelled the family name as "Mackenzie," which is incorrect. See Larpenteur, *Forty Years a Fur Trader*, 298.

7. That is, Buanig, not "eater," in Chippewa (J. N. B. Hewitt).

8. Kurz is probably referring to Denig's brother-in-law, The Light, or Wi-jun-jon, an older brother of Denig's wife Deer Little Woman. George Catlin painted The Light's portrait before his trip to Washington, D.C., in 1832 and after his return, when he was thoroughly Americanized. See Catlin, *Letters and Notes*, 2:194–200. See also Ewers, *Indian Life on the Upper Missouri*, 75–90.

CHAPTER FIVE: OCTOBER 1851

1. "Métis" is the accepted spelling today.

2. Jean Baptiste Moncravie (1797–1885), a native of France, was clerking at Fort Union by 1833. An artist in his own right, Moncravie illustrated the portal painting over Fort Union's south gate. He also painted good-conduct certificates, encouraging Indians to be kind to traders, who would keep tobacco in their pipes. See Ewers, *Plains Indians History and Culture*, 151–57.

3. William Laidlaw was a founding member of the Columbia Fur Company, which Ramsay Crooks of the American Fur Company brought into the fold and renamed the Upper Missouri Outfit. Laidlaw was bourgeois at Fort Union in the winter of 1844–45. See Thompson, *Fort Union Trading Post*, 57.

4. Iron Arrow Point (known as The Great Frenchman) gave the American Fur Company permission to build Fort Union in what was Assiniboine territory. See DeMallie and Miller, "Assiniboine," 574–75.

5. Louis Philippe (1773–1850), the self-styled "citizen king" of France, was from the Orléans branch of the Bourbon dynasty. He acceded to the throne in 1830, spent an uneasy eighteen years as constitutional monarch, was deposed through a coup d'état in 1848, and died in exile in England in 1850.

CHAPTER SIX: NOVEMBER 1851

1. Kurz was either overreacting or ill-informed. David Mitchell, superintendent of Indian affairs, and Indian agent Thomas Fitzpatrick did conclude a treaty with the Teton Sioux, Cheyenne, Arapaho, Crow, Assiniboine, Mandan, Hidatsa (Gros Ventres), and Arikara in September 1851. See Utley, *Frontiersmen in Blue*, 69.

2. Snags are submerged or partly submerged trees capable of ripping the bottom out of a steamboat.

EPILOGUE: COUNCIL BLUFFS TO SWITZERLAND, 1852–1871

1. Kurz, *Journal*, 325.
2. Ibid., 341.
3. Ibid., 341–42.
4. Ibid., 348.
5. Ibid., 273.
6. Eckberg, "Kurz at Fort Union," 12.
7. Kurz, *Journal*, 273.
8. Eckberg, "Kurz at Fort Union," 12.

Selected Bibliography

Barbour, Barton. *Fort Union and the Upper Missouri Fur Trade*. Norman: University of Oklahoma Press, 2001.

Boehme, Sarah E., ed. *John James Audubon in the West: The Last Expedition*. New York: Harry N. Abrams, in association with the Buffalo Bill Historical Center, 2000.

Bushnell, David I., Jr. "[Rudolph] Friedrich Kurz, Artist-Explorer," pp. 507–27 in *Smithsonian Institution Report for 1927*. Washington, D.C., 1928.

Carriker, Robert C. *Father Peter John De Smet: Jesuit in The West*. Norman: University of Oklahoma Press, 1995.

Catlin, George. *Letters and Notes on the Manners, Customs, and Conditions of the North American Indians*, 2 vols. Reprint edition, New York: Dover Publications, 1973.

Chardon, F. A. *Chardon's Journal at Fort Clark, 1834–1839*. Reprint edition, Lincoln: University of Nebraska Press, 1997.

Chittenden, Hiram M. *The American Fur Trade of the Far West*, 2 vols. Reprint edition, Lincoln: University of Nebraska Press, 1986.

DeMallie, Raymond J., and David R. Miller. "Assiniboine," in *Plains, Part 1*, vol. 13 of *Handbook of North American Indians*. Washington, D.C.: Smithsonian Institution Press, 2001.

Denig, Edwin Thompson. *The Assiniboine*. Reprint edition with new introduction, Norman: University of Oklahoma Press, 2000.

———. *Indian Tribes of the Upper Missouri*. Edited with notes and biographical sketch by J. N. B. Hewitt. Forty-sixth Annual Report of the Bureau of American Ethnology, pp. 375–628. Washington, D.C., 1930.

Dollar, Clyde D. "The High Plains Smallpox Epidemic of 1837–1838." *Western Historical Quarterly* 8, no. 1 (January 1977): 15–38.

Eckberg, Scott. *Rudolf F. Kurz at Fort Union: Artist, Clerk, Chronicler*. Reprint edition, Williston, N.D.: Fort Union Association, 2002.

Ewers, John C. *Indian Life on the Upper Missouri*. Norman: University of Oklahoma Press, 1988.

———. *Plains Indian History and Culture: Essays on Continuity and Change*. Norman: University of Oklahoma Press, 1997.

Ferch, David L. "Fighting the Smallpox Epidemic of 1837–38: The Response of the American Fur Company Traders." *Museum of the Fur Trade Quarterly* 19, no. 4 (winter 1983): 2–7; 20, no. 1 (spring 1984): 4–8.

Hafen, LeRoy R., ed. *Mountain Men and the Fur Trade of the Far West*, 10 vols. Glendale, Calif.: Arthur H. Clark, 1965–1972.

Hafen, LeRoy R., and Francis M. Young. *Fort Union and the Pageant of the West*. Reprint edition, Lincoln: University of Nebraska Press, 1984.

Kurz, Rudolph Friedrich. *Journal of Rudolph Friederich Kurz*. Smithsonian Institution, Bureau of American Ethnology, Bulletin 115. Washington, D.C.: Government Printing Office, 1937; reprint edition, Lincoln: University of Nebraska Press (Bison Book), 1970.

Larpenteur, Charles. *Forty Years a Fur Trader on the Upper Missouri*. Reprint of M. M. Quaife edition, Lincoln: University of Nebraska Press, 1989.

Maximilian, Prince of Wied. *Travels in the Interior of North America during the Years 1832–1834*. Cologne, Germany: Taschen, 2001.

McCracken, Harold. *Great Painters and Illustrators of the Old West*. New York: Dover Publications, 1988.

McDermott, John F., ed. *Audubon in the West*. Norman: University of Oklahoma Press, 1965.

Newman, Peter C. *Caesars of the Wilderness*, vol. 2 of *Company of Adventurers*. New York: Viking, 1987.

Pfaller, Louis. *Father de Smet in Dakota*. Richardton, N.D.: Assumption Abbey Press, undated.

Roberts, Robert B. *Encyclopedia of Historic Forts: The Military, Pioneer, and Trading Posts of the United States*. New York: Macmillan Publishing, 1988.

Ross, Alexander. *The Red River Settlement: Its Rise, Progress, and Present State*. Minneapolis: Ross and Haines, 1957.

Schuler, Harold H. *Fort Pierre Chouteau*. Vermillion: University of South Dakota Press, 1990.

Sunder, John E. *The Fur Trade on the Upper Missouri, 1840–1865*. Norman: University of Oklahoma Press, 1965.

Thompson, Erwin N. *Fort Union Trading Post: Fur Trade Empire on the Upper Missouri*. Williston, N.D.: Fort Union Association, 2003.

Utley, Robert M. *Frontiersmen in Blue: The United States Army and the Indian, 1848–1865*. Reprint edition, Lincoln: University of Nebraska Press, 1981.

Wischmann, Lesley. *Frontier Diplomats: The Life and Times of Alexander Culbertson and Natoy-ist-Siksina*. Spokane, Wash.: Arthur H. Clark, 2000. Reprint edition, Norman: University of Oklahoma Press, 2004.

Index